Remembering the Hacienda

NUMBER ELEVEN:
Rio Grande/Río Bravo
Borderlands Culture and Traditions
Norma E. Cantú
General Editor

D0783064

VINCENT PÉREZ

Remembering the Hacienda
History and Memory in the Mexican American Southwest

Texas A&M
UNIVERSITY PRESS
College Station

The paper used in this book meets the minimum requirements
of the American National Standard for Permanence
of Paper for Printed Library Materials, Z39.48–1984.
Binding materials have been chosen for durability.

Library of Congress Cataloging-in-Publication Data

Pérez, Vincent (Vincent Anthony)
Remembering the hacienda : history and memory in the Mexican American
Southwest / Vincent Pérez. — 1st ed.
p. cm. — (Rio Grande/Río Bravo ; no. 11)
Includes bibliographical references and index.
ISBN-13: 978-1-58544-511-0 (cloth : alk. paper)
ISBN-10: 1-58544-511-8 (cloth : alk. paper)
ISBN-13: 978-1-58544-546-2 (pbk. : alk. paper)
ISBN-10: 1-58544-546-0 (pbk. : alk. paper)
1. Southwest, New—History. 2. Mexican Americans—Southwest, New—
History. 3. American literature—Mexican American authors—History and criticism.
4. Southwest, New—In literature. 5. Mexican Americans in literature. 6. Haciendas
in literature. 7. Mireles, Jovita González, 1904–1983 Caballero. 8. Ruiz de Burton,
María Amparo, 1832–1895 Squatter and the don. 9. Carrillo, Leo California I love.
10. Vallejo, Mariano Guadalupe, 1808–1890 Recuerdos históricos y personales tocanta
a la Alta California. 11. Pérez Robles, Francisco, 1908–1994 or 5. I. Title. II. Series.
F786. P399 2006
979—dc22
2006001572

FOR MY GRANDPARENTS,
Francisco Róbles
Pérez
AND
Concepción Herrera
Pérez

"We go into the future facing backward."
—PAUL VALÉRY

CONTENTS

ILLUSTRATIONS

ACKNOWLEDGMENTS

Grateful acknowledgment is made to the following publishers and journals for permission to reprint portions of published material. Sections of chapter 2 first appeared in my essay "South by Southwest: Land and Community in María Amparo Ruiz de Burton's *The Squatter and the Don* and Mariano Guadalupe Vallejo's 'Historical and Personal Memoirs Relating to Alta California,'" in *Recovering the U.S. Hispanic Literary Heritage, Vol. IV,* edited by José F. Aranda and Silvio Torres-Saillant, 96–132 (Houston: Arte Público Press, 2002). A different version of chapter 2 was published in *María Amparo Ruiz de Burton: Critical and Pedagogical Perspectives,* edited by Amelia María de la Luz Montes and Anne Elizabeth Goldman, 27–55 (Lincoln: University of Nebraska Press, 2004). Sections of chapter 3 were included in my essay "Remembering the Hacienda: History and Memory in Jovita González and Eve Raleigh's *Caballero: A Historical Novel,*" in *Look Away! The U.S. South in New World Studies,* edited by Jon Smith and Deborah Cohn, 471–94 (Durham, N.C.: Duke University Press, 2004). Sections of chapter 5 first appeared in my article, "Heroes and Orphans: Testimonial Memory as Resistance and Repression in Francisco Róbles Pérez's 'Memorias,'" *Biography* 20, no. 1 (Winter 1997): 1–54. A different version was published as "Heroes and Orphans of the Hacienda: Narratives of a Mexican American Family," *Aztlán: A Journal of Chicano Studies* 24, no. 1 (Spring 1999): 33–106.

Remembering the Hacienda

INTRODUCTION

The interplay between history and memory in my own family's past first stimulated my interest in Mexican American narratives about the hacienda.[1] One family event in particular—the funeral of my father's aunt, Isabel "Chavela" Róbles in 1992—is the subject of the opening and closing sections of this book. Funerals are perhaps the only social occasions where families are compelled to reflect on their history or at least on the life of one member. All family gatherings provoke historical self-reflection, but only funerals make us remember. That my book originated in family history is a prime example of my engagement with Chicano/a memory and history, and that history, to which I return in chapters 1 and 5, informs my readings of the politics and poetics of the Mexican American past as revealed in five recently recovered "hacienda" literary texts.

After attending the funeral, my parents, Tony and Flora Pérez, and I drove to the cemetery in Santa Paula, California, where Chavela would be buried.[2] Members of both sides of my paternal grandfather's family, the Pérezes and Róbleses, were present. Some Róbles relatives had come from as far away as Zacatecas, a state in central Mexico, to pay their respects to a woman who had immigrated to the United States more than fifty years earlier. After a prayer, my parents and I greeted the Róbles family, some of whom were as unfamiliar to my father as to me. Among them were a couple, Berta and José, who introduced themselves as my father's cousins.[3] While my father spoke with them, I went to greet other members of my family. When I returned a few minutes later, I found myself in the midst of an argument. Confronting my father, Berta had defamed the Pérezes' ancestor, Juan Lira Pérez, my grandfather's father, who died in 1919. Disputing the Pérez family's memory of its patriarch, Berta used the occasion to declare that Lira Pérez had raped a Róbles daughter and disowned the child born to his victim. The Pérez descendants, she suggested, were of the same char-

3

acter as their criminal ancestor. Left speechless, my parents and I watched as Berta and her husband calmly departed.

My grandfather's memory of his father, who died when he was eleven, had more than any other source shaped Lira Pérez's ancestral presence in my family history. As the children and grandchildren of immigrants, we had through two generations fashioned this ancestor into a symbol of our early past, a heroic figure invested with the romantic aura of our cultural heritage. Born in 1854, Lira Pérez was trained as an accountant at the University of Zacatecas. By the late nineteenth century he managed the finances of several haciendas owned by the landed elite in central Zacatecas, near the town of Jerez de García Salinas. Though not a *hacendado* (landowner) himself, by the turn of the century he had become closely associated with the local hacienda oligarchy. As my grandfather wrote in his memoirs, at the outbreak of the Mexican Revolution in 1913 this affiliation led local insurgents to pursue Lira Pérez, marking the conclusion of his storied life and career in Jerez de García Salinas. Over a span of approximately twenty-five years he had six children by four wives. He married his second wife, my grandfather's mother, Juliana Róbles, in 1907. According to the Róbles memory as passed down to Berta, while Juliana recovered from childbirth in 1912, Lira Pérez raped Dominga Róbles, his wife's older sister, who had come to their house to help Juliana recover. He refused to recognize Paulo, his child from that union, as his son. Though my grandfather knew of his half-brother, who was also his cousin, he followed his father's example and never acknowledged Paulo's existence. The memory of the "rape" and of Paulo's rejection by his father, which forms the basis of my interrogation of Pérez family history in chapter 5, was passed down through several Róbles generations, one branch of which immigrated to the United States.[4]

Though evoking an honorable ancestral patrimony in my own family narrative, Lira Pérez played a very different role in Róbles family memory. In the latter he embodied not heritage or tradition but rather, as I trace in chapter 5, aspects of the socioeconomic and cultural currents that contributed to the Róbles family's status in Mexico and later immigration to the United States. Dominga's displaced voice symbolized not only the forgotten history of women within my family's memory of the Mexican past but also the silencing of other groups, such as Indians and *campesinos* (peasants) within my grandfather's mythic rendering of the nineteenth-century hacienda world where his father had lived and worked. Yet what struck me after Chavela's funeral was not only how the silencing of Dominga's voice had in a sense falsified the past. After discovering that other Róbles relatives shared Berta's complaint, I saw how extensively my family's narrative of origins depended on the silencing of contrary memories such as those expressed by Berta.

The silences in the Pérez narrative obscured a conflict-ridden past buried in the unwritten memory of a larger family narrative spanning more than one hundred years. As I explored my family memory, this contested legacy seemed now part of a vast geography that I could never hope to chart, an unknown realm in which history, including the events of my family's past in Mexico's nineteenth-century and revolutionary periods, was imperceptibly impeded by memory, by the stories told about those events.[5] It was a place where oral narratives were the only "truth" but were also a power-ful form of forgetting, and yet it was also where the silenced voices of the past, my Mexican ancestors, called out in the present for their stories to be told. Sifting through the sedimentary layers of my family memory, I discovered in these voices remnants of a community history that reached back to the Spanish colonial era.

I also began to understand how my grandfather's narrative evolved in my family as both a record of the past and as a source of our current identity. For all of its nostalgia, the selective represen-tation of the Mexican past as a story of our origins had served an important purpose in my family, providing a means through which to interpret our existence and sustain our identities in the United States in the face of racial hostility and cultural deracination. De-spite its omissions, the story gave our collective struggle in the United States (perhaps as early as my grandparents' emigration in 1921) a meaning that enabled us to continue on our journey through a world that in my grandparents' day was far from welcoming. At one level an orphaned immigrant's expression of love for his father and nation, at another a potent form of forgetting, and at another, deeper, level my grandfather's narrative painted a portrait of family and community that united and nurtured us as we navigated the present order of things in the United States. Against this alienat-ing modern social order, where my grandfather worked for more than fifty years as a farm laborer, he and his children remembered the hacienda—the pre-modern agrarian community of my grand-father's childhood in pre-revolutionary Mexico and thus an all-embracing symbol of our Mexican (American) origins and identity.

Drawing on my own family history and the writings of a diverse group of authors and theorists, the chapters that follow examine a group of recently recovered novels and autobiographies that span approximately one hundred years and narrate early Mexican Amer-ican history through a set of memories that converge on the ha-cienda. The authors of these works employ the hacienda as a "site of memory," a cultural symbol of a Mexican agrarian (colonial) past set against the landscape of U.S. modernity. Sites of memory, according to Pierre Nora's formulation in *Realms of Memory,* are symbolic representations that embody the interplay between history and memory—that is, the events of a nation or community's past and its (cultural) remembrance of those events. These sites of memory, as emblems of national or group affiliation, include geographical places, monuments, historical figures, literary and artistic objects, commemorations, and other such "spaces" of memory (Kritzman, x). The Alamo, for example, has served as a powerful site of memory within U.S. cultural memory, embodying a frontier myth in which Mexicans were cast as the racial "other."[6] More commonly identified with public history and culture, in which a place, monument, figure, or object symbolizes a nation or group's shared sense of identity and origins, sites of memory in Nora's usage capture the "vestiges of a recovered history constructed in response to a modern world that no longer values memory or tradition." As symbols of the past, they are therefore the ultimate "embodiment of a commemorative consciousness that survives in a [present] history which, having renounced memory, cries out for it" (Nora, 6). Rooted in the present, sites of memory emerge from a sociohistorical landscape that requires them, rather than from the past they embody. Richard Flores, for instance, notes that "those who remember the Alamo . . . do so not primarily to remember the events of 1836 but to re-member a social body through a specific hierarchical and class rubric endemic to the arrival of modernity in Texas" (R. Flores, "Introduction: Adina De Zavala," xviii).

Though I do not offer a study of a single geographically fixed site of public history, Nora's concept points to the intricate bond between memory, identity, and place that forms my book's unifying subject. The chapters that follow examine a set of literary texts that employ the hacienda as a site of social remembrance, a cultural symbol of the pre–U.S. conquest Spanish and Mexican eras that serves in these works to negotiate a path for Mexican Americans during a period marked by racial hostility toward Mexicans as well as the precipitous decline of this population's ancestral ranching economy. If sites of memory are the result of an imaginary process that codifies the historical consciousness of a nation or group, the hacienda, I argue, symbolizes a foundational Mexican American historical identity that Chicano and Chicana scholars and authors have not yet fully explored (Kritzman, x). In place of Aztlán, the legendary homeland of the Aztecs claimed by Chicano cultural nationalism as the mythical place and unitary space of the Chicano "nation," I posit the hacienda as an originary space within Greater Mexico but not one of continuity, unity, or authenticity (Chabram and Fregoso, 204). Rather, in the texts I examine, the hacienda as Mexican (American) memory-place identifies a shared agrarian sociohistorical experience since the Spanish colonial era that simultaneously reveals ruptures, displacements, discontinuities, contradictions, and silences within Mexican American cultural memory.

The hacienda's exposition of difference, discontinuity, and dissonance within Mexican (American) cultural memory and its evocation of a submerged body of (colonial) history that in previous years went unexplored advances the ongoing scholarly endeavor to reframe the notion, inherited from the Chicano student movement, of a singular Chicano cultural identity. Since at least the mid-1980s Chicano/a studies scholars have interrogated this model, rendering its cultural nationalist premises problematic, if not now defunct, at every level. As cultural critics Angie Chabram and Rosa Fregoso noted in an early piece, the "basis of Chicano identity as formulated by Chicano cultural nationalism postulated that collective identity was simultaneity and continuity between the object and its representation" (Chabram and Fregoso, 205). Since little attention was given to examining how specific cultural productions were constructed and excessive emphasis was placed on content, the nationalist model "failed to acknowledge the partiality of representation, the fact that it is an artifice . . . and that representation did not even encompass the complexity of Chicano cultural identity" (206). Chicano identity was conceived instead as a "static, fixed, and one-dimensional formulation," the mirror image of the self-representations of the Chicano studies intellectuals who produced it. It consequently overlooked the "critical points of difference and the experience of rupture and discontinuity" that also "shape [Mexican American] identities in decisive ways . . . [such as] the heterogeneous experiences of migration, conquest, and regional variation," whose histories extend inevitably into the colonial era (205–206).

Though the notion of a transcendental Chicano subject may now be obsolete, the reinstatement of simultaneity and continuity, lapsing into monologic visions of cultural identity reminiscent of Chicano cultural nationalism, continues to haunt the growing body of scholarship about recovered early Mexican American literary texts.[7] Despite noteworthy exceptions, such as Amelia María de la Luz Montes and Anne Elizabeth Goldman's *María Amparo Ruiz de Burton: Critical and Pedagogical Perspectives,* this scholarship too often assumes an equal relationship between history and memory, overlooking the ways in which "ethnic memory is blocked, deflected, and problematically reconstituted according to the over-determinants of ideology and aesthetics, those things that form the very foundation of ethnicity and its mediated representation in literary works," as David Palumbo-Liu explains (213). Disproving such a model, the hacienda as memory-place within early Mexican American narratives reveals that Mexican American (ethnic) identity has always depended upon its social construction and mediation over time and that it has evolved through changing periods in which memory and forgetting have been as important as the unifying myth. In this sense, the hacienda as memory-place attests that even the cultural memories of (ethnic) groups who asserted them outside of or in response to formal history should not be mistaken for a complete or unmediated record of the past (Brundage, 5). To the contrary, as Nora observes, by definition cultural memory "accommodates only those facts that suit it. It thrives on vague, telescoping reminiscences, on hazy general impressions or specific symbolic details. It is vulnerable to transferences, screen memories, censorings, and projections of all kinds" (Nora, 3). Although Mexican American historical literary scholarship informs my readings, I summarize my engagement with this body of criticism as it relates to Mexican American history and memory in my conclusion, where I call for a "poetic" approach to recovered texts grounded in a dialectical understanding of cultural identity within the problematics of memory/history, difference, and positionality.[8]

The works that I analyze draw upon Mexican cultural memory of the agrarian ranching society that existed in much of the Southwest and Mexico until the modern era. If the plantation forms the foundation of U.S. southern society and culture, the hacienda system that dominated the early history of Greater Mexico—that other southern region encompassing present-day Mexico and the Mexican American Southwest—formed a strikingly similar premodern socioeconomic base.[9] Feudalistic, paternalistic, and patriarchal, from the seventeenth through nineteenth centuries throughout most of this region the hacienda's agrarian economic and cultural order shaped the character of all levels of Spanish and Mexican society. Although the hacienda may appear more remote for contemporary Chicanos and Chicanas than the plantation has been for both white and black southerners, the literary works that I discuss remind us of this colonial-era institution's proximity, illustrating its central importance as a site of memory and identity for early Mexican American writers.[10] As my grandfather's stories suggest, the hacienda's ambiguous meaning also indicates the bifurcated historical and cultural experience of Mexican Americans—the descendants of Spanish and U.S. colonialisms—a conflictive and tangible past that forms the subject of the hacienda narratives discussed in this book.

All five of the literary texts that I examine are recently recovered narratives, either published works formerly excluded from scholarly discourse or unpublished manuscripts recently discovered and critically interrogated.[11] Much as these texts foreground the hacienda as a site of social remembrance, the narratives themselves also constitute foundational sites of Mexican American cultural memory. Listed in the order in which they will be discussed in chapters 2 through 5, the works to be analyzed are María Amparo Ruiz de Burton's novel, *The Squatter and the Don* (1885), Mariano Guadalupe Vallejo's memoirs, "Historical and Personal Memoirs Relating to Alta California" (1874), Jovita González and Eve Raleigh's historical romance, *Caballero: A Historical Novel* (written in the 1930s and 1940s and published in 1996), Leo Carrillo's autobiography, *The California I Love* (1961), and my grandfather Francisco Róbles Pérez's autobiography, "Memorias" (written in the 1980s).

As descendants of early colonists of the Spanish and Mexican frontier, the Mexican American authors listed above strongly identified with their colonial-era ancestry and particularly with the landed classes from which they claimed descent. Ruiz de Burton (b. 1831), Vallejo (b. 1807), and Carrillo (b. 1881) were descended from settlers and soldiers who arrived on the Alta California frontier during the period of Spanish colonization.[12] The small number of founding families in this region and intermarriage among those who were landed bound these three authors together as distant relatives. Carrillo's grandfather, Pedro Catarino Carrillo, was the first cousin of Vallejo's wife, Francisca Benicia Carrillo, and Carrillo was related to Ruiz de Burton through her great-grandmother, Doña Isabel Carrillo. Carrillo's great-great-grandfather, José Raimundo Carrillo, came to Alta California from the Baja California town of Loreto, where the Carrillos and Ruizes both resided and where Ruiz de Burton was also born and reared. As Ruiz de Burton, Vallejo, and Carrillo variously portray in their works, Alta California had been settled by Spanish and Mexican colonists and their descendants for almost eighty years prior to being annexed by the United States in 1850 following the U.S.-Mexican War.

Jovita González (b. 1904) was in part descended from the landed Spanish elites who had come to the colony of Nuevo Santander in the eighteenth century (Limón, "Mexicans, Foundational Fictions," 242). González and Raleigh employ this colonial history as both historical subject and geographic setting in *Caballero*. South Texas— the present-day border region between the Nueces River and the Rio Grande that during the colonial era formed the northern portion of the province of Nuevo Santander—had been settled for almost ninety years before it was claimed by the Republic of Texas in 1836, only to be annexed nine years later by the United States.[13] Finally, according to my own family narrative, my grandfather (b. 1908) was descended from early Spanish colonizers of Zacatecas, which in the late 1500s formed the northern frontier of New Spain. Through his father's family my grandfather claimed descent from the rancher class of that region.

I myself compiled my grandfather's life narrative, set in Mexico and Southern California, from memoirs that he wrote during the 1980s.[14] Both the production and recuperation of "Memorias" are therefore mediated by my own involvement as an interviewer, critic, and perhaps more importantly, relative of the author, making this work quite different in form and content from the other narratives listed above. Since my grandfather was not able to complete his original manuscript, the final version will incorporate oral responses to questions that I had posed to my grandfather (who we believe passed away in 1994 or 1995) during tape-recorded interviews.[15] Though I was involved in shaping my grandfather's life story into a narrative even as I struggled to interpret it, I also depended on other family memories as I reconstructed my family's past back to the Spanish colonial era. I relied on the oral stories of not only my grandfather but also his wife—my grandmother, Concepción Herrera Pérez—and other members of my family such as my father, Tony Pérez, my aunt, Esther Doran, and members of my extended family. My family's stories inspired this book by teaching me that the ghosts of our ancestors reside among us in the present—and that we can meet them if we learn where to look. Because my readings of hacienda texts benefitted from my family history, I frame this book with stories from the Pérez narrative and other autobiographical material, including a final chapter on my grandfather's memoirs. In doing so I hope to show that the cultural knowledge contained in family narratives may be more engaging than many formal studies and can therefore creatively serve us as scholars and teachers. Buried in the critical discourse of every formal analysis of Mexican American literature or history is an autobiography, informed by cultural memory, waiting to be written. Similarly, buried in every student essay submitted for a college literature course is a family history often as stimulating and intriguing as the literature taught in the course. As Michel-Rolph Trouillot observes, "We all need histories that no history book can tell, but they are not in the classroom—not the history classrooms, anyway. They are in the lessons we learn at home, in poetry and childhood games, in what is left of history when we close the history books with their verifiable facts" (Trouillot, 71–72).

Chapter 1 presents a historical overview of the hacienda as a socioeconomic institution in Zacatecas, Texas, and California—the three regions of Greater Mexico depicted in the primary texts. To outline the origins of the hacienda system in the early colonial era and its development in New Spain's northern provinces of Nuevo Santander and Alta California, I describe a 1990 trip with my grandfather to visit the rural towns of his childhood in Zacatecas. I define the hacienda's agrarian social order and trace the decline of this institution within Greater Mexico in the modern era, a decline whose socioeconomic and political circumstances form the historical landscape against which the hacienda, as cultural symbol, appears in the texts I have listed.

Chapter 2 examines Mexican Californian class and caste identities as depicted in two late nineteenth-century hacienda narratives: Ruiz de Burton's *The Squatter and the Don* and Vallejo's "Historical and Personal Memoirs." Recalling U.S. southern plantation literature, *The Squatter and the Don* employs the seigneurial identities of the *Californio* (Mexican Californian) gentry to indict the U.S. capitalist social order for governmental and juridical policies that dispossessed most Californio ranchers in the aftermath of annexation. Eleven years before the publication of *The Squatter and the Don*, Ruiz de Burton's close friend Vallejo, the model for the novel's protagonist, narrated his autobiographical testimonial for historian Hubert H. Bancroft's research project on early California history. If placed in relation to Ruiz de Burton's portrait of Vallejo in *The Squatter and the Don*, which displaces the hacienda's internal social contradictions, as I discuss in chapter 1, Vallejo's autobiographical persona in "Historical and Personal Memoirs" serves to expose the circuitous interplay between Mexican Californian history and memory. Ruiz de Burton's historical romance intersects with anti-northern discourse in late-nineteenth-century U.S. southern narrative, whereas Vallejo's work announces the author's status in Alta Californian history as military commander, colonial agent, and *hacendado*.

Chapter 3 extends my discussion of hacienda narrative into the twentieth century by investigating the interplay between history and memory in González and Raleigh's *Caballero: A Historical Novel*. Set on a South Texas hacienda during the U.S.-Mexican War, the novel narrates the story of the rise and fall of a mid-nineteenth-century Mexican landowning family, the Mendoza y Sorías. *Caballero* captures the conflicted cultural and political status of middle-class Mexican Americans and particularly Mexican American women during the 1930s. Its aesthetic and cultural affiliations with U.S. southern fiction illustrate ambiguities within Mexican American cultural memory during this period. Although the novel's romantic unions posit a desired "marriage-of-convenience" between Mexicans and Americans, its hacienda setting and plot structure indicate the work's strong identification with Mexican Texas as a conquered region. Although *Caballero* was written decades after the Californio texts, its use of the hacienda as memory-place is similar to that of the earlier works, with the hacienda serving as a multivalenced cultural symbol of Mexican (American) origins and identity.

Chapter 4 recovers a formerly unknown autobiography written by a descendant of the Carrillo family, arguably the most powerful ranching family of nineteenth-century Mexican California. Written in the late 1950s with the aim of honoring Leo Carrillo's nineteenth-century Californio community, *The California I Love* narrates the history of Mexican California by recounting the Carrillo family's role in the colonization and settlement of the region. Carrillo's status as a film actor, who was typecast as ethnic "other" in more than one hundred Metro-Goldwyn-Mayer motion pictures, complicates his narration of California history. Drawing upon Homi Bhabha's concept of ambivalence, I interpret Carrillo's autobiography and his film career through the lens of cultural politics, particularly the conflict between Anglo Americans and Mexicans in pre–World War II Southern California. Carrillo's fixation on the Spanish past invokes the powerful romantic narrative of Old (Spanish) California. This romantic motif, however, reveals not only Carrillo's nostalgic identification with his ancestral Californio community but also the level of anti-Mexican hostility within pre–World War II Los Angeles. Carrillo's autobiography thus captures the ambiguous meaning of the narrative of Old (Spanish) California for a Mexican American community that after 1920 traced its history to nineteenth-century rural Mexico rather than to Mexican California ranch society.

Finally, in seeking to recover and critically interpret my own grandfather's unpublished autobiography, chapter 5 positions the work in relation to recent criticism on Mexican American life-writing. My grandfather's nostalgic memory of the mythic "colonial" world of his childhood operates as an empowering reassertion of cultural continuity and pride in the face of later sociocultural displacement as a Mexican immigrant in the United States. My family history illustrates how the historical and theoretical issues that I examine in earlier chapters remain a part of the lives of contemporary Mexican Americans, particularly those whose family histories can be traced to revolutionary Mexico.

In my grandfather's narrative the hacienda as memory-place reconstitutes the Mexican agrarian community where he and his father lived before poverty and war forced them to leave, ending his father's career and plunging my grandfather into the capitalist world north of the border. In this sense, in my grandfather's text the hacienda emerges from his experience as a Mexican immigrant, from both geographic displacement and cultural fracture. Similarly, in the other works listed above the hacienda as memory-place develops in relation to social effects associated with the transition to modernity and capitalism and experienced by Mexican Americans in the Southwest in the late nineteenth and early twentieth centuries. As I will describe in chapter 1, in the Mexican American Southwest the most notable of these effects were the replacement of traditional Mexican ranching practices by commercial agriculture, the loss of Mexican ranching lands to the latter, and the racial subordination of Mexican Americans under the U.S. capitalist sociopolitical order. The hacienda as cultural icon thus serves in all five works not only as a socially and culturally fraught symbol of origins set against a racial hierarchy that stigmatized Mexicans but also more generally as a symbolic resolution to the related social and economic contradictions that Mexican Americans faced as their traditional agrarian society eroded under the new industrial capitalist order—or, as in the case of Mexican immigrants like my grandfather, was left behind in Mexico.

This study has been informed and enriched by research carried out through the Recovering the U.S. Hispanic Literary Heritage project. An interdisciplinary venture directed by Nicolás Kanellos at the University of Houston, the project's mission is to identify, recover, interpret, and preserve Hispanic writings from the colonial period to 1960. As noted by one of its distinguished scholars, José F. Aranda Jr., the project's related objective "is the narration of the lives of people of Hispanic descent since the sixteenth century, using such sources as histories, diaries, memoirs, prose, poetry, fiction, and newspapers" (Aranda, 563). Begun in 1990 with the aim of expanding the historical scope of Latino/a studies scholarship, the project has uncovered a wealth of formerly unknown writings, works that would otherwise have remained silenced by racialized academic traditions that consigned some of them to textual oblivion for more than a century. Whether explicitly or implicitly, each of my chapters expounds the recovery project's view that the restoration of early Hispanic American literary texts is always also a political project, one that, as John M. González writes, inherently calls into question "the theoretical assumptions of the academic analysis of 'American' literature through the vectors of power that Chicana/o narrative dissects" (J. M. González, "Romancing Hegemony," 23). The study of early Mexican American literary texts, as another recovery project scholar, Rosaura Sánchez, reminds us, is necessarily concerned "with the politics of identity construction and with the recognition that the bones of 'our dead' have too long lain cluttered in the mausoleum of 'the enemy'" (Sánchez, *Telling Identities*, x–xi). And though I endorse the recovery project's political premises, following González's call for a heightened awareness of our positionings as scholars and critics, I also comment on the type of cultural and political work that the recovery project itself performs, or should perform, in the extension and elaboration of Mexican American and Latina/o culture in the United States (J. M. González, "Romancing Hegemony," 23).

History, Memory, Identity

In recent years scholars in various fields have shown increasing interest in historical memory. Informed by anthropology, literary criticism, psychology, linguistics, and cultural studies, recent studies of historical memory have achieved considerable theoretical and analytical sophistication (Brundage, 3). Although scholarship on the Mexican American Southwest has consistently been engaged with history and memory, few works in this field foreground these concepts in ways that permit an understanding of the relation and distinction among them.[16] Although recovery project scholarship has not exhaustively addressed issues that devolve from the interplay between history and memory, its research on historical narrative always, at some level, wrestles with the nature of these concepts. Following analytical models in ethnic studies and cultural history, scholarship on recovered Latino/a texts assumes that memory is a social rather than individual phenomenon. As the sociologist Maurice Halbwachs posited in the 1920s, since no memory is possible outside frameworks used by people living in society to determine and retrieve their recollections, personal memories are always social in nature (Halbwachs, 43). Whatever their content, they are learned, inherited, or, at the very least, informed by a common stock of social memory (Brundage, 4). Paul Connerton notes that every recollection, however personal it may be, even that of events that we alone witnessed, even that of thoughts and sentiments that remain unexpressed, "exists in relationship with a whole ensemble of notions . . . with persons, places, dates, words, forms of language . . . with the whole material and moral life of the societies of which we are part or of which we have been part" (Connerton, 36). Recovery project research similarly presupposes that as the repositories of personal memories Latino/a literary texts exist in proximity with the material and social life that produced them, with that "ensemble" of people, places, events, and language of which authors and texts are a part. Latino/a authors and narrators remember the past not only as individuals but also as members of families, communities, nations, and other groups with which they identify and also through those geographic places they have lived in and with which they identify.

Models of memory used in ethnic studies and cultural history agree that cultural memory encompasses the shared remembrances through which a society, group, or community imagines and defines itself, giving it a sense of its past and defining its aspirations for the future (Fentress and Wickham, 25). It consists of that body of reusable texts, narratives, and images specific to each society or group in each epoch, whose cultivation serves to stabilize and convey that group's identity and self-image. As Jan Assmann explains, "Upon such collective knowledge, for the most part (but not exclusively) of the past, each group bases its awareness of unity and particularity" (Assmann, 133). Guiding human experience and behavior in the "interactive framework of a society," cultural memory thus enables a nation, group, or community to maintain its nature consistently through generations (125). Drawing upon poststructuralist thought, Stuart Hall observes that the past nowhere has inherent meaning, "only that which is imposed upon it by language, by narrative, by discourse."[17] Against this loss of meaning, cultural memory provides a set of categories through which a nation, group, or community makes sense of its existence, giving meaning to its past and present and projecting that meaning as a shared identity into the future. It is in this sense that U.S. ethnic literature inverts the history-memory relation traditionally assumed in U.S. historiography, imbuing ethnic memory with the status of history and destabilizing formal history, while critiquing its modes of assigning significance. Against the authority of U.S. history, writes Palumbo-Liu, "all notions of ethnic writing as revision of history point to cultural 'memory,' for it is through memory alone, as the repository of things left out of history, that the ethnic subject can challenge history" (Palumbo-Liu, 212–13).

Though cultural memory is commonly invoked in discussions of U.S. ethnic groups excluded from hegemonic history, or more generally of "American" (national) remembrance, in the United States this concept operates simultaneously on many levels, reflecting our nation's sociocultural and ethnic complexity rooted in a conflict-ridden past. "Cultural memory," for example, denotes the historical consciousnesses of groups traditionally erased from formal history (e.g., the counter-memory of African Americans), groups whose collective memory has exerted a dominant influence on formal history (e.g., European Americans), and those whose collective identity has stood in ambiguous relation to formal history (e.g., white southerners). As the interlocking histories of these three communities suggest, the process of cultural memory, like historiography itself, is bound up in complex political stakes and meanings (Sturken, 1). Remembering the past, states W. Fitzhugh Brundage, "becomes implicated in a range of activities that have as much to do with identity, power, authority, cultural norms, and social interaction as with the simple act of conserving and recalling information" (Brundage, 4). How social groups remember the past as a means of constructing identity determines how they relate to each other, to other social groups, and to their own internal subgroups. As Marita Sturken explains, cultural memory "both defines a culture and is the means by which [social] divisions and conflicting agendas are revealed." More crucially, it is a "field of cultural negotiation through which different stories vie for a place in [formal] history" (Sturken, 1).

Models of memory used in cultural history and ethnic studies also generally concur that cultural memory is shared outside the parameters of "history."[18] Both models define the latter in two interrelated senses, first as an investigative process and secondly as a process within a dominant discourse that privileges some groups and marginalizes others. "History" is the practice of reconstructing and codifying historical events based on the documentary traces of an absent past—those "marks, perceptible to the senses, which some phenomenon, in itself inaccessible, has left behind" (Connerton, 13). In contrast to the workings of cultural memory, historians investigate the evidentiary traces of the past "much as lawyers cross-question witnesses in a court of law, extracting from that evidence information which it does not explicitly contain" (13). For this reason, Nora, whose views recall the critique of hegemonic history carried out by U.S. ethnic studies scholars, underscores the ways in which "history" devalues "memory."[19] For him, memory possesses the vitality of living beings and communities because memory is "always embodied in living societies . . . [welling] up from groups that it welds together . . . [and] is rooted in the concrete: in space, gesture, image, and object" (Nora, 3). History, in Nora's model, is close to the opposite: not only static, but "willful and deliberate, experienced as a duty rather than as spontaneous; psychological, individual and subjective, rather than social, collective, and all-embracing" (8). "Suspicious of 'myth' and 'legend' as well as of the vagaries of personal memory," writes Jacquelyn Dowd Hall, "historians take it upon themselves to piece together a plausible narrative from scattered, surviving shards . . . [one] that seems disconnected from living memory" (J. D. Hall, 441). They tend to "position themselves above and beyond memory, which [they] devalue as self-serving and inexact" (440). In Nora's model "sites of memory" embody these differences: memory attaches itself to sites, whereas history attaches itself to events (Nora, 22). Memory is rooted in the concrete and physical, which serves to validate and authenticate its particular version of the past, whereas, as Richard Flores remarks, "official history—intent on unraveling the temporal movement of the past with sources and archives—is only as solid as the narrative it produces" (R. Flores, *Remembering the Alamo*, 21). While "memory needs no validation since it thinks itself complete," he writes, historical narrative can change with the "emergence of new evidence, other perspectives, and possible interpretations" (166).

This distinction between history and memory serves as a fulcrum for my readings. The subject of my study obviously endorses the inherent value of the recovered collective memories of ethnic communities once excluded from formal history. But, aside from this self-evident focus, I am not primarily interested in examining the ways in which formal history (or U.S. cultural memory) effaced the Mexican American past. Rather, beginning with the premise that within (ethnic) cultural memory a dialectic exists between the willfully recalled and deliberately forgotten past, I explore and interrogate Mexican American cultural memory as a source of knowledge through which Mexican Americans reflected on their past and present to help sustain their life-world and make sense of their existence. Each time this tradition was articulated, it was, as Brundage states in relation to U.S. southern memory, "given a meaning appropriate to the historical context in which it was invoked" (Brundage, 9). Hence, rather than focusing on how hegemonic history and "American" collective memory refracted the Mexican American past, I identify the slippages, manipulations, repressions, contradictions, and silences *within* hacienda texts to trace the narrative processes involved in the efforts of this group to construct a reality in and through cultural memory in which to exist.[20] My aim is to situate Mexican Americans in relation to their own traditions, asking how they interpreted their own "ghosts" and used them as a source of cultural knowledge.

I draw upon Jacquelyn Dowd Hall's model of history and memory, which calls for leavening the political dimension in historical literary scholarship with poetics (J. D. Hall, 441). I return to the concept of poetics in my conclusion, where I use it to tie together my chapter readings and bring the full weight of these analyses to bear critically on scholarship in the Recovering the U.S. Hispanic Literary Heritage project. Building on Nora's concepts of history and memory, Hall associates formal "history" with politics and cultural "memory" with poetics. While in literary theory poetics usually refers either to the study of the conventions that inform given texts or to a type of literary criticism associated with New Historicism, following Hall I use the term more generally to evoke the realm of memory, imagination, and difference (442n). Politics, Hall states, "demand that we choose a side, [and] take a stand. Poetics demand that we hold seemingly contradictory beliefs at the same time, that we embrace multiple levels of meaning . . . [and] that we think metaphorically" (441–42). Whereas the politics of history "entail an Olympian stance toward our subjects, who cannot talk back, who are dead and gone," Hall writes, poetics require a different perspective, "one that acknowledges how history is entangled with memory and that implicates us in the history we write" (442). This book is about the politics and poetics of early Mexican American history and memory as revealed in five hacienda narratives. I examine how authors and storytellers remembered the early Spanish and Mexican past symbolically to reclaim a sense of cultural agency, as well as how contemporary critics, like their research subjects, participate in the ongoing fashioning of Mexican American cultural memory. In response to Mexican American historical literary scholarship that would affirm politics at the expense of memory, multiplicity, and metaphor, I posit a poetics of remembrance.

I employ an understanding of (ethnic) identity as a signifying practice, as a positioning and effect grounded in history, memory, and discourse instead of in essence. Rather than a "universal and transcendental spirit inside [oneself] . . . lying unchanged outside history and culture, [suggesting] a fixed origin to which [one] can make some final and absolute Return," as Stuart Hall puts it, (ethnic) identity is better understood as a process through which one's sense of (ethnic) self is continually constructed and reconstructed through memory, narrative, and myth (S. Hall, "Cultural Identity and Diaspora," 53). In the case of narratives and stories about family, kinship, and community, the construction of identity is always a process of people making meaning out of their experiences with whatever tools they have. This does not mean that (ethnic) identity is a mere illusion or trick of the imagination. Though it is "subject to the continuous 'play' of history, culture, and power," (ethnic) identity, as Stuart Hall observes, "has its histories, and histories have their real, material, and symbolic effects" (52–53). Among the *real* effects that have shaped Mexican American cultural identity through time are the variegated sociohistorical processes associated with displacement, dispossession, migration, and conquest. As many recent scholars have also established, the histories of (ethnic) identity find their real and material foundation in the geography of place, the physical locations with which (ethnic) groups identify through time. Echoing earlier theorists of place, Lisbeth Haas, for example, notes that (ethnic) identity is "generally structured in relationship to particular readings of geographic areas, such as are found in the 'imagined community' of the nation" (Haas, 9).

Though I structure Mexican (American) ethnic identity in relationship to the hacienda as it developed within the general spatial geography of Greater Mexico, I do not claim it as the only locus of Mexican American or Chicano/a cultural identity. Such a claim would oversimplify the asymmetrical variation and sociocultural heterogeneity that has characterized Mexico and the Mexican American Southwest since the colonial era. It would therefore contradict the conception of Mexican American cultural identity captured by the metaphor of the border (*la frontera*), a space where different cultures (Mexican, Spanish, European American, indigenous) have converged. A multitude of other Mexican American sites of remembrance have already been the subject of a large body of scholarly and creative writing. Among these are the border, the barrio, the (small) ranch, the home, the (agricultural) field, the factory, the mine, the prison, and so forth, as well as a plethora of current and past historical figures and/or texts from, for example, Gregorio Cortez to Cesar Chavez and, more recently, Sandra Cisneros. But I discovered in my research that the hacienda as employed in early Mexican American narrative sheds light on an early epoch in our collective past—our origins in the Spanish colonial era—that Chicano/a scholarly and creative writings have not yet fully explored and interrogated.[21] If history, as Ramón Saldívar writes in *Chicano Narrative*, is the "decisive determinant of the form and content of . . . [Mexican American] literature," the hacienda embodies that defining sociohistorical determinant in a number of newly recovered Mexican American literary texts (Saldívar, x).

Early Mexican (American) history and memory also cannot be reduced to a single formula within the disparate localities that constitute Greater Mexico—from northern regions such as California, New Mexico, Arizona, Texas, and Chihuahua to southern territories such as Michoacán, Zacatecas, Jalisco, Nayarit, and Oaxaca. Although many areas within Greater Mexico were dominated by the hacienda system for centuries, even those not dominated by this institution were influenced by it. And yet, though I identify a pattern in Mexican American cultural memory across three large geographic swaths of Greater Mexico, I do not claim for my model a uniform applicability throughout this region. Since I have selected texts that foreground the hacienda as a site of memory, I exclude regions where Mexican American cultural memory of a mythic colonial past took a different form, such as in New Mexico. In this region cultural belief in a Spanish origin as well as a land tenure history strikingly different from that of Texas or California seem to have precluded the need for this symbolic form. Also, choosing newly recovered texts as the subject of this study necessarily involved excluding a variety of other Mexican American literary texts that foreground the Southwest's Spanish/Mexican agrarian past, from early works such as the border *corridos* to modern ones such as Ernesto Galarza's autobiography *Barrio Boy* (1971) and Alejandro Morales's novel *Reto en el paraíso* (1983). Finally, as suggested earlier, I do not intend to engage in historiographic debates concerning the nature of nineteenth-century Mexican hacienda and ranch society. Even if some would argue that the hacienda, as conceived in my model, is a grand myth, the works discussed in the ensuing chapters demonstrate that it existed as a potent symbolic form embodying a mythic agrarian past within Mexican American cultural memory. I use historical scholarship on the hacienda system in chapter 1 to advance my argument about the hacienda as Mexican (American) memory-place and symbol of Mexican (American) ethnic origins and identity. In works examined in subsequent chapters I portray Mexican American cultural memory wrestling ambiguously with antagonistic sociohistorical forces to fashion and sustain an empowering Mexican (American) ethnic subjectivity. Let me begin my examination of history and memory as they relate to this subjectivity by describing my visit several years ago to the ranchos of Zacatecas in central Mexico, remnants of what François Chevalier called the great haciendas, where my grandfather spent his childhood.

Chapter

I

The Hacienda
in History and Memory

AFTER the discovery of silver in Zacatecas in 1546, Spanish colonization rapidly engulfed the region's richest mine, Cerro de la Bufa. Over a span of two centuries the Spanish extracted tons of silver ore from this mine's labyrinth of tunnels, a maze one can explore today on a guided tour that includes a visit to a discotheque occupying a gigantic cavern carved out of earth and rock centuries ago by Indian laborers. During a trip in 1990 with my family to Jerez, an outlying rural town from which my grandfather emigrated in 1921, I visited the mine. On top of La Bufa, directly above the mine, three equestrian statues of heroes of the revolution look out over the old colonial city to the valley beyond. Generals Pancho Villa, Pánfilo Natera, and Felipe Ángeles led the revolutionary forces to victory in 1914 in the Battle of Zacatecas. In a recorded interview a year before our trip, my grandfather Francisco Róbles Pérez recounted the battles he witnessed as a child in Zacatecas and Torreón; his wife, my grandmother Concepción Herrera Pérez, also recalled episodes from the war, including the day a procession of triumphant Villista soldiers entered her hometown, Tesorero, a hacienda near Jerez that was one of the destinations of our trip.

The development of the hacienda system in Zacatecas, Texas, and California from the sixteenth through nineteenth centuries illustrates this institution's foundational role in the history of Greater Mexico. Beginning with my grandfather's memories of his childhood in Zacatecas and my self-reflections upon visiting the sites in Mexico that he described in his stories, I draw upon historical scholarship on the hacienda to trace its role in the expansion and consolidation of Spanish colonialism northward from Zacatecas in the seventeenth century. This expansion led in the mid-eighteenth century to the founding of the frontier province of Nuevo Santander, which encompassed present-day South Texas, and in the late-eighteenth century to the colonization of Alta California. I describe the internal character of hacienda society, identifying two central features—paternalism and debt peonage—and present an overview of the socioeconomic processes identified with modernity that led to the decline of Mexican hacienda and ranch society. The calamitous social reorganization of Mexican agrarian society in the modern era, resulting from the economic circumstances that war, displacement, and conquest generated, forms the landscape from which, in early Mexican American writings, the hacienda emerged as a cultural symbol embodying historical origins and ethnic cultural identity. Given the socioeconomic transformation that resulted from the transition to capitalism, the hacienda underpins the thematic foundations of many early Mexican American authors' literary writing, delivering a historical and ethnic counter-narrative to Anglo American conquest and occupation. In the case of immigrants like my grandfather, this counter-narrative was intended to address the pain of both material and cultural losses that resulted from geographic displacement.

The hacienda appeared prominently in a parallel narrative that emerged during the same period in U.S. cultural memory, a narrative whose astonishing popularity would shape cultural representations of the Southwest's history throughout the first half of the twentieth century. As the socioeconomic forces identified with modernity brought an end to the Southwest's Mexican/Spanish agrarian era, this foundational epoch was remembered as Spanish pastoral romance in a flood of literary, artistic, and architectural works by European Americans, many of them transplanted easterners. Soon after its *Ur*-text, Helen Hunt Jackson's *Ramona*, was published in 1884, the romantic narrative of the region's pastoral origins popularized what Carey McWilliams, in *North From Mexico*, termed the Southwest's Spanish "fantasy heritage" (McWilliams, 35). Replacing the United States' conquered Mexican/*mestizo* foes with aristocratic Spanish (hacienda) seigneurs, the rise of the romantic myth within hegemonic discourse chronologically paralleled the material decline of the Southwest's Mexican (agrarian) social order.

MEXICAN MONUMENTS

The Spanish conquest of Aztec society led to the emergence of the hacienda as the dominant mode of production in New Spain in the seventeenth and eighteenth centuries. From the seventeenth century onward, as Enrique Semo observes in *The History of Capitalism in Mexico*, the hacienda "became an increasingly significant phenomenon in the economy" of the colony. Though it emerged as early as the sixteenth century, the hacienda's presence, Semo continues, "became stronger and its influence grew until, in the late eighteenth and early nineteenth centuries, it evolved into the most significant internal element in the social and economic life of the [region]" (Semo, 156). In the northern provinces, which by the late seventeenth century reached beyond the current U.S.-Mexican border region but in the early colonial period extended only to what is now northern Mexico, hacienda boundaries established in the seventeenth century would, as François Chevalier writes, "mark off for several centuries to come properties as big as states" (Chevalier, 184). By the early twentieth century the haciendas of Mexico had borne witness to several centuries of colonial rule, a period of military conflict and internal political strife in the nineteenth century, and a decade of revolutionary war. The ranchos that I visited outside Jerez, whose battered colonial buildings once formed the structures of the haciendas that had dominated the region, offered material evidence of my family's presence in this epochal history.

My grandfather, his daughter (my aunt) Esther Doran, and I traveled to the towns of Tesorero, Víboras, and Esperanza, former livestock haciendas where my grandparents and other relatives lived until the revolution displaced them in 1915. As I detail in chapter 5, my family had constructed its narrative of origins from my grandfather's memory of his father, Juan Lira Pérez, and it was set in the space of Tesorero and other haciendas near Jerez. Before the revolution, when the Tesorero hacienda was a functioning ranch, my great-grandfather had worked there as a bookkeeper and mana-

My grandfather, Aunt Esther, and myself in the city of Zacatecas, 1990.

ger, and he had worked in similar capacities at other local haciendas. His ancestors, according to my grandfather, had helped found the frontier town of Zacatecas in the late sixteenth century.

As we approached Tesorero, the taxi driver asked us why we wished to visit isolated ranching *pueblos* (towns). He was surprised to learn that my grandfather was a son of Jerez whose father had worked for four decades at the haciendas that predated the towns. As he waited in his car, we walked to a tall gate and peered into the property that had been Tesorero. The materiality of the colonial buildings, many standing since the revolutionary era, evoked for me the weight of the Mexican past. My ancestors had been displaced from here when the first phase of the Mexican revolution overturned the hacienda social economy. My grandfather, now in his eighties, was a child when he last saw this location. In 1913 his father had fled with his young son as local insurgents targeted the haciendas where he worked. And yet, the stone buildings at Tesorero could not dissipate the omissions in my own family's narrative of origins. Ancient and impenetrable, the buildings at Tesorero thus serve as a metaphor for the ambiguity of early Mexican (American) history as it will be explored in ensuing chapters. As Michel-Rolph Trouillot comments, "The bigger the material mass, the more easily it entraps us: mass graves and pyramids bring history closer while they make us feel small. A castle, a fort, a battlefield, a church, all these things bigger than we that we infuse with the reality of past lives, seem to speak of an immensity of which we know little except that we are part of it. Too solid to be unmarked, too conspicuous to be candid, they embody the ambiguities of history. They give us the power to touch it, but not that to hold it firmly in our hands—hence the mystery of their battered walls. We suspect that their concreteness hides secrets so deep that no revelation may fully dissipate their silences. We imagine the lives under the mortar, but how do we recognize the end of a bottomless silence?" (Trouillot, 29–30).

Apart from the material symbols of the past, people also embody the ambiguity of history—the immediacy and mystery of the remembered past as described above by Trouillot. Doña Guadalupe Inguanzo, my grandmother's cousin whom we met in the city of Zacatecas, is one among many people I encountered during my trip whose stories reflected this ambiguity. As we rested at our hotel, my aunt informed me that she would try to locate Lupe by telephone, using directory assistance. I told her the chances of finding her were extremely remote: the last time anyone in our family had seen Lupe was in 1915! Fifteen minutes later, Esther returned to tell me that she had just spoken with Lupe and that we were expected at her home in an hour for dinner. Lupe's home was a ten-minute walk from our hotel, a few blocks from the foot of Cerro de la Bufa. She bore a strong resemblance to my grandmother, with large brown eyes set in a face with striking Indian features. In her family photographs were images I had seen in my own grandmother's photo album.

Although none of us had met her before, Lupe embraced us as kin when she learned of our relation. To her, it seems, we were lost relatives who had made our way back to our *real* home after a long journey. As we ate, the shadow of La Bufa fell through a kitchen window. Lupe recounted stories set in the time of the revolution, including the day her teenage cousins, my grandmother and her sisters, left town in a carriage, never to return. A cloud of dust created by the carriage had imprinted itself in Lupe's mind as an image of the loss of her childhood friends and family on that day. When she asked us which tourist sites in town we had visited, I pointed to La Bufa and mentioned the statues. With the innocence of an elderly storyteller whose familiarity with the past annuls the pitfalls of memory—to whom, as William Faulkner wrote, "all the past is not a diminishing road but, instead, a huge meadow which no winter ever quite touches"—Lupe told us that the Inguanzos were *familia* to Gen. Pánfilo Natera and that we also, therefore, were related to one of the famous generals on the mountain.[1] I do not recall the details of the relation, nor do I know whether the tale could possibly be true. The story was all that mattered now.

Scholarship on the early history of Zacatecas fills in my sketch of the origins of the city and its subsequent development of a ranching industry founded on the hacienda mode of production. As Semo explains, "On September 8, [1546], a small detachment of Spanish soldiers, headed by Juan Tolosa, discovered the deposits of Cerro de la Bufa. The exploitation of these deposits, carried out under very difficult conditions . . . quickly fulfilled all expectations" (Semo, 73). King Philip II granted the mining town of Zacatecas the title of "city" on October 17, 1585. Three years later, the king and the Council of the Indies added to this official title the words "noble and loyal" and granted the city a coat of arms. As stated in the royal enactment, the inhabitants of Zacatecas had "served [the King] with faithfulness and care, and defended the city from the Chichimeca Indians . . . as well as [serving] through the benefits accorded by the silver mines on its outskirts, from which have been, and continue to be derived much wealth" (J. Flores Olague et al., 90 [my translation]). By the turn of the seventeenth century, Zacatecas had become the third largest city in the country. A 1620 account mentions "more than 1,000 European families, and a total of 40,000 inhabitants; the city [also] had 25 large *haciendas de beneficio* (livestock haciendas)" (Semo, 73). And yet, as Semo underscores, the region's resources were, in the same era, already dominated by an emergent landed elite. As he explains, "The handful of Basques who embarked on the risky exploitation of the Bufa mine represented the beginnings of a silver aristocracy who appropriated virtually all of the North's resources. Within a few years [after the founding of the mines], they owned large agricultural and cattle properties and commercial and mining enterprises, and they financed, with their own means, expeditions of discovery and conquest" (74).

During the eighteenth century the hacienda system in Zacatecas underwent a period of consolidation. In the late seventeenth century property owners linked to the silver aristocracy took advantage of new laws passed by the Spanish Crown to acquire lands that belonged to Indians. These laws "were a means of justifying the growth and development of large areas of land, confining Indians to smaller and smaller space, and controlling [Indians] economically and socially—along with castes and *mestizos*—so that they would not be able to acquire more land" (J. Flores Olague et al., 88). As a result of these laws, the Indian population became "condemned to dependency on the agrarian structure determined by the hacienda [system], which as it grew increasingly stronger converted them into peons, renters, and later, tenant farmers and salaried laborers" (88–89).[2] By justifying abuses against Indians and lower-class *mestizos* and specifically allowing the occupation of their lands, the laws thus contributed to the formation and expansion of the semifeudalistic hacienda system that lasted in Zacatecas, as in many other regions of Mexico, into the twentieth century. As a host of scholars of have indicated, land policy under the Porfirio Díaz regime (1876–1911) aggravated the hacienda system's social iniquities that had been inherited from the eighteenth century and earlier. In light of these injustices, as Jan Bazant observes in his history of Mexico, on the eve of civil war in 1910 throughout most of the republic "the idea that the existing system of land tenure and agriculture was not satisfactory had been accepted by most responsible Mexicans" (Bazant, 126). The explosion of the military phase of the Mexican Revolution in 1913 thus marked the end of the era of the "great hacienda."

COLONIZATION AND SETTLEMENT ON THE SPANISH FRONTIER

The colonization of Texas and California reveals how the process of conquest and settlement unfolded in much of the Spanish frontier—the colonial region that now encompasses the contemporary Southwest in the United States. The first Spanish incursion into Texas at the end of the seventeenth century was driven by geopolitics as well as the hope of discovering mines like those found in Zacatecas more than a century earlier. Beginning in the late 1600s, the Spanish outposts in eastern Texas blocked the threat posed by the French, whose Louisiana colony bordered New Spain's northeastern province. Similarly, the six thousand colonists whom José de Escandón led to Nuevo Santander between 1749 and 1755 were sent to a region whose settlement would prevent England from seizing a stretch of unpopulated Gulf coast during the War of Jenkins' Ear (Weber, *Spanish Frontier*, 194). Twenty years after the first expedition to Nuevo Santander, Spain, again impelled by global politics, promoted the colonization of Alta California to protect the silver mines of Zacatecas from a feared Russian or English advance (Hackel, 117).

Under the Laws of the Indies, all provincial lands occupied by Spanish settlers belonged to the Crown and were awarded in the form of grants or concessions either to institutions, such as missions and pueblos, or to individuals. In order to establish civilian communities near the new missions and *presidios* (forts), the Crown gave pueblo grants to groups of settlers. Although pueblo grants in Nuevo Santander varied in size, by 1755 these concessions had resulted in the establishment of twenty-three towns, two of which were on the north bank of the Rio Grande, at Camargo (1749) and Reynosa (1749), the first Spanish pueblos within present-day South Texas. By 1755, four other towns had been founded north of the river boundary: Revilla (1750), Dolores (1750), Mier (1753), and Laredo (1755) (Alonzo, 29–32). In Alta California each pueblo grant embraced a tract of four square leagues (*sitios*), the equivalent of 17,712 acres. Designed in part to reduce the military's dependence on the missions, pueblo communities were founded at San José (1777), Los Angeles (1781), and the Villa de Branciforte (1797) (Hackel, 117).

Mission grants played divergent roles in the development of ranching society in South Texas and Alta California. Whereas in South Texas land grants to individuals formed the basis of ranch society, in Alta California ranches were established on mission lands acquired by settlers following the Secularization Act of 1833. This difference reflects the relative failure of the mission system to extend its influence in Nuevo Santander (Weber, *Spanish Frontier*, 121). Although twenty-one missions had been established there by 1755, with four north of the Rio Grande (at Camargo, Mier, Revilla, and Reynosa), by 1772 only nine missions still existed in the province, two of which were located on the Rio Grande (Alonzo, 53). By contrast, mission lands in Alta California would encompass most of the approximately 14 million of acres of arable lands and for more than fifty years constitute the heart of the colonial economy of the region. Claiming the grazing lands along the coast, in the late eighteenth and early nineteenth centuries missionaries from New Spain established a chain of twenty-one missions from present-day San Diego to San Francisco (Hackel, 116). Larger than other land grants, mission grants in Alta California averaged 133,000 acres, though a few encompassed more than a million acres. Following the secularization of the missions, an event that Californio pioneer Mariano Guadalupe Vallejo helped to broker, mission lands were transferred to individual settlers, forming the privately owned hacienda and ranching enterprises that dominated the region until the end of the Mexican era.[3]

Prior to 1848 Spain and Mexico awarded more than 350 land grants in the Lower Valley of Texas, all of which were "given to individuals, with some persons receiving multiple grants" (Alonzo, 264). Although Escandón himself "had not given individual land titles to the colonists who held the lands in common," two of the original pueblos in South Texas were founded by *hacendados*, prominent ranchers with either possession of or rights to extensive landholdings in the form of haciendas. Having established a ranch settlement at Dolores in 1750, Don José Vásquez Borrego "obtained from Escandón rights to approximately 329,000 acres" in present-day Webb and Zapata Counties in South Texas, and his herds "numbered 3,000 cattle, 3,400 horses and 2,650 mules and donkeys" (30–31). One of the founders of Laredo, Blas María de la Garza Falcón, who was descended from a powerful ranching family, played an important role in the early history of South Texas. Although the Garza Falcón family was later displaced by their rivals, which may have contributed to their immigration to the Lower Rio Grande Valley, in the 1740s the Garza Falcóns "had amassed about 457,160 acres of mostly ranching lands" in the current South Texas border region. According to Armando Alonzo, "Their vast holdings consisted of a *hacienda* on each side of the [Rio Grande] river" (32–33). If the mythic *ranchero* historical patrimony described in the prologue (which is labeled "foreword") to González and Raleigh's novel *Caballero* is an indication, it was precisely this hacienda heritage with which the Texas novelist and educator González identified.[4]

Just before the U.S-Mexican War South Texas consisted of "individual properties of the descendants of Escandón's colony and new arrivals from nearby districts in northern New Spain and later Mexico" (Alonzo, 264). The size of these grants ranged from smaller tracts of approximately two square leagues (8,856 acres)—all of which were located along the Rio Grande—to intermediate-size grants of two to four square leagues (8,856 to 17,712 acres), to large grants of five or more square leagues (22,140 acres and up). The large grants "were intended to support *hacienda*-type ranching enterprises involving *ganado de mayor* [bovine cattle, horses and mules]" (39).[5] Between 1757 and 1794, as "unoccupied lands north and east of the Rio Grande towns attracted the attention of the growing population of new *pobladores* whose herds were multiplying at a rapid pace," Spanish officials "granted extensive tracts for stockraising to the citizens of Camargo and Reynosa" (55). Like some of the early grants, a number of these grants were comparable in size to the great estates established between 1834 and 1846 in Alta California by such families as the Vallejos and Carrillos. Between 1778 and 1794, as Armando Alonzo explains, the Hinojosas and Ballís, two ranching families linked by marriage, acquired three grants north of the Rio Grande. These properties measured twenty-five leagues (110,700 acres), thirty-five leagues (154,980 acres), and seventy-two leagues (318,816 acres). "Before the eighteenth century came to an end," notes Alonzo, "a large number of tracts north of the Rio Grande had [similarly] been granted to leading residents of Reynosa and the other river towns" (58).

In Alta California land grants to individuals were of two types: those given prior to 1822 by the Crown and those given between 1822 and 1846 by the Mexican government. During the colonial era only thirty-four such grants were distributed in Alta California. By contrast, with almost eight hundred land grants to individuals approved after the Secularization Act went into effect, by 1840 "the private rancho had replaced the mission as the dominant social and economic institution in California" (Hackel, 132). The size of land grants made after secularization ranged from under ten thousand to several hundred thousand acres.[6] Regional allegiances and political favoritism among anticlerical families determined the process by which, within a span of thirteen years, millions of acres of mission ranching land were sold to the descendants of Californio settlers. As one of the leaders of the secularization movement, Vallejo voiced the argument made by anticlerical Californios who opposed mission control of ranching lands. Citing comments by José María de Echeandía, the former governor of the province, Vallejo points out in his "Historical and Personal Memoirs" that prior to the Secularization Act, "twenty-one mission establishments possessed all the fertile lands of the peninsula . . . and that more than a thousand families of *gente de razón* [people of reason/culture] possessed only that which has been benevolently given them by the missionaries" (M. Vallejo, 2:88).[7]

Following secularization, the politically well-positioned Vallejos and Carrillos each acquired tens of thousands of acres of land, in the north and south, respectively, on which they would establish a number of livestock haciendas.[8] They were among the approximately two hundred Californio families who in 1849 owned the majority of the 14 million acres of arable land in the state (Pitt, 86).[9] In "Historical and Personal Memoirs," Vallejo distinguishes the "haciendas" owned by these families from the many smaller ranchos that also existed there during the Mexican era. He lists the names of some of these California haciendas—"Buriburi, San Antonio, Pinole, San Pablo, Napa, Santa Teresa, Petaluma, Pulgas"— and provides a brief description of these estates. Hacienda buildings, he explains, "were sumptuous": in addition to the main house, they "had a house for the servants . . . a room given over exclusively to the storing of field tools, another for the storage of fresh milk and cheese, and another in which was accumulated tallow and grease" (M. Vallejo, 3:256). Suggesting hacienda society's semifeudal features and seigneurial ethos (described in the next section), Vallejo continues, writing that each hacienda "had thousands of head of cattle and countless bands of mares. Some . . . had more than a hundred Indian servants, to say nothing of the overseers, who were white men. At all the haciendas there were rooms for the accommodation of strangers, they being accorded very good treatment without any remuneration whatsoever being demanded of them" (3:259). Although author María Amparo Ruiz de Burton owned a smaller hacienda property than that of either the Vallejos or actor Leo Carrillo's family, her portrait of the hacienda in *The Squatter and the Don*, as will be discussed in chapter 2, closely resembles Vallejo's above description. Ruiz de Burton arrived in Alta California from her native Baja California in 1848, after the postsecularization land grab, having moved at the end of the U.S.-Mexican War. Her approximately ten-thousand-acre Rancho Jamul, situated east of San Diego, was originally part of a Mexican land grant given to members of the powerful Pico family just before the onset of the war. Much like the struggle faced by the Vallejos and Carrillos after Alta California was incorporated into the United States, Ruiz de Burton's efforts between 1870 and 1890 to prove legal entitlement to her land, as recounted in striking detail in *The Squatter and the Don*, was complicated by the difficulty of validating the original grant that had been given to the Picos several decades earlier.

THE HACIENDA SOCIAL ORDER

In early Mexican American narratives the hacienda embodies what has been lost through war, displacement, and/or conquest. Criticism of U.S. dominance converges in these works with strategies that project the claims of (hacienda) community, whose attributes (e.g., cohesiveness, order, stability, interdependence, honor, etc.) mask its organization of social types along class, racial, and gender lines (Romine, 6–7). The social injustices suffered by the Mexican (American) population merge in hacienda texts with a conception of the hacienda as an organic community in such a way that the two themes become almost interdependent.[10] Historical scholarship on the hacienda sheds light on how these narratives obscure the internal social workings of this semifeudal agrarian institution even as they create from it an enabling Mexican (American) historical (ethnic) subjectivity.

The hacienda was a complex and highly adaptive social institution that developed unevenly in disparate regions of Mexico and the Mexican (American) Southwest over a span of more than three centuries. Although the body of research on this institution points to a "feudal" origin, for decades historians have debated this designation, disagreeing over whether the hacienda possessed a uniform character, as suggested by the term "feudal." Historians also debate whether a concept drawn from European history can capture the complexity of hacienda society in Mexico over a span of several centuries (Miller, 230). The shifting definition of the hacienda in scholarship focused on Mexico, as opposed to the Mexican (American) Southwest, may be summarized as a move away from a view of the hacienda as rigidly "feudal" to one that portrays it as displaying the hybrid features of a traditional institution reacting to new commercial (i.e., capitalist) circumstances. François Chevalier, whose foundational study "brought the great hacienda down from the level of abstraction to that of historical reality," established the feudal nature of the great hacienda as it existed in northern New Spain (Young, 9). Semo, reflecting revisionist scholarship, offers a more complex portrait of an adaptive institution that from the seventeenth through the nineteenth centuries was alternately feudalistic (autarkic) and commercial (mercantile/capitalist), depending on fluctuations in the market.[11] Agreeing with Semo, Simon Miller notes that "[f]ar from being a 'feudal' anachronism of artificial and foreign origins," the Mexican hacienda "was in fact a dynamic and appropriate adaptation . . . and capable of significant capital accumulation" (Miller, 263). Although similar disagreements about the internal character of the hacienda can be

31

found in the scholarship on early Spanish and Mexican ranch society in the southwestern United States, both bodies of scholarship generally concur that hacienda society exhibited semifeudal characteristics.[12] Historians of both regions point to the hacienda's paternalistic social organization and its system of debt peonage as being this institution's most prominent features.

Despite the range of variation in hacienda society observed by historians, in scholarship beginning with Chevalier the patriarchal nature of its social relations draws the traditional hacienda and the feudal European manor together onto common ground (Young, 21). This parallel reflects the scholarly view of hacienda society as hierarchical and oppressive, as the brutal imposition of the Spanish conquerors, a model which implied that the Conquest had "granted the landlord class a monopoly of the land, which in turn had reduced the indigenous peasantry to an indebted peonage, eternally subject to the lord's domination" (Miller, 230). This parallel also suggests the revisionist view that if the traditional hacienda—unlike the European manor—was economically capitalist (or pre-capitalist), it was nevertheless socially feudal (Young, 21). Despite its pre-capitalist character, "[t]he hierarchical and paternalistic social organization of the traditional hacienda, its function as a surrogate community, the mediating role of the patrón vis à vis the outside world, and the affective bonds and loyalty that often bound estate populations together all strongly summon up the image of European preindustrial communities on the land" (Young, 21).

Historians similarly identify paternalism and patriarchalism as key structural features of early Spanish and Mexican ranch society in Texas and California. In his study of Anglo-Mexican relations in the formation of Texas, David Montejano describes early Mexican ranch society in the Texas-Mexican border region as hierarchical and stratified, with a landowning elite "in command of the Mexican communities" (Montejano, 34). Emphasizing the rigid class character of early Mexican settlements, Montejano points out that they were "essentially a three-tiered society composed of landed elite, small landowners (rancheros) and peones" (35). Within this society relations between landowner, or *patrón*, and peon were marked by paternalism, an affective bond of reciprocal obligations between the two without which the social hierarchy could not have been maintained. As in hacienda society elsewhere in Mexico since the seventeenth century, in this relationship the *patrón* was regarded as the "protector, counselor, judge, and dispenser of favors and material rewards," while the *peones* or peons "constituted the loyal work force" (110). The "reciprocal" work arrangement in essence provided the social basis for "loyal workers . . . and an 'organic' understanding of [their] social standing" in relation to their *patrón* (253). And since "owner-worker relations were formal and anonymous," Montejano concludes, "explicit controls by the elite were unnecessary" (253). Historians of Mexican California similarly portray its ranch society as quasifeudal, both hierarchical in the sense that each rancho or hacienda was controlled by a dominant family and patriarchal in that paternalism defined social relations between landowners, vaqueros, and peons.

The concept of seigneurialism has been employed to describe the feudalistic character of the California hacienda during the era of ranching families such as the Vallejos and Carrillos. This term denotes both the quasifeudal nature of this highly class-structured society as well as its paternalistic social relations. Much like scholars of the Mexican hacienda who use the term "feudal" with qualifications, Douglas Monroy argues that in the eighteenth and nineteenth centuries a set of economic and social relations existed in California that "cannot be categorized usefully and accurately as feudal, slave, or capitalist" (Monroy, 102). Although chattel slavery was not practiced in Spanish and Mexican California—that is, Indians were not bought and sold and technically were free to come and go—Monroy's model indicates the striking similarities between the Mexican hacienda and the plantation of the U.S. South. In both systems, landowners possessed a pre-bourgeois "seigneurial" worldview. They did not seek wealth or profit for its own sake but instead valued their land and laborers (slaves in the South and peons in California) as social and cultural capital, a mark of honor that confirmed their social status. Membership in the ruling class took precedence over the accumulation of capital. Accordingly, the *hacendado* and planter did not view the world in capitalist terms such as gain, thrift, or the exploitation of labor. Rather, they interpreted their world through the pre-modern ethos of paternalism. The worldview of Californio culture thus differed fundamentally from that of the Americans who flooded into the region during the Gold Rush and after. Whereas within Californio culture status, honor, reputation, and kinship were interdependent, in U.S. culture social status was determined by an individual's ability to accumulate wealth and property. As in the slave South, in Californio culture, by contrast, "the amount of honor one had made a reputation, not the amount of money" (Monroy, *Thrown among Strangers*, 139). Each Californio therefore "produced only enough wealth for an ostentatious life-style that would establish his social position" by allowing him—within the limits of the hacienda social hierarchy—to "act graciously, honorably, and generously" (100, 139–40).

As in the hacienda system throughout Greater Mexico, in Alta California after secularization a relationship of mutual and personal dependency with the *patrón* attached the laborers to the rancho (Monroy, *Thrown among Strangers,* 102). Owing to traditions of kinship and mutual obligation, the relationship between the Californio landowner and the laborers, as Monroy remarks, was "as personal as it was hierarchical and binding" (100). Although ranchero families such as the Vallejos and Carrillos possessed near-feudal fiefs encompassing up to several hundred thousand acres, an easy familiarity between landowners and peons "may well have characterized much of their day-to-day relationship, given their powerful mutual dependence, in spite of the vast difference in social position. . . . This situation not only suited the labor needs of the [landowners] but made them feel more confident about their socially ascendant selves as well" (154). However contradictory and exploitative, given the laborers' powerlessness within the social hierarchy, the sense of reciprocity between rancheros and their laborers formed the basis of seigneurialism. José Manuel Salvador Vallejo, Mariano's younger brother, captures this seigneurial relationship in his own autobiographical narrative, "Notas históricas sobre California" [Historical Notes on California] (1874): "Our friendly Indians were missed very much, for they tilled our soil, pastured our cattle, sheared our sheep, cut our lumber, built our houses, paddled our boats, made tiles for our homes, ground our grain, killed our cattle and dressed their hides for market, and made our burnt bricks, while the Indian women made excellent servants, took good care of our children, [and] made every one of our meals. . . . These people we considered members of our families; we loved them and they loved us; our intercourse was always pleasant; the Indians knew that our superior education gave us a right to command and rule over them."[13]

As this passage announces, the affective "bond" between laborers and *patrónes* always served the economic and political interests of the latter. But, as will be expounded in chapter 2, it also structured Californio seigneurial-based opposition to (U.S.) capitalism and the intrusion of "modernity" into semifeudal Mexican society.

As in Greater Mexico at large, in Alta California the paternalistic relationship that defined ranch society existed amid profound social contradictions (Young, 21). As the Indians' subjugated status indicates, in Alta California "[t]he Indian servants were very much attached to the hacienda families, but not because of affection. Rather, after the unraveling of their old way of life and the thorough intrusion on their lands the Indians had no choice but to bind themselves to the ranchos. . . . In this personal and seigneurial relationship the patrón took care of his charges' fractured needs for subsistence" (Monroy, *Thrown among Strangers,* 154). The seigneurial bond of reciprocity, moreover, served not only as a means of keeping hacienda laborers consenting to their exploitation; it was also a strategy that protected Californio ranchers from the prospect of rebellion by thousands of Indian warriors (Sánchez, *Telling Identities,* 172). José Manuel Salvador Vallejo confirms that, although the Californios were "guided by the teachings of the good missionaries," they were also "counseled by our forlorn position that made it very plain that in case of a general uprising of the Indians we could not cope with them." Hence Californio rancheros "always did our best to strengthen the bond of friendship that bound the two races together."[14]

Semo points to the revolutionary role that the hacienda and its representatives played in bringing to an end the rule of the Spanish Crown and the vice-regal bureaucracy in the early nineteenth century.[15] But he also notes that the new lords of the Mexican countryside represented an oligarchy whose interests were tied to a quasifeudal mode of production dependent on debt peonage—that is, the system of incurred debt by which landowners controlled the labor supply, consigning generations of hacienda peons to a form of coerced servitude. Since the "revolution" of 1810–21 did not mark the victory of capitalist trends, argues Semo, it did not create the conditions necessary for the transformation of Mexican peons on haciendas into semi-free wage workers. To the contrary, the "revolution" led "to the consolidation of ties of direct extraeconomic coercion between the Indian laborer as an individual and the landowner, ties that were more immune from community or state intervention" than under earlier colonial rule (Semo, 133). This portrait of hacienda society as near-feudal in terms of *hacendado* dominion, with a culture of coercion-cum-paternalism, continues to frame analysis of the Mexican hacienda even as revisionist scholars have refined it to account for the enormous range of variations in the agrarian economy (Miller, 231).

Scholarship on the early history of the Mexican (American) Southwest similarly establishes debt peonage as a defining feature of the agrarian social order.[16] David J. Weber shows that following Mexican independence in this region a number of factors strengthened the institution of debt peonage, including "the influx of capital, its concentration in the hands of a few, and the demand for labor stimulated by the vitality of the economy of the frontier" (Weber, *Mexican Frontier*, 211). Yet, as in Mexico, the character of debt peonage was inconsistent in the Mexican (American) Southwest. Montejano's description of debt peonage in the Texas-Mexican border region provides a case in point. Some historians believe that in this region "peons were reduced to slavery by misery, idleness, or gambling" and that their condition was not hereditary and seldom lasted a lifetime (Montejano, 80): "Sometimes peonage appeared to be the desire of the employer, sometimes that of the employee; and sometimes only the paternalistic shell of peonage remained in practice." This work mechanism, states Montejano, "continued in force long after the mechanism of debt had been effectively discarded" (56). Montejano concludes that the "power of precedent and sedimented tradition was sufficient to keep the character of peon-patrón relations—essentially, labor relations circumscribed by paternalism, reciprocal obligations, and permanency—in place. The sense of belonging to a ranch was another important feature of this relationship" (82).

Peonage was most evident in California, where the newly secularized missions offered rancheros and urban dwellers a windfall of cheap Indian labor (Weber, *Mexican Frontier*, 211). Without the protection of the missionaries, Weber explains, "many former mission Indians fell easily into a system whereby *californios* advanced them goods, money, or liquor, then required them to work to repay their debts." This situation meant that although Indian and Mexican peons in Alta California "were legally free . . . in practice their movement was controlled by the *hacendado* on the basis of debts incurred" (Weber, *Mexican Frontier*, 211). Other scholars similarly underscore the precarious status of Indian laborers in Alta California, describing a harsh system of debt peonage akin to what existed in the hacienda system in the rest of Mexico at the time. While peons were producers, observes Rosaura Sánchez, "the *hacendados* owned the land, the tools, and the animals, and controlled surplus production." Indian and *mestizo* peons hence "became subservient to patriarchal families within the hacienda system, and . . . patriarchal practices provided the exploited and overworked peons with no more than subsistence for their labor" (Sánchez, *Telling Identities*, 54). Confirming the consistent presence of debt peonage in Alta California, Sánchez concludes that the Californio social order "was not an idyllic 'pastoral' society" but rather a "labor-intensive . . . economy with a largely 'unfree' labor force made up of Indian men and women whose ancestors had lived on those lands for generations" (168).

MODERNITY AND THE DECLINE OF MEXICAN (AMERICAN) AGRARIAN SOCIETY

The mine at Cerro de la Bufa, the statues above it, and the hacienda at Tesorero, among other sites that I visited during my trip to Zacatecas, evoked for me the weight of the Mexican past—both its immediacy and ambiguity.[17] Yet the journey itself, to a region from which my grandfather had emigrated as a boy, registered the legacy of that convulsive transformation of Mexican (agrarian) society by the forces of modernity in the late nineteenth and early twentieth centuries. As a participant in the migration of an estimated 1 million Mexicans to the United States between 1900 and 1930, my grandfather's status in Mexico on the eve of his departure was determined by sweeping socioeconomic and political processes linked to global forces identified with the project of modernity.

The transition to modernity in the United States was marked by accelerated social, economic, and cultural change. The terms used to designate this transition—industrialization, the rise of industrial capitalism, urbanization, rationalization, mechanization, bureaucratization, modernization—all suggest the profound socioeconomic upheaval that heralded the advent of the modern age (Marx, 37). Among the effects of modernity, according to Stuart Hall, were the "decline of the traditional social order, with its fixed social hierarchies and religious world-view . . . and the rise of a secular and materialist culture, exhibiting individualistic, rationalist, and instrumentalist impulses" (S. Hall, "Introduction: Formations of Modernity," 5). This process necessarily involved the "redefinition and reinvention of society and self as earlier social rubrics [were] stretched beyond their capacity to recognize, organize, and map emerging relations" (R. Flores, *Remembering the Alamo*, 2). With the rise of the United States to hemispheric dominance in the nineteenth and early twentieth centuries, the forces of modernity—of which capitalism is a primary engine—irrevocably transformed Mexico and the Mexican (American) Southwest. The U.S. seizure of the vast northern territories of Mexico following the U.S.-Mexican War was but one example of many acts of interference in and open aggression toward the old Spanish empire by the industrializing world in the modern era (Robbins, 22).

Despite variations in the effects of modernization in Greater Mexico, taken together the three regions that form the geographic locus of the hacienda narratives discussed in this study illustrate the epochal social transformation that occurred throughout this region in the late nineteenth and early twentieth centuries. In Mexico, Texas, and California the socioeconomic processes identified with modernity brought an end to the agrarian ranch society that had dominated these regions since the colonial era. In Mexico, modernization under the Díaz dictatorship exacerbated the social contradictions of the hacienda system, leading to the onset of a civil war and revolution that toppled the old agrarian order.[18] In Texas and California the Mexican ranch system was displaced through both the fraudulent confiscation of Mexican land by European American settlers and the "more efficient mechanism of market competition" (Montejano, 50). In these regions, as in the western frontier at large, industrial capitalism expanded its sphere of influence following the Civil War, leading to the eclipse of Mexican agrarian society. William G. Robbins describes the processes associated with U.S. industrial capitalism in the U.S. West during this period as "(1) diverse and ever-expanding forms of technology in transportation, communication, agriculture, mining, and lumbering; (2) the emergence of the labor question in the more industrialized sectors; (3) the appearance of sizable ethnic enclaves in virtually every industrial enterprise; and (4) the progressive incorporation and consolidation of the western business world" (Robbins, 85–86).

These developments led not only to the decline of the Mexican ranch economy but also, as Robbins suggests in his third point above, to the proletarianization of much of this region's Mexican (American) population. In the late nineteenth and early twentieth centuries Mexican Americans—most of whom had lived within the structure of a traditional agrarian social order—were incorporated as wage laborers into the U.S. Southwest's commercial agricultural system. With few regional exceptions, by the end of the twentieth century modernization created the economic and political circumstances that led also to the dispossession of the landed Mexican elite of California and Texas. Although freed from the old agrarian order, Mexican (Americans) were plunged into a capitalist world whose market ethos was underwritten in the U.S. Southwest by ideologies of racial and ethnic intolerance that constructed Mexican subjectivity as "subjugated Otherness" (R. Flores, *Remembering the Alamo*, 157, 11).

Díaz has come to personify the contradictions inherent in the project of modernity in Latin America. He seized power in 1876 with the intention of creating in Mexico the spectacular economic and political success of the United States. Led by a group of positivist advisors known as the *científicos* (men of science), the Díaz regime sought to establish a modern nation-state in an overwhelmingly rural society through economic development "based on dictatorial control, a continuing flow of foreign capital, and foreign colonization" (Hart, 437). In its first fifteen years of power, as John Mason Hart explains, the Díaz regime "removed restraints on trade, privatized rural community landholding, brought independent unions under government control, [and] recruited foreign investment to improve industry and technology" (436). Transforming Mexico into a unified nation-state required an assault on traditional social relations. Among the goals of Porfirian modernization, therefore, was the replacement of "traditional [agrarian] society based on local loyalties and forms of knowledge with a modern one grounded in universal, abstract notions of time and space shared by all its members" (Buffington and French, 401).

Despite its stated objectives, Porfirian modernization created a social structure that combined semifeudal and capitalist features. This contradiction was most evident in rural Mexico, where the privatization of land and foreign speculation aggravated the feudal character of the hacienda system, magnifying its longstanding social contradictions and abuses and contributing to the outbreak of war. According to Fernando Henrique Cardoso and Enzo Faletto, because the hacienda system remained the most effective means of keeping the peasant population submissive, Díaz needed to maintain the oligarchy that controlled it (Cardoso and Faletto, 107). Given these circumstances, on the eve of civil war in 1910 the feudal character of the hacienda social order in Mexico was indisputable. In that year, as Michael C. Meyer and William L. Sherman comment, the Mexican census listed 8,245 haciendas in the republic, but a few wealthy families, often tied together by a marriage, "owned ten, fifteen, or even twenty of them . . . [so that] fifteen of the richest *hacendados* owned haciendas totaling more than three hundred thousand acres each" (Meyer and Sherman, 458–59). In the state of Chihuahua, to cite the most egregious instance of land accumulation under the Díaz regime, Don Luis Terrazas owned some fifty haciendas and ranches covering approximately 7 million acres—eight times the size of the legendary King Ranch in Texas (459). Chicano literary works that depict the rural origins of Mexican immigrants to the United States during the Díaz or revolutionary eras portray the brutality of the hacienda's semifeudal labor system. For example, in his autobiography *Barrio Boy*, Ernesto Galarza relates his Mexican rural community's cultural memory of the hacienda on the eve of the revolution: "Old men in the village talked of the time they had worked on a hacienda as if they had served a sentence in prison or on a chain gang. They remembered *capataces* [foremen] who had whipped them or cursed them fifty years before. . . . There were a hundred blood debts of this kind in [town] . . . thousands more of them in all the villages of the Sierra Madre, and millions in all the pueblos of Mexico" (Galarza, 59).

The sociohistorical processes that brought an end to the Porfirian hacienda in the late nineteenth and early twentieth centuries also transformed the Mexican (American) Southwest. South Texas history illustrates how socioeconomic processes linked to the global expansion of industrial capitalism during this period affected the region's Mexican agrarian societies. Richard Flores theorizes the project of modernity in South Texas in relation to the emergence of the Alamo as a cultural symbol. The Alamo as symbol emerged between 1880 and 1920, an era Flores calls the Texas Modern, when modern capitalism transformed the economy of the region, replacing "local" Mexican agricultural and cattle-related practices with large-scale commercial farming (R. Flores, *Remembering the Alamo*, 3). As Flores explains, "Developments in both the railroad and large-scale commercial agriculture were two activities that eroded the traditional, family-based, cattle ranching society of South Texas and reshaped it to the needs and logic of a market economy" (111). By the late nineteenth century, these processes led to an almost complete reversal in the fortunes of Mexican American landowners, a community whose ranching economy, as noted previously, had lasted since the Spanish colonial era (Alonzo, 256). In nearly all districts of the Lower Rio Grande Valley, the combined effects of modernization eroded the dominant position of these ranchers as livestock producers and majority landholders (256). Scholars hold differing views about the role the Mexican landed elite played in these processes and whether a "hacienda" economy like that which existed in Mexico in the same era still survived in South Texas.[19] But all agree that by the early twentieth century capitalist modernization and the hierarchical political and racial structures to which it gave rise had led to the loss of most Mexican (American) ranch lands in the Lower Rio Grande Valley, including both small and large landholdings. José E. Limón describes the effect of this loss as the "rapid transformation of a whole cultural mode of production." The racial subjugation of Mexicans that ensued was thus "the overt manifestation and ratification of the forced transformation of a whole way of life from the generally self-subsistent, vernacularly democratic, political cultural economy keyed on the Spanish language and face-to-face oral communication, to an increasingly mass capitalistic, cash crop agriculture . . . dominated mostly by Anglo-Americans, who controlled the political state apparatus" (Limón, *Mexican Ballads*, 26).

As Limón suggests, in South Texas the project of modernity resulted in the establishment of a class hierarchy structured along ethnic and racial lines. Flores's study reveals how the effects of modernity led in this region not to a model of classic capital-labor relations but rather to a situation much like colonialism, as racial segregation and ascriptive labor segmentation determined the subjugated status of Mexicans (R. Flores, *Remembering the Alamo*, 9). Discursive ideologies of racial and ethnic superiority and inferiority served the socioeconomic changes of the Texas Modern in such a way that the events of the era "[gave] birth to the Alamo while the Alamo as sign [shaped] Anglo-Mexican relations" (11). In short, according to Flores, the socioeconomic changes that took place during the Texas Modern were "made possible by the economic and social displacement" of the Mexican worker (5).[20] As this transformation occurred, "the construction of Mexican subjectivity as 'subjugated Otherness' [was] codified" (11). The cultural memory of the Alamo contributed to this codification, providing "semantic justification for slotting Mexicans and Anglos into an emerging social order brought forth by the material and ideological forces that gripped Texas between 1880 and 1920" (xvii).

If, as Flores argues, the Alamo serves as a "master symbol" of modernity in Texas and the West, the gold rush of 1848–49 served an analogous role in California, delineating a boundary dividing the modern capitalist (U.S.) era from the agrarian period of Mexican and Spanish rule. As the market revolution—that extraordinary economic and industrial transformation that took place in the northern United States during the first half of the nineteenth century—extended its influence into the West, the gold rush marked its arrival in California. Though the calamitous changes ushered in by modernity in California were not completed until the end of nineteenth century, these processes were introduced and established during the gold rush. As the primary engine driving the expansion of market capitalism, explosive population growth, the construction of new railway lines, the development of other forms of industry, and the establishment of U.S. political institutions, the gold rush transformed not only California but the entire western frontier. It also exemplifies the striking rapidity with which this transformation took place between 1825 and 1875. When the first transcontinental railroad was completed in 1869, as Robbins states, "the turbulent forces of an expanding capitalist economic system had wrought a vast continental empire whose productive capacity . . . would astonish the world." In the 1880s "the construction of the remaining transcontinental lines, the settlement of the interior, and the opening up to commercial exploitation of its great mineral wealth were . . . a kind of mopping up in establishing the contours of that new, spacious, but still colonial West" (Robbins, 12).

Though California possesses no geographically fixed "master symbol" of modernity analogous to the Alamo, as in Texas the effects of the expansion of industrial capitalism in this region were the dismantling of traditional Mexican society and its reorganization under a market-based capitalist economic system. The gold rush symbolizes the striking swiftness with which these processes led to the dispossession of Mexican *rancheros* in California and the demise of their agrarian society. Historians such as Leonard Pitt, Mario García, Tomás Almaguer, Albert Camarrillo, and more recently Douglas Monroy and Carlos G. Vélez-Ibáñez have documented the late-nineteenth-century transformation of Californio society that the gold rush set in motion. This process was radically accelerated by the influx of hundreds of thousands of gold-seekers within just a few years, compressing a socioeconomic and political transformation that in Texas took comparatively longer—perhaps because in South Texas the population was, as it remains today, predominantly Mexican American. By contrast, although the Spanish-speaking population had a numerical majority in the south of California until the 1870s, five years after the discovery of gold 300,000 new residents had arrived in a region whose Mexican population had numbered roughly 13,000 in 1848 (Pitt, 131). During the immigration boom of the 1880s the population of Los Angeles increased by 500 percent in two years or so, transforming the electorate into an Anglo American one (274). And yet, as noted previously, in the "antediluvian" days before 1848, as in Mexico before the revolution, the land tenure system in Alta California under Mexican rule exhibited great inequities. With an estimated 200 Californio families owning 14 million acres of land, prominent families such as the Vallejos, Picos, and Carrillos accumulated ranchos encompassing up to hundreds of thousands of acres.

The changes wrought by the gold rush were devastating for the landed Mexican elite, resulting in the piecemeal loss of most of their privately held lands between 1849 and 1880 (Almaguer, 47). But whether the Mexican Californians were former landowners, *mestizos, criollos* (white descendants of early Spanish settlers), or Indians, the restructuring of California during this era "signaled a double shift from ranchos to cities and towns and from property owners to wage labor. This occupational shift or proletarianization meant manual labor in cities and towns and sometimes on farms" (Sánchez, *Telling Identities*, 281). Despite variations in Anglo-Mexican relations in the decades following the gold rush, the project of modernity, having led to the economic collapse of the Californio *ranchero* class, resulted in a class hierarchy in California structured broadly along ethnic and racial lines. By the 1880s, when the majority of Mexican Americans had been integrated as laborers into the new market economy, ethnic and racial relations had developed within the rigid limits of the new class hierarchy. And yet, as Almaguer notes, in California during this era class status mediated social relations between Mexican Americans and European Americans. Almaguer draws a distinction between the "modest structural integration" of the children of the *ranchero* class during this period and the "unassimilable" status of the largely *mestizo* Mexican working class (Almaguer, 65).

Although Mexican Americans faced a class and racial hierarchy that bore a strong resemblance to the Texas model, the demographic shift created by the gold rush and subsequent U.S. immigration to the region in the late nineteenth century highlights a distinction between Mexican American history in California and Texas. In 1850 Mexicans made up only 11 percent of California's total population. But with the arrival of successive waves of immigrants after 1860, by 1900 Mexicans accounted for no more than 1 or 2 percent of the state's population and were numerically surpassed by this time by the Chinese and Native American populations (Almaguer, 70–71). As in Texas, modernity in California resulted in the loss of ranching lands and the consequent transformation of an established "cultural mode of production." But, in contrast to Texas, in California it also led to the near total demographic displacement of Mexican Americans.[21]

Remembering the Hacienda as Frontier Idyll

As the forces of modernity in the late nineteenth and early twentieth centuries eroded the Mexican American Southwest's agrarian social economy, a flood of writings, artwork, architecture, and other cultural products appeared that mythologized the region's Spanish/Mexican history as pastoral romance. Popularizing the image of the Southwest's agrarian origins as Spanish frontier idyll, this romantic revival chronologically paralleled the decline of the old Mexican ranching order. Through its idealization of a pre-modern Spanish epoch of archaic grandeur now existing in the modern era only as wistful (cultural) remembrance, the production of this romantic mythology served symbolically as a cultural eulogy for the passing of the pre-U.S. conquest social order. Although the pastoral myth took root in the same era throughout the Southwest, it developed distinct regional variations in states such as California, New Mexico, and Texas. Southern California produced what is perhaps its single most influential narrative, the mission myth, which achieved renown with the publication in 1884 of Helen Hunt Jackson's historical romance *Ramona*.[22]

Written with the aim of voicing the grievances of California's Indians, *Ramona* tells the story of the star-crossed romance between the title character, a half-blood Indian orphan raised on a Mexican hacienda after the U.S. annexation, and Alessandro, an Indian sheepherder. Though the novel did, as Jackson intended, arouse interest in Southern California's mission Indians, its romantic portrait of Californio ranch society caricatured this population's aggrieved sociohistorical plight. By displacing responsibility for the Indians' status onto the United States, *Ramona* absolved the Spanish/Mexican mission and ranching systems of any role in the Indians' subjugation.[23] Rather than interrogating California's semifeudal Spanish and Mexican origins, the novel instead extolled California's Franciscans and the "fine old Spanish [ranchero] families" who settled the region, groups that, as previously set forth, kept their Indian labor force in semiservitude (McWilliams, *Southern California*, 75–76). By romanticizing the paternalistic bond between Indians and Spanish/Mexicans during the colonial and Mexican eras, *Ramona* erased longstanding social contradictions that marked California's pre-U.S. conquest era.

According to the myth popularized by *Ramona*, agrarian Spanish/Mexican Alta California stood in marked contrast to the U.S. capitalist social order. California's missions were "havens of happiness and contentment for the Indians, places of song, laughter, good food, beautiful languor, and mystical adoration of the Christ" (McWilliams, *Southern California*, 70). Within this space, graceful Indians "knelt dutifully before the Franciscans to receive the baptism of a superior culture" (Starr, *Inventing the Dream*, 58). Pioneer Mexican ranchers who established the semifeudal hacienda system were transformed into "Spanish grandees and caballeros . . . accustomed to the luxurious softness of fine clothes, to well-trained servants, to all the amenities of civilized European living," McWilliams writes. Amid the "green-rolling hills and mustard fields of Southern California," these Spanish seigneurs lived on their ranchos, where "in the coolness of the evening air" they gathered on their spacious patios to "talk of the day's events, sipping gentle wines that revived memories of castles in Spain" (McWilliams, *North from Mexico*, 35). The description of the grand house of the Moreno hacienda in *Ramona* captures this romantic conception of Spanish California's pre-modern seigneurial society: "It was a picturesque life, with more of sentiment and gayety in it, more also that was truly dramatic, more romance, than will ever be seen again on those sunny shores. The aroma of it all lingers there still; industries and inventions have not yet slain it; it will last out its century—in fact, it can never be quite lost, so long as there is left standing one such house as the Senora Moreno's" (Jackson, 15).

Wholly excluded from the Spanish myth were the brutal and insidious elements of colonialism as manifested in the semifeudal mission and hacienda systems. Gone also were any allusions to the actual contemporaneous status of Mexicans and Mexican Americans in the Southwest, either as pauperized descendants of Californio society or immigrant laborers exploited by California's burgeoning agricultural industry. Also gone was any reference to the actual modern-day plight of California's Indians. As captured by *Ramona*, the romantic image of the Spanish/Mexican tradition was "emphasized to the detriment—in fact, to the total neglect— of its realistic latter-day manifestations" (McWilliams, *Southern California*, 80). Such silences mirrored profound contradictions within the progressive ideology of nineteenth-century social Darwinism. As Chon Noriega explains, the Spanish myth's appropriation and romanticization of Californio history "bespoke the inevitable succession of superior 'races' in the pursuit of higher forms of social organization, from nomadic to feudal to small farms to conglomerates: Mexicans over Indians, White (immigrant) settlers over Mexicans, and White (Anglo-Saxon) capitalists over White (immigrant) settlers" (Noriega, 221).

Scholars generally have concurred that economic, cultural, and racial factors contributed to the myth's emergence and popularity. McWilliams notes that the rediscovery of the Spanish/Mexican past occurred between 1883 and 1888, "at precisely the period when the great real-estate promotion of Southern California was being organized" (McWilliams, *Southern California*, 77). During this time, he writes, a "highly romantic conception of the Spanish period began to be cultivated, primarily for the benefit of the incoming tides of tourists, who were routed to the [renovated] Missions much as they were routed to the mythical site of Ramona's birthplace" (77). Jackson in fact modeled the novel's setting after the Rancho Camulos in Ventura County, which she had visited as a tourist and which had once been a part of the Del Valle family's 48,612-acre Rancho San Francisco.[24] Expanding upon McWilliams's model, Kevin Starr traces the interaction of myth-making and crude commercialism during Southern California's Booster Era (1885–1925). He describes how local boosters such as Col. Harrison Gray Otis (owner of the *Los Angeles Times*) exploited the mission myth as a means of promoting economic and real-estate development in the region (Starr, *Inventing the Dream*, 76). Through this promotion, as Mike

Davis summarizes in his reading of Starr, "the mission aura of 'history and romance' would become an even more important attraction in selling Southern California to the nation than weather or movie-industry glamor" (Davis, 27). William Deverell describes how the Old California myth also reflected an Anglo American racial vision of the region's present and future: "The Spanish Fantasy past could work as a regional identifier and as a commodity to lure tourists and consumers precisely because it was about the past. It negated the present. Elite Anglos had embarked on a vision about southern California that was emphatically a racial vision; theirs was a fundamentally Anglo-Saxon plan. Nonwhites had their roles to play . . . but certainly out of the way in well-established places and spaces. In other words, Anglos found Mexicans where they expected to: in 'our Mexico,' in poverty-stricken *colonias,* in *barrios,* and in the laboring hundreds working for the railroad, the citrus farms, or the brickyards. They also found them in the past, where they could be cloaked in the stage directions of fantasy" (Deverell, 248).

Deverell, Starr, Davis, and McWilliams agree with scholars such as Arthur G. Pettit, Douglas Monroy, and David J. Weber that the mission myth also emerged in response to the Southwest's rapid socioeconomic transformation in the late nineteenth and early twentieth centuries. The myth, these scholars indicate, symbolized for white immigrants to the region—and for a wider national audience—an alternative to the social condition of dislocation, alienation, and anxiety that attended the expansion of industrial capitalism during this period.[25] Weber, for example, asserts that Americans embraced the myth as a reaction to the "crass materialism, vulgarity, and rootlessness" that characterized industrial capitalism in the United States (Weber, *Myth and History,* 11). In his view, the myth served to mitigate the psychic fragmentation and alienation that Americans experienced under the effects of modernizing social forces. According to Carolyn Porter, George Lukacs's theory of reification identifies the manner in which the effects of such fragmentation, alienation, and rootlessness "infiltrate the consciousness of everyone living in a society driven by capitalist growth" (Porter, 189). Reification refers to a type of alienation characteristic of modern capitalism in which relations between people take on the character of relations between commodities or objects. The "logic" of the capitalist market permeates the consciousness of individuals to such an extent that it determines how people view and relate to others. With the human bond lost, "all aspects of life are fragmented and instrumentally reorganized to meet the demands of capital" (Marx, 37). The quality of human activity is bracketed, "as all human activity is ruthlessly reorganized in terms of efficiency and sheer 'means'" (Homer, 22).

In California the myth thus reflected deep-seated anxiety among white settlers and immigrants about their own fragmented, atomized, and reified existence. Starr traces this anxiety to a period beginning just after the conquest, decades before *Ramona* appeared. Citing a variety of sources, he notes that the image of Old (Spanish) California grew more appealing as complexities in postconquest California multiplied. For many during this era, Spanish California began to take on the attributes of a lost utopia. Contemporary Anglo American California seemed "opulent, pretentious, and vulgar" compared to the "spiritual dignity" and "simple grace" of quasifeudal Spanish Old California. As Starr explains, "Amidst the American clamor, the myth of pre-conquest contentment remained a haunting alternative" (Starr, *Americans and the California Dream*, 395). McWilliams similarly postulates that the myth represented an attempt to "escape from the bonds of an American culture that neither satisfies nor pleases" (McWilliams, *Southern California*, 82). It gave people "a sense of continuity in a region long characterized by rapid social dislocation" (71). As McWilliams and Starr, among others, all suggest, the myth of agrarian Spanish California embodied for California's white settlers and immigrants what had been lost in the modern U.S. era of reified consciousness.

The myth's evolution in California, however, can also be traced to post-conquest writings by Mexican Californians, who often portrayed the Spanish/Mexican era either in pastoral terms akin to the myth or as a period in which traditional (pre-capitalist) values provided Mexican sociocultural coherence.[26] The Southern California rancher Antonio Coronel is remembered for his distinguished political career, which made him the most renowned citizen of Hispanic Los Angeles (Pitt, 281). But through his friendship with Jackson he played a defining role in the writing of *Ramona* and the popularization of the Old (Spanish) California myth. Along with Vallejo and other Californios, Coronel was interviewed in the 1870s by Hubert H. Bancroft's agents for the historian's research project on early California history. Coronel's testimonial, "Cosas de California" ("California Tales"), presented a detailed account of California history after the 1830s and became one of Bancroft's most prized possessions (Pitt, 281). "Cosas de California" and other Californio testimonials collected by Bancroft form an invaluable body of early Mexican American literary texts that continues to be the subject of inquiry by scholars working on the Recovering the U.S. Hispanic Literary Heritage project. In the early 1880s, Jackson visited Coronel's home in Los Angeles as she did research for a series of magazine articles about California's missions. Coronel's tales about life in pre-U.S. conquest Alta California influenced Jackson's development of a romantic portrait of Mexican Californian society in *Ramona*. Coronel also helped edit the novel, proofreading it for historical accuracy and offering suggestions on local details (Woolsey, 45). Significantly, Coronel's defense of seigneurial Mexican agrarian society, as demonstrated by his attribution of the decline of the mission Indians to the U.S. conquest rather than to Mexican misrule, would find a prominent place in Jackson's novel.[27]

Such representations served deeply contradictory aims in Californio writings. Emerging from the late-nineteenth-century socio-economic setting described earlier, Californio (hacienda) narratives set out to remember and reclaim an agrarian Spanish/ Mexican cultural patrimony as a means of resisting the discursive annihilation of the Mexican American community. In Ruiz de Burton's novel *The Squatter and the Don* and Vallejo's autobiographical "Historical and Personal Memoirs Relating to Alta California" the hacienda as memory-place serves as an answer to the social contradictions lived by Mexican Californians under U.S. dominance. Among these contradictions were the socially and psychologically debilitating effects of nineteenth-century racialism as exemplified by the ideology of manifest destiny. As chapter 2 will describe, the utopian impulse to "true (hacienda) community" in Californio texts constitutes an imaginary and symbolic resolution to sociohistorical and cultural processes that derived from the violent siege of Mexican agrarian society carried out in the late nineteenth century by the forces of (U.S.) modernity.

Remembering the Hacienda
Land and Community in Californio Narrative

María Amparo Ruiz de Burton's novel, *The Squatter and the Don* (1885), and Mariano Guadalupe Vallejo's autobiography of 1874, "Historical and Personal Memoirs Relating to Alta California," are two of the most ambitious Mexican American literary works produced in the post-conquest era.[1] Woven of the social fabric of the Mexican hacienda, together they present a portrait of Alta Californian agrarian society spanning a period of more than one hundred years. As hacienda texts, however, they illustrate the complexity of any effort to employ early Mexican American writings to reconstruct Mexican American literary history.[2] In their cultural and historical convergences with nineteenth-century U.S. southern narrative, they explode Chicano/a studies categorizations that would define such early Mexican American literature as uniformly subaltern, an assumption embraced by numerous recovery project scholars in readings of these and other newly recovered Mexican American texts. The critical reception of *The Squatter and the Don* provides a case in point. Though recovery project scholars such as José F. Aranda Jr. and Manuel Martín-Rodríguez, among others, highlight the problematic nature of this novel's engagement with the U.S. social order, many critics continue to place *The Squatter and the Don* in the tradition of counterdiscursive Mexican American literary production.[3] As Aranda remarks, "[I]n the growing critical industry being built around the reemergence" of Ruiz de Burton, "many have followed the lead of her recoverers, Rosaura Sánchez and Beatrice Pita, in locating a 'resistance' narrative in her life and writings and historicizing her biography as 'subaltern'" (Aranda, "Contradictory Impulses," 554).

Both Aranda and Martín-Rodríguez suggest the need for rigorously historicized studies of early Mexican American literature that would recover a Mexican American literary patrimony without always romanticizing it as already ethnically defined "resistance." *The Squatter and the Don*'s intersection with U.S. southern narrative and its close intertextual kinship with Vallejo's "Historical and Personal Memoirs" present a compelling model for carrying out this project. As hacienda texts, these works demonstrate one means by which nineteenth-century Mexican American writers remembered the Mexican and Spanish past to reclaim their community's history and (re)constitute a Mexican American historical subjectivity. Contesting dominant accounts of the Southwest's history during an era of consolidation of U.S. hegemony, *The Squatter and the Don* and "Historical and Personal Memoirs" examine the repressive impact of conquest that formed a lasting legacy for the region's Mexican American population. Set against the discursive and material threats presented by the forces of (U.S.) modernity, these works at one level find solace by remembering the pre-capitalist Mexican hacienda world. But they also depend on the silencing of memories that would complicate their project to recover the hacienda as a symbol of Mexican American origins and identity.

Resistance to U.S. (capitalist) practices in *The Squatter and the Don* and "Historical and Personal Memoirs" mirrors seigneurial-based anti-industrialist discourse in southern plantation narratives, a body of writings that in the late nineteenth and early twentieth centuries also questioned U.S. economic and political institutions.[4] Much as plantation narrative remembered the "organic" southern agrarian community to counter northern capitalist dominance, Ruiz de Burton's and Vallejo's works both invoke claims to pre-bourgeois seigneurial (Mexican) society as a means of contesting injustice under U.S. rule and the intrusion of modernity into their native region. For dispossessed aristocrats like Ruiz de Burton and Vallejo, the land question thus constituted more than a legal or political dispute with U.S. governmental authority: it represented, rather, a struggle over the claims of seigneurial hacienda community, for centuries the dominant economic and cultural mode of production in Mexico. Remembering the hacienda in *The Squatter and the Don* and "Historical and Personal Memoirs" in this sense serves an "anti-Yankee" ideal broadly analogous to the southern plantation myth, which similarly displaced the coercive nature of an "organic" agrarian community in the interest of opposing U.S. social and political depredations.[5]

In *The Squatter and the Don* and "Historical and Personal Memoirs" the hacienda as memory-place embodies the seigneurial worldview of Mexican Californian culture. As I discussed in chapter 1, seigneurialism dominated social relations within Mexican California and the U.S. slave-holding South.[6] In both regions there existed a hierarchical agrarian socioeconomic system in which status, honor, reputation, and kinship were interdependent and in which traditions of social reciprocity and mutual obligation bound land-owners and their laborers (Monroy, *Thrown among Strangers*, 170). In striking contrast to modern capitalism, within seigneurial society landowners produced neither for the sake of producing nor to accu-mulate wealth. Rather, "social status was the goal of [landowners'] productive efforts," the desire to "elevate themselves to grandeur and aristocracy" (138). Although the elite's social status depended on a coerced, subjugated, and exploited labor force to work the land—slaves in the South and Indian/*mestizo* peons in California—historians such as Douglas Monroy and Eugene Genovese empha-size the anti-market, or "disaccumulationist," nature of the seigneur-ial worldview.[7] Rather than self-interest alone driving landowners' efforts to better themselves socially, honor, obligation, and kinship were also fundamental motivating factors. In seigneurial society money in itself was of less importance to landowners than the amount of honor they were able to bring to themselves.[8] The status-conscious Californios, notes Monroy, accumulated immense tracts of land, but they also gave land away as a means of increasing their status (Monroy, *Thrown among Strangers*, 170). Within the limits of the hacienda social hierarchy, material wealth gave them the where-withal to act honorably and generously (139–40).

By contrast, Americans imbued with the spirit of capitalism viewed land above all as a commodity, its value measured in money. Unlike the Californios, according to Monroy, the Americans "held no discernible sense of reciprocal obligation to the people on the landscape with respect to the Americans' entitlement to what was to them mere property." Whereas American business owners and speculators in California gave free rein to their accumulationist desires, the Californios were "accustomed to financial dealings based on honor and kin ties rather than the rigors of the contract and the impersonality of the market" (Monroy, *Thrown among Strangers*, 170). Hence, in the Californio view, Americans instilled with the ethic of individualism and commercialism acted unethi-cally because they had no conception of honor or obligation that bound them to a community within which public morality super-seded individual wants and desires. As Vallejo remarked about Americans whom he encountered in New York in a letter to his wife Francisca in February 1865, "Every one is money mad; it seems to me that the people are crazy. Friendship is for the sake of self inter-est alone and I have not regarded it so up to now and it makes me unhappy, just to think about it. The madness they have is desperate madness."[9] Eleven years later in a letter to his son Platón, Vallejo similarly wrote, "[T]o be an honest man among so many [American] scoundrels is practically impossible. The world is bedevilled. One can't live in it without being a rogue, through and through."[10]

After the U.S. conquest, these sociocultural differences led Californio landowners Ruiz de Burton and Vallejo to reassert their precapitalist seigneurial values and identities. In their writings the hacienda therefore becomes a space not only of Mexican ethnic origins and identity but also of the pre-bourgeois seigneurial culture of hacienda society, one in which the accumulation of money was not the primary raison d'être and where, as the Californios believed, human relations had not yet been corrupted by modern (commercial) values. In this way the hacienda symbolizes a cultural ethos strikingly similar to what the plantation does in late-nineteenth- and early-twentieth-century southern agrarian narrative.

The origins of the depression-era southern agrarian critique of industrial capitalism sheds light on this cultural ethos, capturing the Californio elite's own seigneurial outlook vis-à-vis modernity and U.S. dominance. Southern agrarianism, as Richard Gray explains, assumed that "[r]ural, and more particularly Southern, society is natural; urban society . . . is artificial, mechanical. Southern life is peaceful, idyllic, having made allowances for human nature and reached an accommodation with its natural surroundings; whereas Northern life is warlike, with its people interminably engaged in destructive and self-destructive activity." Recalling Ruiz de Burton's and Vallejo's portraits of Mexican agrarian society, U.S. southern agrarians asserted that "[s]outhern life is in harmony with things . . . [and] is sane, balanced, and healthy . . . [offering] the possibility of human affection and contact. Northern life, by contrast, is unbalanced, unhealthy, characterized by disharmony and fanaticism, and denies all bonds and connections other than the economic" (Gray, 154).

Gray's further comments on the origins of the southern agrarian critique mirror the Californios' own historical condition under U.S. rule. "The Agrarians had begun with a profound sense of historical displacement," states Gray, and with "the suspicion that an accelerating process of change was threatening to destroy not merely the contours of their physical world but their modes of being and perception, the solidity of their social and moral selves and the terms in which they interpreted things" (Gray, 164). In the context of a modernity identified with the capitalist North, the agrarians "had found in Agrarianism a kind of nucleus, and a catalyst: something around which they could gather their feelings of unease and which, in addition, could help transform those feelings into a coherent aim. Quite simply, the Agrarian idea seemed to offer balm to their divided minds, to allay some of their anxiety about the immediate moment by discovering possible redemption in yesterday and tomorrow; the present might be confused, their belief was, but with the help of the regional codes a bridge over it might be built, uniting a past apotheosized by memory to a future transfigured by hope" (164).

The southern agrarians of course drew upon the anti-industrialist polemic in the works of early southern domestic and plantation writers such as Caroline Gilman, Augusta Evans, John Pendleton Kennedy, and Thomas Nelson Page, an argument premised on the seigneurial ethos that dominated nineteenth-century plantation society.[11] Mounting a "defense of their native or adopted region," these early southern writers, as Elizabeth Moss notes, portrayed "the South as an ordered, harmonious society governed by the aristocratic code of noblesse oblige . . . [and by a] system of recip- rocal relationships that made southern society the moral superior of the individualistic North" (Moss, 29). Both southern domestic fiction and plantation narrative, Moss continues, "tapped into readers' apprehensions about the precarious state of southern affairs, stressing the stability of the South and the instability of the North; both lamented the materialism of the modern day; both designated the home, with woman its custodian, as the bedrock of southern civilization; both projected the South as the bastion of national virtue and the North as the nation's ruin." Perhaps most important, both the plantation novel and the southern domestic novel "were quickly enlisted in the service of the southern cause as southern writers became increasingly convinced that their culture was under attack from northerners" (21).

Though scholars have explored how the Californios' racial and ethnic consciousness shaped their recalcitrance to the new U.S. so- cial order, the seigneurial cultural origins of Californios such as Ruiz de Burton and Vallejo—both of whom strongly identified with the landed Creole elite from which they claimed descent—have been overlooked. Ruiz de Burton (1831–95) and Vallejo (1807–90) were descended from settlers and soldiers who colonized the California provinces and acquired land grants there during the Spanish and Mexican eras. The daughter of Isabel Ruiz and Jesús Maitorena (also spelled Maytorena), María Amparo Ruiz de Burton was the granddaughter of Don José Manuel Ruiz, commander of the Mexi- can northern frontier and governor of Baja California from 1822 to 1825. His brother, Capt. Francisco María Ruiz, was the commander of the San Diego presidio, or military fort (1801–13 and 1817–18). Each brother received a land grant for his military and govern- ment service. Don José Manuel received two *sitios* (square leagues) comprising 8,856 acres of land that became the Rancho Ensenada de Todos Santos, which encompassed what is now the Baja California city of Ensenada and its environs. Don Francisco María received the first land grant distributed in San Diego, and the resulting Rancho Los Peñasquitos covered 8,484 acres. Ruiz de Burton chose to use her mother's family name over her father's to link herself to these landed ancestors. Through her great-grandmother, Don José Manuel's mother Doña Isabel Carrillo Millar, Ruiz de Burton was also related to "two prominent Carrillo families in Alta California and [was] consequently tied by blood or marriage to

Leonardo Barbieri, *Portrait of Francisco Pacheco,* Californio rancher, 1852, oil on canvas, 39½ x 31½ in. Courtesy of the de Saisset Museum, Santa Clara University permanent collection, Gift of Monserrat Roca, 1.757.

Leonardo Barbieri, *Portrait of Feliciana Estrada Pacheco*, wife of Francisco Pacheco, 1852, oil on canvas, 39½ x 31½ in. Courtesy of the de Saisset Museum, Santa Clara University permanent collection, Gift of Monserrat Roca, 1.759.

other leading Californio families" (Sánchez and Pita, introduction to *The Squatter and the Don*, 8). The names of these prominent ranch families included Vallejo, Guerra y Noriega, Alvarado, Pacheco, Castro, Pico, and Estrada. Ruiz de Burton arrived in Alta California from her native Baja California in 1848, having moved at the end of the U.S.-Mexican War. From the powerful Pico family, which in the pre-conquest era acquired numerous Mexican land grants in Southern California, she purchased her approximately 10,000-acre Rancho Jamul, located east of San Diego.

Twenty-four years older than his friend and distant relative Ruiz de Burton, Mariano Guadalupe Vallejo, the son of Ignacio Vallejo and Maria Lugo, also strongly identified with his storied colonial-era forebears. As Madie Brown Emparan writes, "[T]he ancestral threads of the Vallejos are woven into the tapestry of America from almost the time of its discovery" (Emparan, 1). Vallejo's paternal ancestor, Adm. Alonzo Vallejo, served the Spanish Crown at the inception of the colonization of the new world. His military career included service in the colonial outpost of Santo Domingo (Hispaniola), where he was sent in 1500. Two of Alonzo's brothers were soldiers in Hernán Cortés's expedition to Mexico in 1519. After the Spanish conquest, they settled in New Spain. One brother, Don Pedro Vallejo, "became one of the governing officials of the province of Panuco on the Gulf of Mexico where he was lord of great silver mines and master of peons innumerable" (2). Don Pedro Vallejo's descendants resided in the province of New Galicia (Jalisco) for more than two hundred years. One of them, Ignacio Vicente Vallejo (b. 1748), enlisted as a soldier in the 1773 expedition that led to the first Spanish settlements in Alta California. Don Ignacio Vicente eventually acquired the Rancho Bolsa de San Cayetano, an 8,881-acre land grant approximately twenty-three miles north of present-day Monterey, California. His eighth child, Mariano, built upon his father's landholdings following the secularization of Alta California's missions. Don Mariano acquired ranch properties in Napa, Sonoma, and other northern Alta California counties that would make him the most powerful *hacendado* in the region. At the height of his career in the years preceding the U.S. conquest, Vallejo's landholdings would encompass at least 175,000 acres and perhaps as much as 225,000 acres. Several of his nearly contiguous grants stretched all the way from Mendocino County in the west to the Carquinez Straits northeast of the San Francisco Bay (Rosenus, 64).

Rather than examining how this ancestral sociocultural patrimony contributed to the formation of Californio selfhood, many literary and historical scholars have instead focused on how Californio aristocrats such as Ruiz de Burton and Vallejo negotiated a new (white) cultural identity within the socioeconomic constraints and racial hostility of the post-conquest era. In the case of Ruiz de Burton's *The Squatter and the Don*, critics generally have agreed that it does not oppose capitalism per se but only the predatory type identified with the Gilded Age, as embodied by Leland Stanford and his railroad monopoly. Since the novel depicts Californios participating in a number of entrepreneurial ventures, its criticism of Yankee business practices must not be construed as a blan-

Mariano Guadalupe Vallejo, ca. 1850s. Courtesy of the Bancroft Library, University of California, Berkeley.

ket condemnation of capitalism. As John M. González explains, the "approbation is for a government-corrupting monopoly corporate capitalism that would chaotically erase racial distinctions in the pursuit of profit" (J. M. González, "Whiteness of the Blush," 160). By upsetting the Californios' business endeavors, González argues, monopolistic capitalism prevents the projected union of

Anglo and Californio families, undermining the Californios' racial and class positioning within the new (capitalist) social order.[12]

Though correct in problematizing Californio resistance to capitalism, González's argument dismisses Ruiz de Burton's anti-capitalist argument by portraying it as emerging from the equivocations of disgruntled Californio protocapitalists. Much as in Vallejo's "Historical and Personal Memoirs," in *The Squatter and the Don* the Californios' desire to be included within the new capitalist social economy represses but does not erase the seigneurial-based aversion to capitalism that historically defined the Californio oligarchy's sociocultural identity. If Californios had become successful capitalists under the new social order, Vallejo's and Ruiz de Burton's texts both indicate that they would have embraced an entrepreneurial finance capitalism that offered paternalistic control of the lower classes, for both portray unfettered monopoly capitalism as creating chaos at both ends of the class hierarchy (Luis-Brown, 817). However, when it becomes clear in both texts that members of this group will *not* be accepted as (white) equals within the post-conquest (capitalist) social order, Ruiz de Burton and Vallejo increasingly fall back on the Mexican Californian elite's pre-bourgeois agrarian ethos to expose the injustices perpetrated by U.S. social institutions. Rooted in the anti-industrialist culture of semifeudal Mexican (agrarian) society, Ruiz de Burton's and Vallejo's criticisms thus constituted for these heirs of the seigneurial agrarian tradition a meaningful argument against the values of modern capitalism, whether monopolistic or not.

Although *The Squatter and the Don* and "Historical and Personal Memoirs" do not foreground the old order in precisely the manner of plantation narrative and despite the fact that the ambiguous meaning of race in the Californio texts complicates the analogy, like plantation writings both works depict the hacienda as an organic "true community" set against the landscape of a capitalist modernity hostile to this community's values and beliefs. Having lost their land and social status, Ruiz de Burton and Vallejo drew upon their community's sociocultural patrimony to mold a distinctive Mexican American historical subjectivity in the post-conquest period. Their engagement with U.S. dominance constitutes a defense of the hacienda in both a literal sense, as the material inheritance of family or community, and as a cultural ideal founded on the seigneurial ethos of this semifeudal institution. It is in this pre-bourgeois context that Californio resistance to U.S. capitalist practices in both works must be placed. Rather than conveying primarily an ethnicity-based engagement with U.S. institutions, passages such as the following in *The Squatter and the Don* must be understood as emerging from the Californios' pre-capitalist worldview. In chapter XX, for example, the narrator contrasts a modern secular (capitalist) morality with the (Christian) seigneurial ethos identified throughout with the Californios: "Would that the power, the wisdom, the omniscience of God had not been repudiated, discarded, abolished, by modern thinkers, so that now but few feel any moral checks or dread of responsibility; for if there is to be no final accounting, morality ceases to be a factor, there being no fear of any hereafter; and as a natural sequence, there is no remedy left for the terrible '*palsy.*' For it is a well demonstrated fact that *sense of justice* or pure *philanthropy*, alone, is but frail reliance. Fatally has man elevated his vanity to be his deity, with egotism for the high priest, and the sole aim and object of life the accumulation of *money*, with no thought of the never-ending tomorrow, the awakening on the limitless shore! No thought of his fellow-beings here, of himself in the hereafter!" (Ruiz de Burton, *The Squatter and the Don*, 206; emphasis in original).

Rather than reflecting the progressive thought of the era, recurring "anti-market" passages such as this one in Ruiz de Burton's novel condemn the new "secular" capitalist order by invoking the traditional values and beliefs (e.g., religion, morality, responsibility, honor, etc.) of seigneurial Mexican agrarian culture.

South by Southwest

In the introduction to Ruiz de Burton's first novel, *Who Would Have Thought It?* (1872), Sánchez and Pita note that the displacement of the plantation ruling class in the South after the Civil War would have triggered "memories of what had taken place in Alta California, where after occupation the ruling Californios were reduced to a subaltern minority" (Sánchez and Pita, introduction to *Who Would Have Thought It?*, ix). More recently, Sánchez and Pita draw from Ruiz de Burton's correspondence to conclude that the author "sympathized with the defeated Confederacy, seeing in the South's defeat a mirror of the defeat of Mexico in 1848, and in Reconstruction, a clear imposition of Yankee hegemony on the Southern states" (Sánchez and Pita, *Conflicts of Interest*, 195). But Sánchez and Pita's earlier readings of Ruiz de Burton's fiction diminish the author's identification with the conquered white South in *The Squatter and the Don* and *Who Would Have Thought It?*, both of which provide ample evidence of the author's contempt for Reconstruction and all groups, such as the Radical Republicans, that supported it. In the period following the Civil War, Radical Republicans called for the dismantling of the white power structure in the South and campaigned for equal rights for African Americans. Despite Ruiz de Burton's portrait of racial hostility toward Mexican Americans in *The Squatter and the Don* and her call for constitutional rights for this aggrieved ethnic minority in the Southwest, her novels clearly opposed the same approach to the African American "problem" in the South.

Among Californios, Ruiz de Burton was not alone in expressing sympathy for the Confederacy. Leonard Pitt traces the long political relationship between the Californio elite in Southern California and pro-slavery Democrats from the South, a relationship that created a Democratic majority that withstood the shifting tides of California politics (Pitt, 133). In the 1850s, when Mexican Americans were still a demographic majority in Los Angeles, the city was considered a pro-slavery and Democratic town (194). The head of the Democratic County Committee, Antonio Coronel, was a wealthy Californio rancher who in 1853 became mayor. In the presidential election of 1860 Democrats were able to keep the city's total number of votes for Abraham Lincoln to a mere 356.[13] When the South seceded, one of the Californios' closest allies in Los Angeles, Joseph Lancaster Brent, enlisted in the Confederate army and went to Louisiana for front-line duty. Servulio Varela, a Californio rebel hero of the U.S.-Mexican War, followed Brent's example and also joined the southern war effort as a soldier. Another Californio and also a longtime colleague of Coronel, Tomás Sánchez—veteran of the Battle of San Pasqual, prominent *ranchero,* bandit fighter, and Democratic boss—also enlisted in the Confederate army, as a second lieutenant, although he never left town for active duty (234).

Although Vallejo was not a Southern California native, he too was a lifelong member of the Democratic Party. When the South seceded, however, Vallejo supported the war measures of the federal government, for which he was branded a "Black Republican" by fellow California Democrats—an epithet used by opponents of abolitionists to attack those who were perceived as anti-slavery or anti-southern (Emparan, 135). Reflecting her own southern sympathies at the outset of the Civil War, this same term of opprobrium appears in a letter that Ruiz de Burton wrote on February 2, 1860, to condemn U.S. congressional opponents of the McLane-Ocampo Treaty, which was viewed as an effort by the South to annex additional pro-slavery territory.[14] Similarly, Ruiz de Burton's identification with the fallen southern planter class is apparent in chapter III of *The Squatter and the Don,* entitled "Pre-empting the Law," in which the narrator makes note of the "carpet-bags" carried by immigrant/settlers flooding into California (Ruiz de Burton, *The Squatter and the Don,* 71). This reference obviously recalls the popular usage of the term "carpetbagger," coined by white southerners to condemn northerners moving into the war-ravaged South during the Reconstruction period.

Along with the pro-southern Democratic political views that dominated Civil War–era Southern California, Ruiz de Burton's motivation for identifying with the fallen southern planter class could only have become more urgent during the thirteen years between the publication of *Who Would Have Thought It?* in 1872 and *The Squatter and the Don* in 1885. Her fortunes declined rapidly during this period as she borrowed money to wage a legal battle to regain control of her rancho near San Diego. According to Frederick Bryant Oden's master's thesis, after 1870 "[f]irst the squatters, and then the rival claimants" ensured that if Ruiz de Burton "were ever to regain the rancho, it would be . . . after a long and hard-fought struggle" (Oden, 164). After more than a decade of litigation, by September 1882 Ruiz de Burton, in debt to two groups of creditors, faced financial ruin. As *The Squatter and the Don* indicates through its tale of Californio (read: Spanish) landed aristocrats being reduced to common (read: Mexican) laborers through dispossession, the loss of Ruiz de Burton's landed status subverted her own class and racial positioning within post-Reconstruction U.S. society.

Vallejo, Ruiz de Burton's close friend upon whom she would model *The Squatter and the Don*'s protagonist Don Mariano Alamar, faced an equally precipitous financial crisis in the same period.[15] By 1875, when Vallejo presented his "Recuerdos históricos y personales" to Hubert Howe Bancroft, he "had been despoiled so extensively that he had been forced to sign away most of his land" (Padilla, *My History, Not Yours,* 78).[16] Forced into litigation with squatters and speculators, Vallejo's hacienda empire had been lost except for a small ranch in Sonoma. Like many other Californio rancheros, Vallejo had been mistreated, swindled, and robbed, often by the very people he had befriended (Emparan, 122). At the time of his greatest despondency, he had written to his son Platón about the conflict he faced between his sense of honor and the insurmountable debts that he owed: "There are very exceptional situations in life which are not in the reach of all. . . . Mine for instance—an accumulation of bitterness and vexation in every sense, weary of struggling against Fate for a long time now, despairing sometimes of life itself, in a sea of difficulties which embitter it at every instant; exasperated always; the soul uneasy and the heart hardened, disgusted at many men (almost against humanity). With unavoidable debts which Honor, Duty and Society demand, I have been held in anxiety, hellish, frightful and therefore unusual. . . . [I am] burning in an abysmal inferno of griefs that have poisoned my blood."[17]

Significantly, in light of *The Squatter and the Don*'s biographical premise, in the ten years between the formal presentation of Vallejo's autobiography and the publication of Ruiz de Burton's novel, Vallejo's fortunes continued to spiral downward without surcease (Padilla, *My History, Not Yours,* 103). In another letter to Platón, dated January 11, 1877, Vallejo refers to the "difference between the present time and those that preceded the usurpation by the Americans." Given the new circumstances, he continues, "if the Californians could all gather together to breathe a lament it would reach Heaven as a moving sigh which would cause fear and consternation to the Universe. What misery! And it is much more intense than when everyone without exception lived in abundance. This country was the true Eden, the land of promise where hunger was never known."[18] As Genaro Padilla observes, a year later Vallejo "saw his own material and physical condition represented in a photograph of his once beautiful home in Petaluma, now in ruins" (Padilla, *My History, Not Yours,* 103). In a letter written in 1878, not long after losing a large sum of money in a failed business venture, Vallejo compares "that old relic with myself and the comparison is an extant one; ruins and dilapidation. What a difference between then and now. Then Youth, strength and riches, now Age, weakness and poverty."[19] Throughout his work Vallejo's autobiographical persona evokes, as in the above self-references, a simultaneous disillusionment with the U.S. "present" and solace through nostalgic remembrance of the pre-conquest Mexican era. Vallejo's fierce identification with his 66,622-acre Petaluma rancho, however, suggests as well his ideological and cultural investment in the hacienda identities of the landed Californio elite.

The Squatter and the Don's plot reflects the parallel biographical experiences summarized above. The novel depicts the decline of the Alamars, a Californio family whose 47,000-acre cattle ranch forms part of a land grant ceded to its ancestors more than fifty

Ranch house at Vallejo's Petaluma hacienda, which by the 1870s was a relic of the Mexican era. Hanging sign at left center reads "Old Adobe." Courtesy of The Society of California Pioneers, San Francisco.

years earlier. From 1872 to 1876 the Alamars lose their land and ranch as a result of laws that favor Anglo American settlers and squatters over Mexican families who had acquired their ranches during the Spanish and Mexican eras. The novel narrates this story through the Alamars' relationship with the Darrells, a white settler/squatter family newly arrived on the Alamar ranch. The squatter/rancher conflict develops through a series of interethnic romances involving the children of these two families.

William Darrell relocates his family to San Diego in the belief that the Alamar grant, ostensibly rejected by the courts, is public domain and therefore open to legal settlement. His wife Mary, however, had learned otherwise and directed their son Clarence to purchase a tract from the Alamars before the family moves. Because of William's well-known pro-squatter sentiments, neither has informed William that he and his family already own the land on which they have settled. Just as Mrs. Darrell had feared, after the family moves William's pro-squatter views blind him to the legitimacy of the Alamars' complaint against scores of illegal squatters who have not purchased their land. Significantly, Clarence and his mother's motivation for sympathizing with the Californio ranchers is influenced by Mary's Creole descent, which shapes Clarence's view of "Latin" people. The marginal presence of Tisha, Mary's African American servant, moreover, serves to remind the reader that, as a white southerner after the Civil War, Mary would be sensitive to the uncompensated and unlawful seizure of property, which is the way plantation owners viewed emancipation. Hence Mary's determination to provide legal compensation for Don Mariano's land comes not merely out of the kindness of her heart but also from what Ruiz de Burton characterizes as a historical recognition of the homologous position the Californio *hacendados* and the white ex-planter class shared during this period.[20]

While he is disabused of his misconceptions, William Darrell finds himself drawn into the sphere of genteel Mexican American society through Clarence's romantic relationship with Mercedes, Don Mariano's daughter. The squatter/rancher land entitlement conflict threatens to rend the romantic union between these two characters. Clarence's sympathy for the Alamars' plight, along with the shock of preemption by Mrs. Darrell, however, compels William to confront his beliefs and renounce squatterism. Although Clarence and Mercedes are in the end married and the Alamars are saved from destitution by Clarence's newfound stock market wealth, the resolution of the clash between the Darrells and the Alamars does not save the Californio ranchers. With countless settlers and squatters refusing to embrace Mr. Darrell's example and still more arriving to stake claims on Californio land, the era of the "Spano-American" ranchers is rapidly coming to a end. As Don Mariano reluctantly acknowledges, "I am afraid there is no help for us native Californians. We must sadly fade and pass away. . . . We must sink, go under, never to rise" (Ruiz de Burton, *The Squatter and the Don*, 177). Don Mariano dies of an illness as he realizes that his family's hacienda estate will be lost. A final attempt to save the family's land through the construction of a railroad, a project which the don and other San Diego ranchers hope to broker, is thwarted by Leland Stanford and his monopolistic railroad trust, representatives of the new capitalist order.

The Texas Pacific Railroad project serves in the novel to establish a sociopolitical and cultural kinship between Mexican California and the U.S. South, a solidarity based on a shared condition of military defeat and subjugation by the Yankee North. As a striking symbol of modernity, the railroad's destructive impact in the novel also functions to unite two seigneurial cultures, those of Mexican California and the U.S. South, in common cause against Yankee industrial capitalism. Several passages illustrate this kinship by portraying northern monopolists victimizing both the already besieged Californios and the conquered South at the height of Reconstruction. The narrator explicitly links the plight of Mexican California to the South in two chapters that depict Californio support for construction of the railroad. Connecting Southern California to the South, the railroad, according to the novel, would have benefitted both regions. But in chapter XX the Californio ranchers' representatives in Washington, D.C., hear "strange rumors about Congressmen being *'bribed with money'* and in other *ways improperly influenced by a 'certain railroad man,' who was organizing a powerful lobby to defeat the Texas Pacific Railroad*" (Ruiz de Burton, *The Squatter and the Don*, 210; emphasis in original). Confirming the rumors, the railroad monopoly controlled by Stanford manages to terminate the Texas Pacific Railroad in favor of its own Central Pacific line. This machination is, in fact, what occurred despite U.S. congressional action against the monopoly, the actual text of which appears in chapter XX listing the frauds "perpetrated by Messrs. Leland Stanford, Huntington, Crocker and Hopkins, under the name of 'Central Pacific Railroad Company'" (209). Conflating the contemporaneous plights of the South and Mexican California, a Californio supporter in Washington, D.C., concludes, "There never can be any better argument in favor of the Texas Pacific than are now plain to everybody. So, then, if in the face of all these powerful considerations Congress turns its back and will not hear the wail of the prostrate South, or the impassionate appeals of California, now, *now*, when there is not one solitary reason under heaven why such appeals and entreaties should be disregarded, is there any ground to expect any better in the uncertain future? Certainly not" (216; emphasis in original).

Voicing his identification with the South's condition under Reconstruction, Don Mariano decries the tactics used by Stanford's monopoly, particularly its political manipulations. The monopoly, he now recognizes, has deceived southerners into believing that the Texas Pacific Railroad was being built for the benefit of northern interests. Significantly, as in other sections of *The Squatter and the Don*, the seigneurial concept of honor serves to buttress Don Mariano's critique of political corruption under the new social order. As he states, "[I]f [the monopoly's representative] had been sent to deceive the North, to fool the Yankees, the errand would have been—if not more honorable—at least less odious for a Southerner, not so treacherous; but to go and deceive the trusting South, now when the entire country is so impoverished, so distressed, that act, I say, is inhuman, is ignominious. No words of reprobation can be too severe to stigmatize a man capable of being so heartless" (Ruiz de Burton, *The Squatter and the Don*, 308–309). Similarly, Don Mariano declares that the Yankee monopolists "should be stigmatized . . . as corrupters, as most malignant, debasing, unscrupulous men . . . men who are harmful to society, because they reward *dishonorable* acts; because they reward, with money, the blackest treason" (309; emphasis added). Chapter XXXIII, which depicts Don Mariano's meeting with Stanford, further illustrates the seigneurial basis of the Californio rancher's criticism and southern sympathies. Stanford, whose unabashed devotion to a market ethos leads him to assert that "corporations have no souls" (318) and that "everyone is in [business] for himself" (316), peremptorily rejects Don Mariano's business proposal. In response, Don Mariano's friend and fellow rancher, Mr. Holman, voices the Californios' seigneurial-based argument: "[C]ommercial honor [and] business morality should be based on strict rectitude, on the purest equity. . . . [S]o soon as any one in the pursuit of riches knowingly and willfully will injure any one else . . . he then violates the principle upon which commerce should rest" (317).

It is in this context that Californio opposition to the amoral practices of Yankee capitalism, as expressed memorably by Don Mariano's wife, Doña Josefa, near the end of the novel, must be read. Doña Josefa's elegy to her husband represents both a statement of the claims of seigneurial Mexican (hacienda) society (e.g., its "rectitude," "dignity," and "equity") and an eloquent critique of the morally corrosive modern capitalist order: "In a mild and dignified way, her mind rebelled. She regarded the acts of the men who caused her husband's ruin and death with genuine abhorrence. To her, rectitude and equity had a clear meaning impossible to pervert. No subtle sophistry could blur in her mind the clear line dividing right from wrong. She knew that among men the word BUSINESS means inhumanity to one another; it means justification of rapacity; it means the freedom of man to crowd and crush his fellow-man; it means the sanction of the Shylockian principle of exacting the pound of flesh. . . . Doubtless they say that they earned the money in BUSINESS . . . that one word justifies in the pursuit of riches everything mean, dishonest, rapacious, unfair, treacherous, unjust, and fraudulent" (Ruiz de Burton, *The Squatter and the Don*, 363).

In the final chapter, entitled "Out with the Invader," the narrator revisits the southern analogy. Calling for a "Redeemer" who will "emancipate the 'white slaves' of California," she binds the plight of the Californio ranchers (and particularly those in heavily Democratic Southern California) to the sociohistorical status of the southern states during and after Reconstruction (Ruiz de Burton, *The Squatter and the Don*, 372). The railroad monopoly and its handmaiden, the U.S. Congress, once again serve as symbols of both U.S. political hegemony and the forces of industrial capitalism. As the narrator concludes in the book's final lines, "But these [events], as well as the blight, spread over Southern California, and over the entire Southern States, are historical facts. All of which, strung together, would make a brilliant and most appropriate chaplet to encircle the lofty brow of the great and powerful monopoly. Our representatives in Congress, and in the State Legislature, knowing full well the will of the people, ought to legislate accordingly. If they do not, then we shall—as Channing said 'kiss the foot that tramples us!' and 'in anguish of spirit' must wait and pray for a Redeemer who will emancipate the white slaves of California" (372).

"Redeemer" contemptuously recalls the memory of Lincoln, the savior of the North and emancipator of the slaves. But it is also a not-so-veiled statement of support for the South's Redeemers, a political party that in the 1870s and 1880s worked to undermine Reconstruction. As Eric Foner explains, the Redeemers "included secessionist Democrats and Union Whigs, veterans of the Confederacy and rising younger leaders, traditional planters and advocates of a modernized New South. They shared . . . a commitment to dismantling the Reconstruction state, reducing the political power of blacks, and reshaping the South's legal system in the interests of labor control and racial subordination" (Foner, 588). By equating the "white slaves" of Mexican California with whites in the South during Reconstruction, the novel reasserts a sociohistorical and political kinship between the two regions—simultaneously conferring "whiteness" on the Californio elite—based on a common cause against Yankee oppression. As David Luis-Brown observes, the novel in this way "calls for these victimized regional classes, white Southerners and Californios, both of whom embody old money, honor, traditional values, and a stable social hierarchy, to redeem the nation morally by displacing the monopoly capitalists" (Luis-Brown, 817).

FENCING IN COMMUNITY

In *The Squatter and the Don* and "Historical and Personal Memoirs," the marking of boundaries serves a community-defining function strikingly similar to strategies that Scott Romine identifies with southern plantation narrative. In *The Narrative Forms of Southern Community* Romine examines a group of works spanning the 1830–1940 period that attempt to posit an organic "true community" held together by "manners and morals deriving from a commonly held view of reality" (Romine, 1). Rather than exposing the contradictions "inherent in these [works'] attempts to legitimize the existing order," Romine focuses on "the more specific issue of how these narratives register resistance to their own symbolic function." Working against their overt purpose, plantation narratives depict a community "whose ostensibly self-evident organization into class or racial types threatens to be exposed as a matter of coercion rather than consent" (18). Romine's conception of community dispatches southern fetishizations of "true community." Rather, Romine defines community as "a social group that, lacking a commonly held view of reality, coheres by means of norms, codes, and manners that produce a simulated, or at least symbolically constituted, social reality," adding that a community "relies not on what is there so much as what is, by tacit agreement, not there" (3). Community, in his model, is enabled by practices of avoidance, deferral, opposition, and evasion. Romine stresses, for example, the important role that the drawing of boundaries plays in "defining a community's inside and outside, and more importantly, its conditions of insiderhood and outsiderhood" (4). Boundaries in plantation works circumscribe the plantation, the local network of plantations, the region or state, and the South (5). It is not simply that boundaries in plantation narratives privilege "insiderhood" over "outsiderhood" but rather that they mark the "insider" as one who is "located within a network of social relationships and obligations that does not extend indefinitely." In this sense, boundaries "tend to be drawn in such a way as to divide order from chaos, internal security from external threat." Consequently, the communal boundary "marks not merely an already ordered social space, but a space inside of which order can and must be actively maintained" (6).

In *The Squatter and the Don* and "Historical and Personal Memoirs," the drawing of boundaries similarly serves to redefine Mexican (hacienda) community as a social unit as a defense against U.S. material and discursive threats to its existence. Although these boundaries may shift, in both texts they possess a geographic analogue. Whether they are the boundaries marking the borders of individual ranchos, Mexican and Spanish land grants, Alta California, or Mexican territory, in *The Squatter and the Don* and "Historical and Personal Memoirs" such demarcations serve to circumscribe and reconstitute Mexican (American) community. Since boundaries form the foundation of land entitlement claims, the mapping of these lines forms a central trope in both works. But the drawing of boundaries also functions as a way of marking a community's inside and outside and, more importantly, its conditions of inclusion and exclusion (Romine, 4). By marking boundaries between the Californio community and the encroaching Yankee world—that is, between, as the novel's title announces, the Mexican "don" and the American "squatter"—Ruiz de Burton's book reconstitutes cultural identities rooted in the region's seigneurial ranching community.

The novel's land argument rests on establishing the legitimacy of boundaries based on Spanish and Mexican entitlement claims. When the narrator cites the 1848 Treaty of Guadalupe Hidalgo, which recognized geographic demarcations established during the Spanish and Mexican eras but did not validate pre-conquest land grants, she thus references the decades-long history of colonization of Alta California and other northern territories by settlers from New Spain and Mexico. The novel adduces the treaty to document prior boundaries circumscribing the conquered region as well as proof, therefore, of the injustice of U.S. land policy, which refused to recognize Mexican and Spanish land grants.[21] Or, as Don Mariano explains to Clarence in chapter XVI, "It ought to have been sufficient that by the Treaty of Guadalupe Hidalgo . . . the nation's honor was pledged to respect our property. The treaty said that our rights would be the same as those enjoyed by all other American citizens. The [government] never thought of that. With very unbecoming haste, Congress hurried to pass laws to legalize their despoliation of the conquered Californians, forgetting the nation's pledge to protect us" (Ruiz de Burton, *The Squatter and the Don*, 175). Similarly, throughout "Historical and Personal Memoirs" Vallejo cites legal and political documents to establish the legitimacy of Mexican and Spanish entitlement claims and thus prove the *illegitimacy* of U.S. land policy that negated such documents. Quoting, for example, from "Title Eleven of the Regulation and Instruction for Presidios set up by the Spanish monarch in the *cedula* of September 10, 1772," he notes that "since the regulation and its provisions had always been in force in California since the founding of San Luis Obispo Mission and since no laws were or had been passed in conflict with its provisions, it is clear that the [U.S.] California state courts acted lightly when they handed down decisions which were in open conflict with that Regulation" (M. G. Vallejo, 5:186).

Don Mariano's efforts in chapter II to require that fences be constructed around the homesteads of squatters on his ranch illustrate the role that the marking of boundaries plays in *The Squatter and the Don*. The fences represent both a physical and figurative demarcation. They will physically block Alamar's cattle from squatters who are shooting or capturing them when they wander onto their homesteads—a widespread problem for Californio ranchers whose land was occupied by squatters. The fences also symbolically separate the "inside" seigneurial community of ordered space from the outside threat of disorder embodied by the squatters. Don Mariano comments on the absurdity of the "no-fence" law, a California statute ostensibly passed to protect agriculture but that in fact permits Alamar's livestock to be slaughtered or stolen by squatters who do not yet possess a legal claim to their homesteads: "By those laws any man can come to my land[,] . . . plant ten acres of grain, without any fence, and then catch my cattle which, seeing the green grass without a fence, will go to eat it." As with the piecemeal appropriation of his land, the injustices mount, for the squatters may then "put the cattle in a 'corral' and make me pay damages and so much per head for keeping them, and costs of legal proceedings and many other trumped up expenses, until for such little fields of grain I may be obliged to pay thousands of dollars" (Ruiz de Burton, *The Squatter and the Don*, 66). As the novel here and elsewhere discloses, under the new U.S. social structure, the law does not serve the interests of justice and "order"; on the contrary, by lending its authority to the squatter movement, it legitimizes injustice and "disorder."

Don Mariano attempts to resolve the conflict by offering to cede the squatters their homesteads and provide them with cattle on the condition that they no longer grow a single commercial crop (monoculture) but, rather, become cattle ranchers and (subsistence) farmers like himself. But the don invites them to adopt the hacienda mode of production not because he believes the squatters are worthy of inclusion within the Mexican hacienda community. On the contrary, the squatters personify all of those qualities—individualism, selfishness, greed, disorder, and so forth—identified with capitalism and modernity that stand in opposition to seigneurial Mexican culture. It is not simply that the squatters are of a different race and class but rather that they possess no appreciative understanding of Mexican seigneurial beliefs and values. That Don Mariano would "invite" such outsiders to become ranchers when they have clearly transgressed the boundaries of the Californio social order reflects his growing desperation in the face of his community's imminent financial and sociocultural ruin. Clinging to his traditional value system by acting honorably in offering to give the squatters their homesteads, Don Mariano must face a group of men for whom the concept of honor appears archaic. Unabashedly, one squatter tells the don that "the 'no fence law' is better than all the best fences," since it protects the squatters' interests at the expense of the don's (Ruiz de Burton, *The Squatter and the Don*, 95). When the suspicious squatters jocosely announce that they "don't want any cattle" because they "ain't no *vaquero* to go 'busquering' [searching] around and lassoing cattle" (94), the don's tone becomes increasingly desperate. "All I want to do is to save the few cattle I have left," he explains. "I am willing to quit-claim to you the land you have taken, and give you cattle to begin the stock business, and all I ask you in return is to put a fence around whatever land you wish to cultivate, so that my cattle cannot go in there" (92).

The don's advice in the remainder of this scene mirrors Vallejo's own strategy in "Historical and Personal Memoirs": to celebrate subsistence farming and self-sufficient production with multiple industries at the (autarkic) haciendas as a means of validating the mode of production and property relations that existed in pre-1848 California (Sánchez, *Telling Identities*, 177). As in Vallejo's text, in *The Squatter and the Don* this argument represents one of many veiled defenses of pre-invasion California and its semifeudal hacienda system (177). Agricultural and ranching products function metaphorically in this scene, with hacienda products a figuration for Californio ranch community and grain or (commercial) crops a metonym for the threat posed by the squatters. The don recalls the pre-capitalist "old times" of agrarian Alta California when he says that on the Mexican ranchos "we raised all the fruits we needed for our use, and there was no market for any more . . . [and] we raised cattle and sold hides and tallow every year" (Ruiz de Burton, *The Squatter and the Don*, 93). Along with recommending stock raising, the don pleads with the squatters to diversify their agricultural production by planting "vineyards, olives, figs, [and] oranges" and making "wines and oil and raisins" (92). Diversification, the don insists, will make the squatters self-sufficient, protecting them from fluctuations in market prices as well as unpredictable weather. The novel's defense of the hacienda takes more obvious forms as well. The two interethnic marriages between children of the Alamars and their Anglo American neighbors, the Mechlins, posit a symbolic union not with Anglo capitalist society but, rather, with those Anglos who have at least nominally embraced the seigneurial agrarian culture of the Alamars.

The threat posed by the squatters throughout represents that of a contrasting (modern) conception of production as much as it does the threat of a differing nation, race, or class. Since it is clear to Alamar that without fences, or boundaries, between the two communities, the (modern) Yankee world will engulf Californio hacienda community, the don continues his argument promoting traditional hacienda industries. It is "a mistake to try to make San Diego County a grain-producing county," Alamar replies to the resistant squatters. "It is not so, and I feel certain it never will be. . . . This county is, and has been and will be always, a good grazing county—one of the best for fruit-raising on the face of the earth. God intended it should be." He pleads with the squatters to "devote your time, your labor and your money" to producing diversified (hacienda) products, "raising vineyards, fruits and cattle, instead of trusting to the uncertain rains to give you [commercial] grain crops" (Ruiz de Burton, *The Squatter and the Don*, 91).

When the squatters accuse Clarence of "favoring the aristocracy" because of his planned marriage to Don Mariano's daughter Mercedes, Clarence defends the don's proposal by pointing to the futility of efforts to do away with the Californios' traditional industry and community. "Plant wheat," he insists to the squatter Gasbang, "if you can do so without killing cattle. But do not destroy the larger industry with the smaller. If, as the Don very properly says, this is a grazing county, no legislation can change it. So it would be wiser to make laws to suit the county, and not expect that the county will change its character to suit absurd laws" (Ruiz de Burton, *The Squatter and the Don*, 96). As in the above passage, in which the existence of the semifeudal hacienda mode of production is ordained by God, here the immutability of geography confirms for Clarence the historical continuity of Mexican hacienda community in the face of its imminent destruction by "absurd" laws implemented by outside (U.S.) forces. As in the previous passages, both Clarence and Don Mariano, like Vallejo himself, endorse a pre-capitalist mode of production as more sensible and therefore desirable for Alta California (Sánchez, *Telling Identities*, 176).

The novel's hacienda setting, where gentility and romance thrive as modernity steadily encroaches, forms a bastion of the pre-1848 Californio community in a region now controlled by the United States. The hacienda's boundaries therefore serve, as in the above passages, to mark a line dividing the outside world of capitalism and modernity from the seigneurial "true community" of the rancheros. And yet the hacienda also provides a genteel space for the flowering of romantic unions between Californio and Anglo, figuring the possible integration of the ("Spanish") Californio elite into the new (white) American social order. Scholars generally have concurred that despite the novel's express denunciation of (monopolistic) capitalism, the assimilation of the upper-class "Spanish" Californios into white American society is one of the novel's central concerns, written as it was "after the Californios' whiteness had been threatened by their lowered class status, the two being contingent categories" (Tuttle, 62).[22] Clearly, the many interethnic romantic unions in the novel, which are identified with the pastoral hacienda setting, express an anxious (Californio) desire for integration into post–Civil War U.S. (white) society—and hence acceptance by the landed Mexican elite of those U.S. social institutions that had displaced pre-1848 seigneurial society. But these romances also serve a wider purpose, reinstating the seigneurial cultural and caste identities of the landed Mexican elite to advance the novel's anti-capitalist and "anti-modern" polemic. At the beginning of chapter VIII Alice Darrell and her brother Clarence pay a visit to the Alamar rancho, where their respective partners, Mercedes Alamar and her brother Victoriano, wait to receive them. In contrast to the sordid money-centered world of the squatters and other representatives of the new order, such as the robber baron Leland Stanford, hacienda boundaries in this scene demarcate a realm of manners, romance, and leisure. In much of the novel the pastoral motif is disrupted by the brutal reality of occupation by squatters, whereas in this passage the hacienda, framed by the grandeur of its physical surroundings, mirrors the idealized romantic unions between Californios and Anglos.

As Alice and Clarence approach the hacienda, they discern "[t]he golden rays of a setting sun" which "were vanishing in the west" and "a silvered moon" that "was rising serenely over the eastern hills." When their carriage "reaches the foot of the low hill where the Alamar house stood," the "French windows opening upon the veranda sent broad streams of light across the garden and far over the hill." As if to extend the pastoral motif to the great house of the hacienda itself, sounds of music and singing greet the two visitors. When the initial singing ceased, "the prelude of a Spanish song

Lithograph of Vallejo's ranch, Lachryma Montis (Tears of the Mountain), at Sonoma, ca. 1840s. Vallejo used this pastoral image on one of his letterheads. Courtesy of The Society of California Pioneers, San Francisco.

was begun. . . . A lady at the piano arose and selected another piece of music, and began the accompaniment of [an] old and well known [song]." As the two watch the singer from outside the house, Alice asks her brother who the woman at the piano is: "'She is Mercedes,' whispered Clarence, glad of the excuse to whisper, and with a preparatory checking of breath and swallowing of something that seemed to fill his throat always, when her name was mentioned" (Ruiz de Burton, *The Squatter and the Don,* 112). Mercedes sings a second song with so much feeling that "it seemed to Clarence that he could not have listened to the simple melody before now attentively enough to appreciate its pathos, for it sounded most sweetly touching to him" (112–13).

This passage recalls a scene in chapter II that similarly marks the space of the hacienda as one of romance and gentility, attributes of seigneurial "true community" diametrically set against the intruding outside capitalist forces that frustrate Don Mariano. Troubled by the arrival of more squatters on his land, the don is first depicted in this scene as a disconsolate figure "silently walking up and down the front piazza of his house at the rancho." He hears the "sounds of laughter, music, and dancing [that] came from the parlor, [where] the young people were entertaining friends from town with their usual gay hospitality, and enjoying themselves heartily." The threat posed by the "outside" world, however, prevents the don from participating in the possible union of (Anglo American?) young people "from town" with the children of the Californios.[23] As much as he would like to join the festivities and fulfill his role as seigneurial patriarch, the don is preoccupied with the squatters and must forgo the celebration. The narrator points out the contrast between community "insiderhood," symbolized by the hacienda house itself, and the disruption threatened by the squatters by noting that Don Mariano "was as fond of dancing as his sons and daughters, and not to see him come in and join the quadrille was so singular that his wife thought she must come out and inquire what could detain him" (Ruiz de Burton, *The Squatter and the Don*, 64).

One discerns the gravity of the don's dilemma at the end of the scene: the squatters are arriving in increasing numbers to stake claims on his rancho, physically and symbolically transgressing the boundaries of hacienda community. Driven to denounce a government whose democratic principles he embraces in theory, Don Mariano's ensuing comments identify the marriage of U.S. law and the racialized politics of land entitlement under the new capitalist order. This "marriage" appears all the more abhorrent to the don given his faith in the efficacy of seigneurialism, which, in his eyes, promotes the very essence of "public morality" (Ruiz de Burton, *The Squatter and the Don*, 174). The Treaty of Guadalupe Hidalgo, he remarks, "said that our rights would be the same as those enjoyed by all other American citizens. But, you see, Congress takes very good care not to enact retroactive laws for Americans; laws to take away from American citizens the property which they hold now, already, with a recognized legal title. No, indeed. But they do so quickly enough with us—with us, the Spano-Americans, who were to enjoy equal rights, mind you, according to the treaty. . . . This is what seems to me a breach of faith, which Mexico could neither presuppose nor prevent" (67).

Elsewhere Don Mariano employs the seigneurial concept of honor to condemn the U.S. juridical order. In chapter XVI he laments not only the "sapping . . . of public morality" and the loss of "all respect for the rights of others" under the new sociopolitical order but also the larger loss of U.S. "national honor" due to the subversion of the treaty, which, he emphasizes, "was pledged to respect" Mexican property (Ruiz de Burton, *The Squatter and the Don*, 174–75). To act dishonorably by breaking a solemn pledge, in the don's view, undermines the foundation of "public morality" on which traditional Mexican (seigneurial) culture rests. By contrast, the concepts of "honor" and "public morality" appear alien to the Americans depicted in *The Squatter and the Don*, the best example being Stanford, who personifies the amorality that in the novel lies at the heart of U.S. capitalist culture. As one Californio supporter remarks about Stanford's railroad monopoly, speaking also of the monopolist himself, "[I]t has no soul to feel responsibility, no heart for human pity, no face for manly blush—that soulless, heartless, shameless monster" (320). Mirroring the seigneurial-based argument made against the law, the narrator warns Californians that the monopolists will "contaminate the public press and private individual until thy children shall have lost all belief in honor, and justice, and good faith, and morality. Until honesty shall be made ridiculous and successful corruption shall be held up for admiration and praise" (304).

The squatters thus embody, like Stanford, the destructive social forces identified in the novel with (outside) Yankee dominance, including the new cultural ethos of individualism and commercialism. The Californios' seigneurial-based attack on this new outlook is perhaps best captured by the narrator's response in chapter XXXV to the squatters' defense in court of its legally sanctioned appropriation of the Mechlins' ranch: "The answer to Mrs. Mechlin's complaint [against the squatters] was a masterpiece of unblushing effrontery that plainly showed it had originated in a brain where brazen falsehood and other indecencies thrived like water-reptiles growing huge and luxuriating in slimy waters" (Ruiz de Burton, *The Squatter and the Don*, 338).

Constructing Community in "Historical and Personal Memoirs"

Although it continues to serve as a foundational source on early California history, Vallejo's five-volume autobiography, "Historical and Personal Memoirs Relating to Alta California," has attracted little in the way of comprehensive scholarly study.[24] The work's subtitle, "A Political History of the Country from 1769 to 1849. Customs of the Californians. Biographical Notes Concerning Notable Individuals," announces its expansive historical breadth. Among its many subjects, Vallejo's work includes detailed descriptions of the indigenous cultures of Northern California, an equally meticulous recounting of the processes of colonization and settlement, and an extensive account of the long political battle to secularize Alta California's missions and open church lands to Californio ranchers. In passage after passage, Vallejo's prominent role in the history of the northern region of Alta California—as Indian fighter, colonial agent, military commander, *caudillo* (boss), *hacendado,* and patriarch—stands out. Read in intertextual relation to Ruiz de Burton's *The Squatter and the Don*, Vallejo's narrative highlights the novel's absences and exclusions.[25] In setting forth Californio grievances over land entitlement, Ruiz de Burton's work suppresses not only Vallejo's status as landed patriarch but also his position as military commandant and director of colonization for the northern frontier. It thus represses Vallejo's pivotal role in the

Vallejo with his niece Carmelita Kune, 1887. Courtesy of The Society of California Pioneers, San Francisco.

politics of secularization, a struggle that led to the founding of Alta California's hacienda economy. Although Don Mariano Alamar in *The Squatter and the Don* rarely deviates from his role as hacienda seigneur—a figure for whom honor, status, reputation, and kinship are interdependent—Vallejo himself was well acquainted with the world that existed outside the boundaries of the Mexican hacienda.

Padilla's study of early Mexican American autobiography, *My History, Not Yours*, which devotes much of its first half to Vallejo's life and writings, has informed my reading of "Historical and Personal Memoirs." Padilla proposes a sociohistorical interpretation of Mexican American autobiographies that refuses to treat reductively the range of cultural and ideological meanings his seminal study reveals in these texts. *My History, Not Yours* urges contemporary Chicano and Chicana critics not to dismiss nineteenth-century Mexican American autobiographies simply because their authors, as the products of a social elite dispossessed by Anglo American conquest and colonialism, often nostalgically embrace early Mexican (hacienda) society instead of providing examples of "heroic narrative resistance" (Padilla, *My History, Not Yours*, 39). Padilla argues that when colonized by the United States after the U.S.-Mexican War, Mexicans "immediately gave utterance to the threat of social erasure" at the hands of a foreign culture and imposed political system (4). Critics dealing with narratives of that era must "examine the various ways in which autobiographical expression emerged from social rupture and was formed within a matrix of dislocation, fear, and uncertainty" (10). Calling their works "narratives of dispossession," Padilla convincingly asserts that "nostalgia for an earlier world produced not a non-critical reaction to loss, but an oppositional response to displacement, albeit a response often deeply mediated by a language of accommodation" (x).

My History, Not Yours thus uncovers a "retrospective narrative habit" in nineteenth-century Mexican American autobiographies that "goes beyond reconstructing an individual life." Instead, such a life "is measured within a communitarian configuration and against the disruption of identity as identity is situated within an imagined cultural community of the past" (Padilla, *My History, Not Yours*, 232). For the Vallejo family, for example, U.S. annexation of Mexico's northern region meant economic and political disenfranchisement under Anglo American hegemony. This disenfranchisement brought with it cultural fragmentation and displacement for the Vallejos as well as for the entire Mexican American population. As Padilla remarks about Vallejo's "Historical and Personal Memoirs," "[T]he autobiographical act, therefore, becomes a tense ritual of gathering and sorting the relics of the communal past, narratively reifying the cultural legacy while rearranging the national one, proclaiming a desire to become an American but doing so in a language and discourse of opposition" (89).

My History, Not Yours shows that while Mexican history has been reified in autobiographical accounts such as Vallejo's, they nevertheless represent an honorable Mexican American historical and cultural legacy preserved for, and available to, later generations. What is missing from Padilla's model is an explanation of how and why key aspects of this history were mythologized or suppressed. Though *My History, Not Yours* does disclose the gendered omissions and biases within Vallejo's patriarchal narrative in two chapters devoted to Mexican American women's autobiographies, a particularly notable absence is an interrogation of the seigneurial class and caste identities from which Vallejo's patriarchal authority emerged.[26] With the recovery of a portion of the encoded "parchments" of Mexican American history and their acceptance as true documents of that culture, the task that remains is to decipher and interpret the remainder of Vallejo's text. Looking at Vallejo's life and memoirs in relation to the space of the Mexican hacienda serves to further historicize *The Squatter and the Don*'s representation of Vallejo's life as Californio seigneur.

"Historical and Personal Memoirs" employs many of the same community-defining strategies identified in my comments on Ruiz de Burton's novel. Like *The Squatter and the Don*, the work is broadly concerned with valorizing seigneurial Californio (hacienda) community to serve the landed elite's allied sociocultural and political impulses in post-conquest U.S. society. As in *The Squatter and the Don*, in "Historical and Personal Memoirs" this project is contingent upon the inscription of boundaries that serve to draw distinctions between Californio "true community" and all of those outside groups that at one point or another threatened it (e.g., native peoples, and later, Americans and other immigrants who arrived during and after the gold rush). Although these boundaries may shift, they are always at some level geographic. Depending on the period covered, they variously circumscribe individual ranchos, land grant territory, Alta California, the Spanish northern frontier, and the Mexican nation. In the first two volumes of the narrative, which delve at length into the decades-long military campaign by colonists to subjugate Alta California's native peoples, the boundaries demarcate a border separating Spanish "civilization" (order) from Indian "barbarism" (chaos, disorder).

Sánchez notes that constructs of dispossession, enslavement, and extermination of the Indians in "Historical and Personal Memoirs" frame its "subsequent policies toward 'emancipated' neophytes [mission Indians]," serving to constitute Californio identities as *gente de razón* (people of reason/culture) (Sánchez, *Telling Identities*, 55). Like other Californio autobiographers, Vallejo employs this term to distinguish "Spanish/Creole" Californio ranchers from Indian and *mestizo* peons. To be a member of the *gente de razón* meant to be not like Indians or dark-skinned *mestizos*. The racialized other "served not only as a labor force on the ranchos, but also as the ontological antithesis to 'us,' the 'civilized' and cultured Hispano gentry" (Monroy, *Thrown among Strangers*, 136–38). The Indians' "irredeemable nature not only ordained their servitude," explains Monroy, "but qualified [them] to serve as caricatures of everything that the [*gente*] *de razón* thought they themselves were not. Ascendant Californios, though often mestizos, were, in other words, *gente de razón* because they were not Indians" (191).[27] Vallejo's many allusions to California's "heathen barbarians" thus serve to constitute the Californio gentry's identity as Spanish/Creole, legitimizing its own privileged position within the hacienda social economy. For this reason, although the anticlerical Vallejo criticizes the mission system for exploiting and oppressing California's Indians, he is willing, as Sánchez observes, "to set aside [his] critiques and praise the missionaries' dedication to the project of Christianization as well as their effectiveness in organizing an Indian labor force." Sánchez continues, "The mission's practical function as a civilizing, pacifying, disciplining, productive institution thus overrides all criticism of the mission as an enslaving, coercive, abusive apparatus of the Crown" (Sánchez, *Telling Identities*, 66).

Although Vallejo constructs the California Indian as racial "other," his strategy to employ the Indian to demarcate the boundaries of Californio (hacienda) community is throughout fraught with contradictions. Like other Mexican and Spanish intellectuals of his era, Vallejo shared a humanistic tradition that since the sixteenth century "argued against the natural inferiority of Indians and in favor of the equality of Indians with other men," according to Weber. In the "glow of the Enlightenment, eighteenth-century Spanish liberals rekindled the spark of humanism and combined it with an anticlericism" (Weber, *Mexican Frontier*, 45). In the Spanish colonial setting of North America, this anticlericalism spelled a troubled future for the missions. But for liberal intellectuals of Vallejo's epoch, the triumph of republicanism in the American and French revolutions, and later in the Spanish-American independence movements, represented the fulfillment of Enlightenment philosophy. Michael J. González writes that "[p]olitical documents such as the United States Constitution or the French Declaration of the Rights of Man crowned the individual, or the ideal of what an individual should be, with inalienable rights" (M. J. González, 154). While the Mexican Constitution of 1824—to which Vallejo devotes a lengthy passage in which he criticizes its failure to address the plight of the Indians—"affirmed the equality of all Mexicans without mentioning Indians specifically," documents such as the 1821 Plan of Iguala proclaimed that "all Mexicans, 'without any distinction of European, African, or Indian, are citizens'" (Weber, *Mexican Frontier*, 47).

Although Ruiz de Burton's portrait of Don Mariano Alamar captures Vallejo's own philosophical liberalism, the novel depicts the political views that emerge from this liberalism as naive, weak, and ineffectual in defending Mexican interests against "Yankee" aggression. This weakness is often figured by the physical illness of male Californio characters, particularly by Don Mariano's ailments, which include a bout of pneumonia, a "congestive chill," and finally a nervous collapse that leads to his death (Tuttle, 68). Sánchez and Pita read these illnesses as a central theme in the novel, asserting that "the crippling and freezing of the Californios" serves "as a metaphor for the political disempowerment and economic choke-hold brought down upon" them (Sánchez and Pita, introduction to *The Squatter and the Don*, 21). While Don Mariano Alamar's philosophical liberalism proves debilitating, when put into practice by republican political entities such as the U.S. government liberalism serves in the novel as an ideological mask for predatory Yankee capitalism, as illustrated by the actions of Stanford's railroad monopoly. The U.S. government and its juridical system do not serve the "people," as the nation's republican precepts proclaim, but rather the interests of capital, whose representatives control Congress. Republicanism espouses liberty and justice, but as the handmaiden to capitalism its noble claims are unfounded and its effects insidiously *unjust*.[28] This polemic conforms closely with Ruiz de Burton's remarks in several letters that she wrote to Vallejo in the late 1860s. In a letter of February 27, 1868, for example, she writes that "[i]t is impossible for me to approve of such *republics*. . . . I love '*the truth*' too much to see it insulted in such a cruel and crude way and not regret it . . . in the name of truth, why name despotism 'liberty' and tyranny 'justice'—oppress, tyrannize, but do not lie . . . the lie is what shocks one more, what I find disgusting and repugnant."[29]

Unlike *The Squatter and the Don*, in which Indians rarely appear either as individuals or as a population, Vallejo's portrait of the native peoples of Alta California in "Historical and Personal Memoirs" at one level reflects the author's faith in republican ideology and its liberal precepts.[30] As citizens of the Mexican republic, Vallejo affirms, Indians possess the same rights granted to all of its citizens by Mexico's Constitution of 1824. This document, he proudly states, "guaranteed equal rights to all citizens, and identical privileges and rights to all the states" (M. G. Vallejo, 2:33). He continues, "Faithful observance of all the articles of this document, abounding in sane principles of equality, would have lifted the inhabitants of the Republic to the height of felicity . . . [raising] the Mexican Indian to the dignity of a free man" (2:33–34). In "civilizing" the Indians of Alta California, Vallejo advises in volume 2, the first step should be "to let them understand their property rights" in accordance with the "principles of the rights of peoples" (2:253).

Unfortunately, in Alta California, argues Vallejo, Catholic missionaries and their benighted institutions have denied Indians these rights. The California missionaries are thus first impugned for having failed to "inculcate in their neophytes any principles as to the rights of free men" (M. G. Vallejo, 1:68). Under the missions, Indians, Vallejo insists, were at the mercy of "evil spiritual fathers" who established "at will and without consulting any other *law* than their own convenience the increasing numbers of settlements of converted Indians" (3:108; emphasis added). Vallejo summarizes his broader grievances against the missions at the end of volume 1, implicitly delineating his philosophical liberalism and republican political ideals. Sánchez lists these grievances as "exploitation of the Indians (forced labor through coercion), oppression (excessive cruelty . . . and excessive labor demands), enslavement (neophytes as unfree labor), cultural alienation (interdiction of their communal practice), monastic rigidity (no comforts), ideological and material manipulation (creation of consumer desires), and [repression of] resistance (escape from the mission)" (Sánchez, *Telling Identities*, 66). The Franciscan missionaries' despotic institution, Vallejo alleges, oppressed and exploited California's Indian population and impeded social and political progress in the region.

Despite his philosophical liberalism and devotion to republican ideals, Vallejo's narration of the political struggle leading to the 1833 secularization of the missions reveals profoundly contradictory sentiments toward California's Indians. Secularization resulted in the distribution to settler families of millions of acres of mission lands *and* thousands of Indian laborers who had formed the missions' work force. It also resulted in the pillage of "immense wealth in cattle, sheep, horses, mules, and the ruin of vineyards, orchards, gardens, and fields of corn and wheat" (Sánchez, *Telling Identities*, 157). The process unfolded during the thirteen years between secularization and the American possession, when "the Mexican governors made a stunning eight hundred land grants, mostly to Californios" (Monroy, "Creation and Re-creation," 180). The distribution of land, laborers, and property was hardly equitable. Though it appeared as if individuals simply applied to the governor for a grant, in reality "intense political intrigue had positioned only certain people to benefit from the largesse" (180). This intrigue forms the subject of countless pages in Vallejo's narrative, as the author's "advocacy for revindication of Indian rights serves as a strategy to affirm the rights of the [Californio] 'native sons' to the land" (Sánchez, *Telling Identities*, 138). Over the span of a few years, politically well-positioned Californio families such as the Vallejos in the north and Carrillos in the south acquired enormous tracts of land on which they established livestock haciendas. Even if prominent liberals like Vallejo had "sincerely supported justice for the Indians, by the late 1830s the prospect of acquiring and developing church territory had obscured all other emotions" (M. J. González, 163). Vallejo became the dominant "seigneur" of the northern frontier, where he already ruled as military commander, acquiring tens of thousands of acres of land on which he would eventually husband twenty-five thousand cows, twenty-four thousand sheep, and two thousand horses (Monroy, "Creation and Re-creation," 182).

During the period following secularization, Californio affection for the former neophytes withered. As Michael J. González comments, although liberal Californios like Vallejo "once hailed the natives as fellow citizens before secularization, after 1834 they only saw laborers who could be controlled to reap the land's riches" (M. J. González, 162–63). Vallejo's polemic against the tyranny of the missions thus conflicts with his seigneurial social status as a *hacendado* whose ranchos had hundreds of former neophytes at his service. While he advocates freedom and liberty for California's neophytes, as the dominant seigneur of the northern frontier, Vallejo "made use of a large [Indian] labor pool . . . and was able to keep his peons at his disposal by offering subsistence and little else" (Sánchez, *Telling Identities*, 163).

For these reasons, the image of California Indians that Vallejo constructs depends entirely on the context. In the sections that praise the mission's early civilizing function, when Vallejo describes his military exploits as a commander in battles against the native peoples of northern California, the vocabulary of the Enlightenment shifts to the racialized language of difference. And yet because Vallejo always employs the language of difference in his paternalistic portrait of Indians, the "secularization" and "colonization" passages at times converge to depict Indians collectively as "brutes" who have been "kept in a condition of barbarism and ignorance" (M. G. Vallejo, 2:34). Such a description justified the Indians' deliverance from mission tyranny but also naturalized their subordination under colonial rule and the post-mission seigneurial hacienda system, the latter of which Vallejo studiously avoids referencing other than as an institution that displaced the despotic mission. As Sánchez observes, in such passages "paternalistic and positivistic frameworks conceal the coercive nature of these civilizing strategies and instead sanction them for enabling a demonstration of the Indians' capacity to appropriate new ideological discourses and be regenerated" (Sánchez, *Telling Identities*, 65).

Vallejo's conflicted consciousness as (modern) liberal ideologue and (colonial) feudal seigneur reflects the failure of nineteenth-century Mexican liberalism to address longstanding social injustices inherited from the colonial era. In Alta California, as in Mexico, Sánchez explains, "liberal discourses would be primarily linked to economic liberty and private property rather than to a defense of equality, for the caste system was still operative and the subordination of Indians crucial for [the hacienda] mode of production" (Sánchez, *Telling Identities*, 99). Weber's comment about the role of "race" in this process is that "despite the egalitarian spirit of the liberal thought that informed the Mexican Constitution and the Plan of Iguala, in practice these strokes of the pen did not eliminate racial distinctions, which continued to appear in public documents, nor did they eliminate discrimination or exploitation" (Weber, *Mexican Frontier*, 47). For these reasons, as Michael J. González points out, while the Californios "hardly merit a defense for subjugating and then taking advantage of the Indians," as liberals they "had little incentive to respect the native Californians after secularization." He adds that their own "standard of liberal conduct allowed them the luxury to excuse any abuse they heaped on Indians." In one sense, liberalism and republicanism assumed progress: "In a world supposedly free from the influences of church, caste, or any other impediment, all individuals had a chance to rise according to their own talents. Also, as reformers had argued in Mexico, in a liberal society the individual regulated his own behavior. Therefore, when the ex-neophytes reputedly squandered their liberty on a round of cards or drinks, they faced the contempt of many *gente de razón* who could claim that by rejecting the progress the Indians deserved to sink into misery" (M. J. González, 165).

The politics of secularization in Alta California sheds added light on Vallejo's conflicted consciousness. California Franciscans opposed the conversion of missions to "secularized" parishes because, as Weber explains, they believed "Indians were not yet prepared to assume the role of citizens and needed the protection of the padres, or [settlers] would exploit them" (Weber, *Mexican Frontier*, 60). At the same time, even as anticlerical settler families coveted the rich ranch lands of the missions, "Indians themselves displayed contempt for the [mission] system that had kept them forcibly institutionalized" (67). As Vallejo's experience indicates, however, secularization in Alta California always had more to do with control of California's rich grazing lands and native population than it did with Enlightenment ideals or liberal ideology. The economic interests and property rights of Californio settler families, moreover, also coincided with economic and political processes then occurring in Mexico. As Weber observes, "[E]conomic forces in Mexico which sought to expand private property at the expense of communal property played a greater role in secularization" than did the liberal ideas of the day. "Californios and federal officials alike saw missions as an obstacle to the economic development of the province. The missions' near monopoly over California's coastal strip and over the indigenous labor force hindered badly needed immigration and retarded growth of private ranches and farms" (62). Amid Vallejo's grievances against the missions, he too sometimes takes this pragmatic tack. The "demoralization" of Mexican Californians, Vallejo believes, resulted "from the fact that the best buildings, the most fertile countryside haciendas and the most fertile country estates were under the control of priests who did not derive from those valuable properties all the returns they would have produced under private administration. . . . It turned out that [their tenants] could not turn in and make those improvements which were indispensable for the furtherance of agriculture, since in view of the short period of time for which the unalienable lands were rented to them they only engaged in superficial labor of little account which did not have the permanent character so necessary for agricultural progress" (M. G. Vallejo, 3:265).

Despite such passages, in which Vallejo appears to be an emissary of progress, rarely can he repress his contradictory relation, as liberal "father" and colonial "master," to California's native peoples. In the closing passage of the first chapter in volume 1, for example, he first affirms the humanity of the region's Indians by arguing that indigenous religions were not unlike those of some European societies. "If I have called attention" to the "stupidities . . . believed and practiced by the French and Germans," he states, "it has been to prove the unfairness of writers who condemn the rites and idolatrous beliefs of the Indians of Alta California." Like Europeans, Vallejo notes, the native peoples of California, "guided by their natural instinct alone and with no other monitor than their own conscience, rendered homage to the Supreme Creator and had faith in the immortality of the soul" (M. G. Vallejo, 1:13). But in the ensuing paragraph, Vallejo's liberal conception of Indians as members of the human community stands in marked contrast to his role and identity as military commander and colonial administrator of California's northern frontier. In this passage, Vallejo feels compelled to justify to an audience who may disagree with his "liberal" view of Indians why he has chosen to "[sketch] some of [their] peculiarities and customs": "Since in the course of my narrative I shall have occasion to describe the wars and campaigns I have waged against them, as well as the treaties which I signed with them, I have felt it imperative to call attention to a few prominent characteristics of the tribes with which my countrymen and I have fought in order to assure the safety of the settlers who had come from across the seas to people this then virgin soil, as well as to protect the neophytes, upon not a few occasions the object of attacks by heathen warriors who, thirsting for gain and revenge, very frequently made daring incursions and violent assaults upon the missionaries, the neophytes and their possessions" (1:14).

As the above passage suggests, Vallejo participated in battles in which hundreds of Indians were killed, and he thus stands in sharp contrast to the avuncular image of Don Mariano Alamar in *The Squatter and the Don.* Drawing in part on Californio accounts, Sherburne F. Cook traces the salient battles of Vallejo's military career in his study of California's Indian wars. In 1829 Vallejo "led a military campaign with cavalry, artillery, and all the panoply of war against the Miwok tribe and their legendary leader, Estanislao. Though the campaign took a heavy toll of life and did the Miwok great damage, it failed to subjugate them" (Cook, 109). In 1834, in the midst of the political battles over secularization, "Vallejo led Mexican soldiers against the Satiyomi, a subtribe of the Wappo; after two battles, 200 Indians were killed and 300 captured." In 1837 "Vallejo was skirmishing with the Patwin under the leader Zampay." In 1841, five years before the arrival of U.S. troops in California, "Vallejo is described by W. H. Davis as going to Clear Lake and slaughtering 150 Indians as they emerged from a *temescal,* the so-called 'Clear Lake Massacre.'" Two years later, his brother Salvador Vallejo went to the Gulf of Mendocino and "by means of rapidly constructed boats, attacked the natives who lived on islands, slaughtering 170" (9). Though, as Cook contends, "exaggeration is to be expected in accounts of these battles . . . there is reason to believe that the figures were not excessively inflated" (10).[31] Cook's portrait conforms with James Sandos's description of Vallejo as a *caudillo* (landed boss) who "carved out [a] personal fiefdom in the wilderness" (Sandos, "Between the Crucifix and Lance," 216). Such *caudillos,* as Sandos comments, were "men of some cunning and ruthlessness, cruelty in dealing with Indians, boldness in striking out into uncharted terrain, [and] strong desire for personal wealth" (217–18). Given the virtual state of war that existed between Mexican settlers and California Indians as late as the American possession, it should not be surprising that most tribes in the region favored the United States in the U.S.-Mexican War.

THE GOLD RUSH AND THE HACIENDA

Vallejo's narrative also constructs notions of Californio (hacienda) community inclusion and exclusion through its rendering of the gold rush. As discussed in chapter 1, the gold rush of 1848–49 serves as a "master symbol" of modernity in California history, delineating a boundary dividing the modern capitalist (American) era from the agrarian period of Mexican and Spanish rule. The demographic transformation during the years following this event serves as a reference point for considering the claims of Californio community in Vallejo's work. When Vallejo narrated his life story in 1874, he and most other Californio ranchers had already been dispossessed. But the Mexican American population had also become a minority amid a burgeoning immigrant population arriving from all parts of the United States and the world. In 1841, there were between 6,500 and 7,000 Mexicans and fewer than 400 foreigners of all nationalities in Alta California. Of the 10,000 Mexicans in the region in 1850 when it became a state, only 3 percent owned large ranches, illustrating the division between landed and poor Mexicans established during the post-secularization land grab. With the flood of immigrants brought by the gold rush, by 1851 Mexican Americans made up only 11 percent of the state's population. Between 1860 and 1900 the total number of Californians rose from 380,000 to nearly 1.5 million. During this period, Mexican Americans increasingly became subject to racial discrimination in public institutions, objectification in popular culture, and violence in the form of lynchings. By the turn of the twentieth century, ten years after Vallejo's death and five years after Ruiz de Burton's, Mexicans accounted for no more than 1 or 2 percent of the state's population (Almaguer, 70–71).

Vallejo's desire to invoke the claims of Californio agrarian community derived from the reality of a proportionately diminishing population, the concomitant loss of community land to arriving immigrants, and the loss of Californio power that these processes wrought. His response, much like Ruiz de Burton's, however, expresses both his fear of these changes and his need to (re)assert his conception of seigneurial Californio (hacienda) community. By projecting the social disorder he perceived onto outsiders (i.e., onto gold rush immigrants), Vallejo posits pre-conquest Californio agrarian society as a "true community" in the sense of one held together by manners and morals deriving from a commonly held view of reality (Romine, 1). Framing his "Historical and Personal Memoirs" with the idea of a "patriarchal," "healthy," and "moral" Californio community corrupted by the invading (capitalist) forces of the gold rush, early in volume 1 Vallejo cites the harmful influence of immigrant outsiders on "our young people." This passage and subsequent ones from Vallejo's text must be placed in the same seigneurial context used to interpret Doña Josefa's elegy to Don

Mariano, and other similar passages, in *The Squatter and the Don*. Like Doña Josefa's comments, Vallejo's remarks directly reference the values and beliefs of Mexican seigneurial (hacienda) culture: "How fine it would have been, had the vaunted enlightenment which the Americans have brought to California not perverted our patriarchal customs and let down the bars surrounding the morality of our young people. For, however much it may grieve us, we cannot deny that our progeny have to a great extent forgotten the healthy maxims we taught them. This relaxation of healthy morality may be attributed to the contact they have had with people of slight scruples who emigrated to California in the first period of the discovery of the rich gold deposits which caused such a pleasant surprise throughout the world" (M. G. Vallejo, 1:48).

Vallejo's comments represent more than a revisionist reading of an event in U.S. history that had already been transformed into myth by the time Vallejo narrated his story—and one that would be romanticized by hegemonic historians such as Hubert Howe Bancroft and Frederick Jackson Turner. The passage also constitutes a statement of community self-definition in the face of the all-encompassing crisis in Californio hacienda society brought about by the U.S. conquest and its aftermath.

Vallejo returns to the same point in an extended passage at the end of his narrative. Although he acknowledges that the "change of government which took place . . . has resulted in benefit to the commerce and agriculture of the young state," he emphasizes that it damaged the "morale of the [Mexican] people, whose patriarchal customs have broken down little by little through contact with so many immoral persons who came to this my country from every nook and corner of the known world" (M. G. Vallejo, 5:189). Like the previous quotation, Vallejo's grievance projects disorder onto the "outside" societies and particularly the United States, thereby affirming the attributes of the pre-1848 seigneurial (hacienda) community. (The United States, of course, had become the dominant foreign influence in California, the final arbiter of community within the former boundaries of agrarian Mexican Alta California.) Initially, the passage discusses the treatment of the insane during the early period of U.S. rule as a means of constructing community inclusion and exclusion. "Insanity" serves here as a metaphor for the chaos and disorder that Vallejo identifies with the forces and representatives of capitalism as epitomized by the gold rush.

In California in 1849 "there was no asylum in which to care for the insane," notes Vallejo. "[M]iners and emigrants who lost their reason during the first years of North American rule in California were treated more like wild beasts of the desert than like human beings. The raving maniacs were fastened with chains to trees or posts in the stables," he writes, "and the harmless lunatics were locked up on deserted ships in the harbor." If one interprets this comment not as historical truth but rather as an effort to assert the differences between community insiders and outsiders, one finds less surprising Vallejo's subsequent claim that "with the exception of two lunatics whom the general government had sent from Mexico," insane persons "had been unknown among us [Californios] since the settlement of Alta California" (M. G. Vallejo, 5:188). Although this proposition seems unlikely, in the context of a lengthy passage listing each gold rush immigrant group with the respective social malady that it supposedly introduced to California, these comments instead represent an attempt to reconstitute the pre-1848 (hacienda) social order by reestablishing the community boundaries that once circumscribed it. Vallejo continues that it was with "much wonder among us born in the country that two native-born Californios were later deemed insane," since within the "true community" of Vallejo's hacienda social order this problem never existed. "It is in truth with profound sadness," he reflects, "that from '48 until '52 the sick and insane received at our hands treatment that very ill befitted the boasted civilization of the century and our humanitarian sentiments" (5:188). While this final passage may refer to a new American California collectivity, given the context it seems clear that "we" and "our" instead express the moral vision of the Californio community. Within the organic "true community" of the pre-U.S. conquest era, Vallejo suggests, the sick and insane were cared for according to traditional values and customs, whereas under the modern U.S. (capitalist) social order, in which such community values no longer apply, they were mistreated (e.g., the insane were tied to trees or locked up on ships).

By positing the Americans as only one among many immigrant groups that brought social ills to the region, the remainder of this passage illustrates this point by representing the Californio (hacienda) community as being quite literally under siege by outsiders *in general.* Given the charged politics of land entitlement, one might expect Vallejo's concluding passages to draw a bead on the Americans. Instead, Vallejo constructs a model of difference focused on establishing opposition between the pre-conquest Californio (hacienda) community on the one hand and all of those foreign societies that were represented in California during the gold rush on the other (i.e., those who had crossed the boundary marking "inside" from "outside"). The following passage may be read as a list of grievances as well as a statement of the apocalyptic decline of the Californios by the mid-1870s. While the Mormons, according to Vallejo, "professed a religion which is in open conflict with good taste and with moral and political soundness," immigrants from other countries introduced more serious problems to California: "Australia sent us a swarm of bandits who . . . dedicated themselves exclusively to robbery and assault," Peru "sent us a great number of rascals, begotten in idleness and schooled in vice," and Mexico "inundated us with a wave of gamblers who had no occupation save that of the card table." France, continues Vallejo, sent "several thousand lying men and corrupt women," Italy, "musicians . . . who lost no time in fraternizing with the keepers of gambling-houses and brothels," Chile, "laborers . . . [of whom] many were addicted to drink and gambling," and China, "clouds and more clouds of Asiatics and more Asiatics . . . [who were] very harmful to the moral and material development of the country" (M. G. Vallejo, 5:184).

Conflating insanity with alcoholism to complete his model of the decline of traditional Californio community, at the end of this passage Vallejo points out that the "great supply of liquors" brought by foreigners created social havoc in the post-1848 era. As he puts it, whereas "before the coming of Fremont, we drank only pure liquor, and that in small quantities, and everyone enjoyed good health, tenacious memories, and lively intelligence," after the war and especially during the gold rush the situation was very different. "From France and Germany were introduced great supplies of liquor made up of chemical ingredients and noxious herbs," writes Vallejo, "and these affected the nervous system, clouded the intelligence, and undermined the most robust constitutions, sowing the fatal seeds of a multitude of diseases which were not long in sending to premature graves young men in the flower of their lives" (M. G. Vallejo, 5:188–89). This statement adds a new ingredient to Vallejo's discussion. Unlike the earlier comparisons, here "outsiders" not only contributed to the moral decline of community but also undermined the "memories" and "intelligence" of post-1848 Mexican Californians. Members of the pre-1848 California community possessed sound memories and intelligence whereas post-1848 society must confront a tragic loss of both. Given this circumstance, Vallejo's multivolume historical autobiography thus serves the important function of defending the community against this threat to Californio memory, intelligence, and history in the post-1848 era.

In "Historical and Personal Memoirs" the Americans embody a composite of the social maladies listed above and something more, for they have not only permitted this invasion by outsiders but also controlled the institutional apparatus that by the mid-1870s had caused the eclipse of the Californio ranchers. The Americans are thus "legal thieves, clothed in the robes of the law, [who] took from

us our land, and our houses and without the least scruple en-
throned themselves in our homes like so many powerful kings." As
Vallejo concludes, "It was our misfortune that these adventurers
of evil law were so numerous that it was impossible for us to defend our rights in the courts, since the majority of the judges were
squatters and the same could be said of the sheriffs and the juries."
Justice for them "was only a word used to sanction robbery" (M. G.
Vallejo, 5:185). Earlier, Vallejo had reminded readers once again of
the fundamental differences between modern (U.S.) capitalist values, which he believed are driven by individualism and commercialism, and the traditional morality he identifies with seigneurialism, in which community supersedes individual desires and honor,
status, reputation, and kinship are interdependent. Lamenting the
loss of another of his ranchos to squatters, Vallejo states,

> I cite this isolated incident in order that those who read my
> narrative may form some idea of the way in which the Ameri-
> cans treated the Californians when they took possession of
> this region. This unjust and rapacious conduct contrasts very
> unfavorably with the kind of treatment we extended to the
> Americans when our numbers were so great and we could put
> forty men in the field for each two they had capable of bearing
> a gun. We took great pleasure in making them gifts of land,
> livestock and agricultural implements. We acted in this man-
> ner because our upbringing and our religion taught us to do
> unto others as we would have them do unto us. No sooner did
> the Americans find themselves in a majority, however, than
> they treated us not as brothers, but like a conquered people.
> From the day on which California was delivered, bound hand
> and foot, to the sons of the "Great Republic" by the "grand-
> sons of Cain," the former have done everything they could to
> deprive the Californians of the lands belonging to them by
> law, justice, and right. (4:294)

Like *The Squatter and the Don*'s engagement with capitalist practices, these passages carry deeply contradictory meanings. At one
level, Vallejo points to the Americans as the embodiment of amorality and disorder because of the very *real* socioeconomic and cultural threat that the new Yankee order posed to the Californio
community. As discussed earlier in this chapter and in chapter 1,
the gold rush *was* a period marked by social conflict and upheaval
and particularly so for the landed Californios whose agrarian society was within the span of a few years inundated with tens of thousands of landless "foreigners." As *The Squatter and the Don* accurately depicts, after leaving the mines, immigrants who had arrived

during the gold rush became land-hungry squatters who, with the sanction of the federal and state governments, staked claims on land already occupied by Californio ranchers. Protracted litigation by squatters and their supporters in the government would eventually bankrupt Vallejo, Ruiz de Burton, and most of their fellow Californio ranchers.

But, as in *The Squatter and the Don,* the communal boundary in "Historical and Personal Memoirs" at another level plays a role analogous to that inscribed in southern plantation texts in that it marks an "already ordered social space . . . inside of which order can and must be actively maintained" (Romine, 6). According to Robert Brenner, the desire to maintain the existing social order is characteristic of pre-capitalist producers who have direct access to their full means of subsistence. As he explains, this group's "rationally self-interested activity will, as a rule, have as one of its goals maintaining those precapitalist property relations, which structure non-development."[32] Preserving the hacienda social economy, of course, also meant for Vallejo a return to traditional "premodern" gender roles and relations. As Padilla observes, Vallejo's autobiography "discloses a deeply embedded patriarchal consciousness in which wives, daughters, and sisters are remembered as virtuous and obedient before 1848, recalcitrant and foolish after. Respect for, obedience to, honor of, deference toward the patriarch were, for Vallejo, signs of familial and general social well-being before Americanization; after the displacement of the patriarch, the children fell away from the code of behavior and the patriarchal world collapsed" (Padilla, *My History, Not Yours,* 113).

Despite his deeply conflicted consciousness, like Don Mariano in *The Squatter and the Don* Vallejo was as bound to the seigneurial ethos of his traditional agrarian community as were most authors of plantation narratives. As this chapter has argued, however, this connection should not diminish the viability and eloquence of his depiction of U.S. (capitalist) practices in post-U.S. conquest California. But, let us recall, southern plantation and domestic fiction, and the southern agrarian movement which in the 1930s drew upon this literary tradition, formulated a critique of northern "industrialist" (capitalist) ideology and praxis as trenchant as that which characterizes Vallejo's "Historical and Personal Memoirs" or Ruiz de Burton's *The Squatter and the Don.*[33]

Vallejo's project to restore community boundaries separating "inside" from "outside" reminds us, in another way, of the contradictory political and ideological impulses underlying Californio claims to "true community." After reconstituting community boundaries in the above passages, Vallejo announces his willingness to integrate into the new social order if the United States would live up to the ideals that had attracted him to its republican form of government. Noting that "in spite of the Treaty of Guadalupe Hidalgo, the Americans have treated the Californians as a conquered people," Vallejo couches this grievance in rhetoric expressing a desire for conciliation with, and thus inclusion within, U.S. society. In mistreating the Mexican Californians, he argues, the Americans have refused to recognize them "as [U.S.] citizens who willingly became a part of that great family which, under the protection of that glorious flag that proudly waved at Bunker Hill, defied the attacks of European monarchs who, seated upon their tottering thrones, were casting envious eyes toward California and the other regions embraced within the great federation of the sons of liberty" (M. G. Vallejo, 5:190).

Despite such "integrationist" passages in "Historical and Personal Memoirs" and *The Squatter and the Don*, in both texts the hacienda functions broadly as a mimetic image and icon of pre-1848 Californio community. In both, the hacienda not only serves to circumscribe and define the lost seigneurial agrarian social order but, as the landed Californio elite's symbol and icon of landownership and social power, it also constitutes the overarching image onto which all of the supposed attributes of genteel Californio community have been projected. The hacienda as icon and myth emerges from the devastating social effects of U.S. dominance in much the same way that the pastoral icon develops in U.S. southern writing through regional conflict with the North. In Californio texts the impulse to "true community" as symbolized by the hacienda constitutes an imaginary resolution to antagonistic socioeconomic processes deriving from the violent siege to traditional agrarian (hacienda) society carried out by the combined forces of capitalist modernity.

Building upon the southern analogy posited in this chapter, chapter 3 traces this study's examination of hacienda narrative to the U.S. South, where a shared Mexican/southern history of defeat and conquest by the "Yankee" North, fixed in the former Confederate geography of Texas, bound Mexican American hacienda narrative to southern plantation writing. Set in South Texas during the U.S.-Mexican War, Jovita González and Eve Raleigh's *Caballero: A Historical Novel* invokes the hacienda as a site of Mexican (American) historical origins as a means of negotiating a social path for Mexican Americans in pre-1950s Jim Crow–era Texas. Extending and complicating Californio themes, it illustrates the shifting meanings of the hacienda as an agrarian ideal within Mexican American cultural memory.

Chapter

3

History and Memory
in Jovita González and Eve Raleigh's
Caballero: A Historical Novel

WRITTEN more than four decades after Ruiz de Burton's *The Squatter and the Don* and Vallejo's "Historical and Personal Memoirs," one of the most recent discoveries of the Recovering the U.S. Hispanic Literary Heritage project is *Caballero: A Historical Novel*, by the Mexican American educator and folklorist Jovita González and her Anglo American coauthor Eve Raleigh.[1] A historical romance about Mexican-Anglo conflict and conciliation, *Caballero* is set on a South Texas livestock hacienda during the U.S.-Mexican War (1846–48). Much like its Californio counterparts, *Caballero*'s convergences with the southern literary tradition problematize Chicano/a studies models that identify early Mexican American literature either as subaltern or as emerging uniformly from within the Mexican/Hispanic literary tradition.[2] Contradicting ethnic cultural nationalism through its depiction of unions between Mexicans and Anglo Americans, *Caballero* simultaneously upsets a narrowly defined Chicano/a literary recovery model through its striking southern historical and aesthetic affinities. While it diverges sharply from the Californio texts by depicting the hacienda as a socially complex institution with internal contradictions and competing interests, like Californio hacienda texts it works to overturn a number of assumptions underlying the recovery project's reconstruction of Mexican American literary history. Ambiguously affirming a common historic identification based on a shared sense of (Mexican American) ethnicity while displacing much of what the semifeudal hacienda came to symbolize for its authors, like the hacienda narratives examined in chapter 2 *Caballero* speaks to the heterogeneity of Mexican American culture and history and the multiplicity of current and past (Mexican American) identities shaped by this myriad experience. One means by which a Mexican American (literary) history can be recovered without being romanticized a priori as ethnically constituted resistance can be found by exploring the dual postcolonial origins of the Chicano/a population—Spanish and U.S.—as captured in the space of the hacienda in González and Raleigh's novel.

The southern analogy for *Caballero* draws on several recent literary models. The plantation novel's political strategies parallel the nation-building project of nineteenth-century romantic fiction in Latin America as explicated in Doris Sommer's *Foundational Fictions*. Sommer views the Latin American romance as a novelistic projection of, and device for, national political consolidation in a period of internal intersectional conflict in the newly ascendant nineteenth-century republics. It is in this interpretive context that José E. Limón, who with María Cotera recovered and edited *Caballero*, observes that marriages between representatives of opposed groups in the novel symbolically resolve interethnic and regional conflict, projecting a consolidated U.S. nation into which Mexican Texans have been integrated. The modern (capitalist) U.S. nation, in Limón's reading of *Caballero*, can be understood as being the destiny of Mexican Texas, and Mexican Texas may be seen as a part of the United States' pre-modern (and pre-capitalist) agrarian past (Fox-Genovese, 411). Though Limón does not repeat the subaltern argument, he does point to the possible influence of the Latin American, and particularly Mexican, historical romance on *Caballero*, suggesting that the novel emerged from the Mexican and Latin American literary tradition. However, the plantation narrative, particularly Margaret Mitchell's *Gone with the Wind*, was just as likely a source, a possibility that would overturn a Chicano/a recovery model by placing González at the center of discourses typically associated with Anglo America.[3] This broader comparative interpretation would account more fully for the novel's focus on nineteenth-century hacienda history as well as the work's foregrounding of (modern) Anglo America over (semifeudal) Mexico. That the Missouri-born Raleigh "had some large role probably in crafting the overall romantic narrative development of the plot" makes the argument for a southern influence even more compelling (Limón, introduction to *Caballero*, xx). Limón identifies Raleigh's role in "crafting González's contribution into the form of the romance novel" (xix–xx). Correspondence between the authors also makes clear to Limón, however, that this creative process occurred "with the active participation of González" (xxi), whose "familial-ancestral background" provided the source of the novel's historical context and setting (xx). Finally, although a strict Chicano/a recovery model perhaps cannot be expected to identify González as a southerner, as a native-born Texan she grew up in a state with strong historical and cultural ties to the South that often overshadowed the different historical and cultural heritage of western Texas and the South Texas borderlands.[4]

My analysis of *Caballero* differs from Limón's reading of the novel in another fundamental way. Mexican integration into U.S. society, as depicted in *Caballero*, is itself bifurcated along a North and South divide and is therefore more complicated than Limón's criticism suggests. Reflecting a not-always repressed identification of Mexican Texas as a conquered region, the novel presents the conjugal union of two central characters—María de los Angeles Mendoza (Angela) and Alfred "Red" McLane—who represent opposing sides in the war, as a marriage of convenience, even as this romance metonymically acknowledges benefits to the Mexican population in an imagined future U.S. Texas.[5] In a parallel interethnic union, however, the idealized "true" love between Angela's sister, Susanita Mendoza, and the southern planter Robert Davis Warrener contrasts markedly with the pragmatic union of Angela and Red. Whereas Limón uses Angela and Red's marriage of convenience as a primary frame of reference, both of these parallel romances must be examined in order to understand how the novel defines a path for Mexican-Anglo relations during the 1930s and 1940s, when the novel was written. Much like Mitchell's novel, which, as Elizabeth Fox-Genovese argues, served to establish a "historical pedigree" for the New South during and after the region's post–World War I integration into the industrial capitalist United States, *Caballero* pragmatically projects Mexican American inclusion in the New South(west) by remembering the rise and fall of this subordinated population's landed rancher elite (Fox-Genovese, 394).

Just as one cannot remove Mitchell's historical romance from the plantation literary tradition, one cannot critically approach González and Raleigh's novel without "remembering" the nineteenth-century history that it recovers.[6] Although, like Mitchell's novel, *Caballero* employs nineteenth-century history to explore and resolve social and cultural dilemmas of the modern (i.e., post–World War I) era, as in *Gone with the Wind* this early history does not serve merely as an empty canvas devoid of cultural and ideological meaning. Much like plantation narratives that remembered the Old South, *Caballero* recovers the Southwest's own pre-modern agrarian socioeconomic institution—the semifeudal hacienda—to negotiate a cultural and political path in the modern era for a population that, like the Old South's, had been conquered in the mid-nineteenth century by the United States. Even if the novel diverges in important ways from early plantation writings, *Caballero* evinces cultural, ideological, and political preoccupations strikingly similar to those of later plantation works produced by white southerners—particularly Mitchell's celebrated text. Most importantly, like *Gone with the Wind*, *Caballero*'s attack on patriarchy as a metonym for the semifeudal old order asserts the benefits of integration within the modern (capitalist) U.S. social order. Interethnic romance in *Caballero* thus projects Mexican American inclusion within a liberal and modern New South(west), an imagined bicultural society in which the pre-modern agrarian culture of its Mexican (i.e., southern) minority has not been lost but has ideally served to enrich and transform a modern Anglo American society driven by individualism and commercialism.

Incorporating the countermemories of disenfranchised groups such as women and the lower classes, the hacienda as memory-place operates in *Caballero* in a more complex fashion than it does in either Ruiz de Burton's *The Squatter and the Don* or Vallejo's "Historical and Personal Memoirs." But much as in other early Mexican American narratives, in *Caballero* the hacienda as memory-place functions broadly as an ethnic cultural icon, one that emerges amid the socioeconomic transformation that occurred with the arrival of modern capitalism in the Mexican southwest as described in chapter 1. In Texas this change took place between 1880 and 1920, a period that Richard Flores has labeled the Texas Modern, when commercial agriculture was able to replace traditional Mexican farming and ranching practices. "The effects of the Texas Modern on the lives of the local Mexican population were severe," notes Flores (R. Flores, *Remembering the Alamo*, 5). These effects included "underemployment that ensured poverty; little access to public institutions, enforced by practices and policies of segregation; and loss of political power" (5). The new economic conditions identified with the Texas Modern were in this manner formalized into "segregated, prejudicial, and devalued social relations between Anglos and Mexicans" (10). It was from within these changing material conditions that the cultural memory of the Alamo, which functioned to codify Mexican subjectivity as "subjugated Otherness," emerged (11).

As these social conditions developed between 1880 and 1920, the myth of the pastoral Spanish Southwest, as set forth in chapter 1 in relation to the socioeconomic processes identified with modernity, was gaining national prominence through such writings as Helen Hunt Jackson's historical romance *Ramona* (1884). Popularizing California's mission myth, *Ramona* sparked a decades-long romantic revival mythologizing the Southwest's Spanish/Mexican past as pastoral romance. In the decades following *Ramona*'s publication this cultural movement influenced the lives of an entire generation of Americans, including, perhaps, González and Raleigh. As Leonard Pitt notes, during this period "ethnologists, poets, novelists, health seekers, and refugees from Eastern urban turmoil sought the solace of unspoiled wastes, discovered the pre-Yankee culture of the Southwest, and immersed themselves in it" (Pitt, 288). As discussed in chapter 1, the rise of this Hispanophilic agrarian cultural movement would mark the extinction of the old Mexican ranching order. Through its idealization of a pre-capitalist Spanish epoch of seigneurial grandeur now existing only as nostalgic remembrance, it served as a cultural eulogy for the passing of the pre-conquest (Mexi-

Jovita González, San Antonio, Texas, 1934. Courtesy of E. E. Mireles and Jovita González de Mireles Papers, Special Collections and Archives, Bell Library, Texas A&M University–Corpus Christi.

can) social order. Although the plantation narrative clearly informs *Caballero*'s portrait of early Texas history, the romantic narrative of the Southwest's (Spanish) agrarian origins as popularized by *Ramona* also circulated widely within pre–World War II U.S. culture, serving as a type of western analogue to the southern plantation myth. By wedding the two great agrarian mythologies of the era, González and Raleigh sought in *Caballero* to exploit the astonishing popularity of these myths within U.S. culture. It was in this seemingly contradictory cultural, literary, and sociohistorical setting that González and Raleigh, seeking to give voice to the silenced historical memory of Mexican Texans, wrote *Caballero*.

Constructing the Hacienda

The hacienda's ambiguous meaning in *Caballero* illustrates the heterogeneous historical experiences of Mexican Americans—descendants of both Spanish and U.S. dominance—a history that *Caballero*, more than other early Mexican American narratives, succeeds in capturing. Set on a livestock hacienda in South Texas, the border region between the Nueces River and the Rio Grande, *Caballero* opens in 1846 with news of the 1845 U.S. annexation of the Republic of Texas. Reflecting both Mexico's refusal to recognize the seizure of its northern territory and regional *tejano* (Mexican Texan) resistance to Anglo American aggression, Don Santiago de Mendoza y Soría, the patriarch of Rancho La Palma de Cristo (Palm of Christ), expresses shock and indignation at the news of the arrival of U.S. troops. Other Mexican Texans close to him agree. "We laughed at their Republic of Texas," his neighbor Don Gabriel tells him, "and at the flag they made and turned our backs to it and said 'We are in Mexico'" (J. González and Raleigh, 11). "We do not choose to be dirty *Americanos*," his sister, Doña Dolores declares. "We are Mexicans, our mother land was Spain. Not all of their laws can change us." (9) The novel is set during the two-year war that followed and ends in 1848. But the prologue (which the authors labeled "foreword") hearkens back to the colonial era of the previous century, establishing both the Mendoza family's genteel Hispanic/Creole pedigree and its almost mystical identification with the family hacienda, established in the 1740s by the Mendozas' pioneer ancestor, Don José Ramón. The hacienda buildings, the narrator remarks, were an obsession with Don José: "[H]e loved every bit of mortar and every wooden pin that bound it" (xxxviii). Decades later when Santiago is a young man his dying grandmother tells him that he will some day inherit the hacienda property and cultural legacy. The hacienda, she says, was "your grandfather's dream, which he built into reality. It was my entire life. . . . [B]e worthy of Rancho La Palma, and the things for which it stands." Those things were "religion, traditions, . . . [and] gentility" (xxxix).

Just as its semifeudal agrarian setting recalls the plantation landscape, *Caballero*'s sentimental plot, set amid the backdrop of war, mirrors the storytelling style of the historical romance as it developed in the U.S. South. The novel abounds in the melodrama of romantic unions between star-crossed young lovers of opposed backgrounds as it depicts the tragedies of war and intrigues of genteel agrarian society. The themes of conflict and conciliation between Anglo American and Mexican develop through a central romantic union between Lieutenant Robert Warrener, a soldier in the U.S. army—and a Virginia planter and slaveholder—and Susanita, Don Santiago's youngest child. Although the military conflict threatens to end this romance, the narrator throughout identifies the cause of Don Santiago's opposition to this relationship as Mexican patriarchy, thinly disguised as patriotism. In keeping with seigneurial cultural tradition, the don wishes to maintain his unquestioned authority in the domestic sphere. Whereas, for example, Don Santiago and his son Alvaro uphold arranged marriages, Mexican women oppose such unions as an archaic custom of the premodern (hacienda) era. In *Caballero* Mexican nationalism and patriotism in this manner go hand-in-hand with patriarchal privilege. It is in this fundamental regard that the hacienda world of *Caballero* is neither the Eden of the romantic colonizer nor the pastoral idyll of plantation lore. As María Cotera comments, in its "unflinching depiction of patriarchal values . . . [and] its deconstruction of the idealized male hero" *Caballero* "forecasts the cultural production of women of color" that emerged in response to "nationalistic male-centered discourses" (Cotera, "Hombres Necios," 340).

Two other romances between Mexican women and American men complete the novel's effort to predict, symbolically, the integration of Mexicans into U.S. Anglo society in Texas, thus displacing Mexican patriarchy. Susanita's sister, Angela, also against their father's wishes, marries Red McLane, a transplanted Yankee entrepreneur who hopes to enhance his political career through marriage to an established Mexican family. Rejecting Alvaro's marriage proposal, Susanita's friend Inez Sánchez elopes with Johnny White, a member of the Texas Rangers, a paramilitary unit that fought against Mexican guerrillas during and after the war. Other pairings drive home the theme of interethnic union. Befriending an American military physician, the don's other son, Luis Gonzaga, leaves the hacienda for the East to study art. For these perceived transgressions of Mexican custom and nationhood, the don unhesitatingly disowns both Susanita and Luis. As the United States takes control of Mexican South Texas, even the don's trusted peons, who are portrayed as exploited victims of the hacienda social order, leave Rancho La Palma to pursue the American way. One peon, Manuel, whose family had worked on the Mendoza hacienda for several generations, joins Warrener, with whom, as he later writes, he is *"muy contento"* (very content) (J. González and Raleigh, 205). Cotera points out that Don Santiago's peons "reject the slave-like system of the hacienda in order to explore their identities as labor in a world of capital" (Cotera, "Hombres Necios," 341). In this way, "the power base that Don Santiago has been consummately unaware of, yet which has held his hacienda together, begins to erode beneath him" (341).[7]

The novel traces Don Santiago's growing isolation from family and community and his concomitant decline as patriarch, a process that symbolizes the eclipse of Mexican (hacienda) ranching society in the region and the emergent consolidation of U.S. rule in the late nineteenth and early twentieth centuries. Portrayed early in the novel as the personification of his community's genteel culture and history, as the primary obstacle to Mexican-Anglo union, Don Santiago becomes the narrative's unexpected antagonist. The novel's other antagonist, Alvaro, carries out his father's beliefs through his guerrilla activities against the U.S. army and his misogynistic relations with his sisters and other women. The novel's title is therefore ironic in every conceivable sense, suggesting that although the don is, in the eyes of his community, an honorable gentleman-rancher—the literal translation of *"caballero"*—he is also a patriarchal relic of the semifeudal Mexican colonial era. He embodies both the genteel seigneurial Mexican/Hispanic past and, but more crucially, its social contradictions and iniquities. As a prisoner to cultural tradition, the don continues to uphold a patriarchal code even as his hacienda world collapses under the influence of what the novel portrays as a more progressive and egalitarian (modern) U.S. society. The last *"caballero"* in the Texas border tradition, Don Santiago becomes a tragically enervated figure, an anachronistic patriarch in a conquered and occupied homeland. After Alvaro is killed by the Texas Rangers, Don Santiago dies alone, an image symbolic of the don's loss of family, community, culture, and nation. This end, the narrative warns, represents the likely fate of Mexicans who, rather than pragmatically looking to the modern capitalist U.S. future, stubbornly cling to the semifeudal Mexican past. At the end of the novel Warrener discovers the don's body at the foot of a cliff overlooking Rancho La Palma, where he had often retreated. He dies on same the day that Roberto and Susanita, seeking to reconcile with him, have returned with his first grandchild.

Veiling a political message in romantic unions set in a semifeudal agrarian landscape, *Caballero* recalls nineteenth-century southern domestic (plantation) fiction as practiced by such writers as Caroline Gilman, Augusta Evans, and Maria McIntosh—as well as works in the same tradition by such twentieth-century writers as Margaret Mitchell.[8] Although the nineteenth-century southern domestic novel espoused the notion that the (white) South was inherently superior to the North, it imagined a desired resolution, through metonymic romantic union, to regional divisions. In the typical domestic novel northern men who became romantically attached to southern women were invariably converted to the southern cause in the process—a scenario that, interestingly, *Caballero* inverts, with the United States now *favored* over the (Mexican) "South" (Moss, 27). The projection of sectional rivalries into sexual politics also occurred through the marriage of a northern woman to a southern man, with the virile or southern party being dominant.[9] Once again, *Caballero* reverses this strategy in order to assert the benefits of the modern U.S. "North" over the semifeudal Mexican "South." But regardless of the outcome of such unions, in southern domestic fiction, as in *Caballero*, these romantic pairings were consummately political. As Moss notes, in them "intersectional rivalries initiated by interfering Northerners eventually separate lovers, split families, and destroy lives. Imported Northern values (temporarily) debase the moral currency of southern society and throw the community into disarray" (Moss, 13). But in the end romance resolves regional rivalry to the inevitable advantage of the southern (plantation) community. This pattern of resolution reflects the conservative political and cultural perspective of southern domestic novelists and their mostly native-born audience, an agrarian-based politics that *Caballero*, like *Gone with the Wind*, clearly rejects. "Distressed by the spread of individualism and materialism," southern domestic novelists associated these so-called evils of modernization with the North and "sought to protect their region from infection through their fiction" (Moss, 28). If placed in this comparative context, *Caballero* appears less a novel of conciliation with the new capitalist social order than a progressive attack on not only the pre-modern patriarchal traditions embodied by the hacienda but also their modern cultural and social legacy. In this sense the novel can be productively construed as "subaltern," as Cotera's analysis demonstrates.

Just as Scarlett O'Hara establishes her role as a nontraditional plantation heroine by transgressing gendered southern codes of conduct in *Gone with the Wind*, in *Caballero* female characters such as Susanita, Angela, and Doña Dolores defy the rigid gender codes and social conventions of seigneurial hacienda culture.[10] One extended scene in *Caballero* illustrates this theme.[11] After Susanita and Warrener rescue Alvaro from the Texas Rangers—who will soon execute him for his participation in a guerrilla insurgency against the U.S. army—Alvaro accuses his sister of using "his plight as an excuse to go to her lover" (J. González and Raleigh, 274). Don Santiago agrees, noting that by going out accompanied by a peon rather than by a man from the hacienda aristocracy, she brought dishonor upon herself and her family. Susanita has transgressed the code of honor that forms the foundation of seigneurial hacienda culture. "A true lady," the don tells her, "knows that her honor must be kept unsoiled above all else, because it belongs also to her family, is part of a proud name and the first obligation to the master of the house." Better that Alvaro, or Susanita herself, had died than that the latter bring shame to the Mendozas. "Death is nothing," Don Santiago declares, "be it for herself or for another, if she but save her honor. Alvaro's death . . . would have been a glory to our name as against the shame you have put upon it by dragging it in the dust" (279). He announces that Susanita has "forfeited [her] rights as a daughter" and that he "will never see . . . or speak to [her] again" (282).

The don's actions recall the defining influence of the code of honor on gender relations within seigneurial southern plantation society. Bertram Wyatt-Brown explains that this code created "[t]he familiar stereotyping of Southern ladyhood—the glorification of motherhood, the sanctity of virginity, and the noble self-sacrifice of the matron." The code of honor had a very important social purpose in plantation culture, ensuring at least outward female submission to male will (Wyatt-Brown, 14). After Don Santiago disinherits his daughter, the narrator of *Caballero* emphasizes this very point in a Mexican (hacienda) cultural context: "Honor! It was a fetishism. It was a weapon in the hand of the [hacienda] master, to keep his woman enslaved, and [he had] his fingers . . . twisted upon it so tightly he could not let go." The narrator continues, "Ironically, the Mexican *caballero* gave stern codes of honor to his women— waiting but the chance to dishonor them." The caballero "made an inflexible law of chaperonage, to protect [women] from himself." Linking the Mexican code of honor to the novel's larger allegorical union of Mexicans and Americans, the narrator notes that it was unthinkable "that men of an inferior race, as the Americans were viewed, could treat a girl with greater courtesy and gentleness than a Mexican *caballero*" (J. González and Raleigh, 280).

The Hacienda as Southern Space

Although *Caballero* symbolically resolves interethnic conflict through integration rather than retreat to a pastoral (i.e., patriarchal) hacienda past, it portrays the elite Mexican families of the border region in a manner that mirrors the portrait of southern culture found in plantation narrative, including the modern and more progressive *Gone with the Wind*. Whereas the Americans are "strong, powerful, fearless, and seem to have unlimited wealth," declares the hacienda priest Padre Pierre in chapter 5, they lack what (landed) Mexicans have: "dignity, self-respect, pride, nobility, traditions, and an old and sound religion" (J. González and Raleigh, 54). Given that González counted some of these landowning families among her ancestors, such a passage cannot be regarded as ironic, despite the don's later role as antagonist. Of the many American characters in *Caballero*, only Warrener, a southerner, will prove to be an exception to the don's rule distinguishing Mexicans from Americans. Despite the novel's attempt to promote a resolution to this interethnic conflict, *Caballero* makes it clear that the seigneurial "organic" community of the pre-modern Mexican hacienda rests on a "doctrine of traditionalism" according to which "religion, gentility, family rank, and patriarchalism" take precedence over modern (U.S.) values such as individualism and the quest for money (21). This idea recalls the description of traditional seigneurial southern culture as "nonaggressive [and] noncommercial . . . one in which people were not grasping, always in a hurry, greedy to make more and more money" (Conkin,

86). *Caballero* makes reference to other supposed U.S. southern traits to such an extent that Paul K. Conkin's summary of the agrarian view of southerners applies just as well to the Mexican gentry of *Caballero*. Southerners, Conkin remarks, "have a special relationship to the land, to local space, to roots. They are closely tied to immediate family or to networks of kin. They love leisure . . . [and] finally, southerners [are] more religious than people in other sections of the country" (86).

It therefore does not seems coincidental that González and Raleigh chose to include the scion of a southern planter family as a countervailing romantic protagonist. As a southern gentleman, Warrener embraces a traditional seigneurial doctrine not unlike that of the Mexican elite. In contrast to Red, Warrener, as a southern planter-aristocrat, possesses the "dignity, self-respect, pride, nobility, [and] traditions" that early in the novel are associated with the hacienda oligarchy. Luis Gonzaga at one point describes him as "an *hidalgo* [nobleman] in his country as [the Mendozas] are here [in Texas]" (J. González and Raleigh, 108). When Angela informs her sister Susanita about her plan to marry Red, the latter immediately draws a distinction between the two Americans. Unlike the honorable southerner Robert Warrener, Red, who is originally from New York, "bribes" Mexicans with "nonsense like helping [our] people. . . . [He] can't be anything but repulsive," Susanita tells her sister (213). When Red tells "Roberto" Warrener that they'll soon be "brothers," "Warrener's answer was a grunt. Brothers, he and McLane!" (244). At the end of the novel, Warrener even sympathizes with Don Santiago's plight as a fallen patriarch, seeing the don's lifeless body as a symbol of the sociohistorical status of border Mexicans. He recalls that his wife had told him that Mexicans had "been in Texas close to a hundred years," and that "the men piling into [Texas] were asserting their rights as 'Americans' . . . wearing the rainbow of the pioneer as if it were new and theirs alone. Already talking loudly about running all Mexicans across the Rio Grande from this 'our' land" (336). These sympathetic words, however fraught with the patriarchal seigneurial ethos, could never have come from the don's other future son-in-law, Red, who, though prefiguring the new U.S. order, is often portrayed as a southwestern version of a carpetbagger.[12]

In *Caballero* (hacienda) pastoralism symbolically serves the "southern cause" of marking Yankee (capitalist) difference, a not unexpected consequence of interethnic romantic unions that symbolically unite the two seigneurial "Souths" as much as they do Americans and Mexicans. Mirror-image pastoral descriptions of the plantation and hacienda consummate the regional "marriage."

The hacienda pastures, states the narrator in chapter 3, "dipped and rolled and swelled in a mighty sea of green, finally to break into mists of blue against the infinity of space" (J. González and Raleigh, 32). The "long limitless" plain surrounding the home "ran into a reddening, gold-painted sky." The land on which Rancho La Palma de Crist was built was "[a]s enchanting, as beckoning and beautiful . . . as it had been nearly a hundred years ago, when Don José Ramón had stood there." The hacienda home was "[l]ike a romantic dream . . . the patio a brilliant jewel in the setting of white [plain]. . . . The white thread of a stream blocked off gardens, orchards, fields of ripening maize like oddly striped aprons of green and brown and yellow" (33). *Caballero* includes a sketch of the floor plan of the "House of Mendoza y Soría," which conforms to the narrator's description of the hacienda home in chapter 2: "[a] thick stone wall [that] was built around approximately an acre of ground and rooms built against it through the years, opening into the outdoor living room, the patio" (20).

Warrener's nearly identical pastoral description of his family's Virginia plantation serves to "make clear" to Susanita's mother that Americans "have gentle ways of living also, and that [Susanita] will be a queen in the [plantation] setting" (J. González and Raleigh, 227–28). Rather than a patio in the Spanish architectural style, the Warrener plantation has "verandas, and they are wide open porticos with high pillars painted white." There is "grass thick as a carpet, and it is watered to keep it green." The plantation trees "are much larger than [the hacienda's] cottonwoods, and they have wide branches that throw heavy shade over both lawn and house." As one continues, one drives "under these great branches and there are flowers also and shrubs and vines that bloom, and ahead . . . is this big white house with green grass like a rug all around it" (227). The home is large and high, "with bedrooms and the ladies' *salas* on the second floor. A wide and open stairway leads to them from the *sala* downstairs, so that . . . the ladies can look like beautiful queens as they come down the steps" (227).

Caballero also incorporates numerous overtly "anti-Yankee" passages, recalling the southern plantation romance's political premise, from references to atrocities committed against Mexicans by the Texas Rangers to passages that depict the usurpation of Mexican land by American squatters.[13] At times, the pastoral motif facilitates this commentary, as when, for example, the narrator counterposes the green space of the border (haciendas) to the invading Americans who have violated Mexican territory: "Americans roamed over the land in groups, looked for places where the grass was the greenest. . . . Coveting. Visioning homes. Building dreams of empire. Not caring—too many of them not caring that homes had stood here for a hundred years" (J. González and Raleigh, 301). At one point, the narrator describes the arrival of Americans in South Texas as an invasion, overtly contradicting the novel's conciliatory premise. "'Remember the Alamo!' [the Americans] shouted and visited the sins of Santa Anna upon all his countrymen, and considered themselves justified in stealing the lands of the Mexicans," the narrator states. "They pillaged and stole, and insulted, and called themselves a sword of the avenging God, and shouted their hymns to drown their consciences." This scene was "repeated in variation for many years to come, until an empire of state would rise on land that had scarcely a square yard of it that had not been wet with blood" (195). As a result, native-born "Mexicans formed wagon trains and fled [the region] dominated by the invading peoples they considered inferior" (301).

Throughout *Caballero* the hacienda subject and setting work in this manner to establish the historical and cultural primacy of Mexican over Anglo Texas, countering the discourse of U.S. colonialism by recovering a minority community history that during the 1930s and 1940s, and earlier, had received little public or official recognition. In the "Authors' Notes" section that serves as an introduction to the novel, González and Raleigh indicate the importance of recovering this forgotten regional history. "[S]eeing the need to cover a phase of history and customs heretofore unrecorded," they first sent *Caballero* to publishers in 1939, the year the release of the movie version of *Gone with the Wind* reflected the southern romance genre's mass cultural appeal (J. González and Raleigh, xxx).

After being conquered by the United States, southern whites and Mexican Texans separately resisted "Yankee" intervention, in part, by remembering their pre-conquest society and (re)defining themselves in the aftermath of defeat by imagining their pre-bourgeois agrarian values and beliefs as fundamentally distinct from those of the new socioeconomic order. Although this process has more commonly been associated with the South, Genaro Padilla's research on the role of nostalgia in early Mexican American literature demonstrates that in the aftermath of the U.S. conquest in the Mexican Southwest a similar form of cultural remembrance emerged. Yet the post-Reconstruction plantation myth developed from the need to justify white supremacist support for Jim Crow segregation in the 1880s and 1890s, not simply from white southern desire to recover the social world of the Lost Cause to resist Yankee intervention. It was because the freed slaves represented a substantial political and social threat to the privileges of whiteness that a concerted cultural and political movement developed to disenfranchise them. Even the liberal affirmation of the New South in *Gone with the Wind* cannot alter the racial legacy that this 1936 novel inherits from the plantation literary tradition—and which it reinstated during the pre–World War II Jim Crow era. As a text that draws upon the same literary tradition, *Caballero* similarly emerged from the racially charged context of the Jim Crow South. But in stark contrast to southern literature's use of the plantation myth to justify the entrenched racial hierarchy, in *Caballero* the hacienda theme and particularly the unions between Anglos and Mexicans instead would have functioned—had the novel been published in the era in which it was written—as an argument *against* Jim Crow segregation. Quite unlike southern plantation and domestic fiction, a literary genre that Mark Twain satirized in *The Adventures of Huckleberry Finn* and which González and Raleigh also seek to turn on its head, *Caballero* would have been published at a time when racism in the United States was directed against the very community of Mexican elites whose early history was the subject of its sentimental story.[14]

After Mexico and the Confederate states of the South were defeated by the United States, "the subaltern sectors of north Greater Mexico and the South . . . experienced the worst effects of Northern capitalist domination, a domination always deeply inflected with and complicated by racism" (Limón, *American Encounters*, 18). Although the late-nineteenth-century decline of Mexican ranching society in South Texas ideally should have led to greater freedom for its laboring population, by the turn of the twentieth century Mexicans were instead relegated to a subordinate status that closely resembled the African American experience in the South. In racial and socioeconomic terms, Mexicans in Texas and elsewhere in the territory annexed by the United States became the southwestern equivalent of freed slaves who, despite being released from the plantation, had not yet achieved real freedom and equality.[15] "The most striking aspect about the new social arrangement [in Texas]," as David Montejano explains, "was its obvious racial character," adding that "[t]he modern order framed Mexican-Anglo relations in stark 'Jim Crow' segregation. Separate quarters for Mexican and Anglo were to be found in the farm towns of South Texas" (Montejano, 160).

Born in 1899, González spent her childhood in one such community, Roma, situated on the present-day border, the heart of the old Mexican ranching society of South Texas.[16] She describes the racial hierarchy that existed there, and throughout the border region, in her 1930 master's thesis: "Segregation of the two races is practiced in every town north of the counties bordering the [Rio Grande]. After [World War I], when the boys returned from France, a fraternal spirit animated by a common bond made the Texas-Mexicans hope for a change. But this superficial outburst of enthusiasm and emotion was not lasting. Many incidents which occurred lately have disgusted the Texas-Mexicans to such an extent that some have changed from the most loyal American subjects to the most bitter anti-Americans" (J. González, "Social Life," 108).

As González suggests above, within the South Texas farm order of that era "[s]pecific rules defined the proper place of Mexicans and regulated interracial contact. . . . The separation was so complete and seemingly absolute that several historians have described the farm society as 'castelike'" (Montejano, 160). Although, as Montejano points out, the notion of caste applies poorly to Jim Crow segregation in the United States, "it suggests, nonetheless, the degree to which race consciousness and privileges permeated social life in the [South Texas] farm order" (160).

By 1910, the Mexican Texan gentry whose culture and history González and Raleigh had meticulously documented in *Caballero* had been displaced by Anglo American ranchers and farmers and a new socioeconomic hierarchy had been established. The process by which Mexican rancheros in Texas were dispossessed was complex and varied. As Montejano explains, "Mexicans in Texas, especially above the Nueces [i.e., outside of South Texas], lost considerable land through outright confiscation and fraud" (Montejano, 52). Below the Nueces, "the experience of displacement was more complex. While fraud and coercion played an important part, the more systematic, more efficient mechanism of market competition also operated there. The accommodation between American mercantile groups and the Mexican upper class was, from a financial standpoint, inherently unequal" (50). The "peace structure" between the two elites—as *Caballero*'s interethnic romantic unions suggest—saved some upper-class Mexicans, but it did not forestall the outcome of the competition between the two (52). After the turn of the twentieth century, the landed upper class to which González traced her ancestry and with which she closely identified was extinct except in a few border enclaves.[17] "Not only did the new American law fail to protect the Mexicans" Montejano writes, "but it also was used as the major instrument of their dispossession" (52). Perhaps as a result of this socioeconomic upheaval in the region, in 1910 the González family's "fortunes had changed for the worse, and they moved to San Antonio, drawn by better opportunities, including a good education in English, and by the gradual emergence there of a small but stable Mexican middle class" (Limón, "Mexicans," 242).

The former Mexican ranching industry had its origin in the Nueces–Rio Grande area, where *Caballero* is set, with the livestock establishments of the Rio Grande rancheros. As noted in chapter 1, this industry can be traced to a group of founding hacienda estates established by colonists from New Spain in the mid-1700s, precisely the lineage outlined in *Caballero's* prologue/foreword. As Armando Alonzo notes, "Under Spanish and Mexican rule, ranching and commerce became the principal economic activities of the settlers, especially in the Lower Rio Grande Valley. . . . While the towns served as centers of local government and trade, stock-raising developed in the surrounding territory, especially in the north bank area." Of the two key enterprises, "stock-raising easily became the more popular occupation of the Hispanic settlers, who not only took advantage of the benefits provided by the virgin plains but also utilized a long history of ranching to develop stock-raising" (Alonzo, 67). As Limón notes, *Caballero's* "historical material, the plot of ethnic ćonflict, and the characters . . . [were] based on González's professional research and cultural background" (Limón, "Mexicans," 243). Her family history, as stated earlier, was apparently a key source. Members of the González family "were in part descended from [the] landed Spanish elites who had come to southern Texas in the eighteenth century" (242).

As Flores's study of the Alamo demonstrates, during the "Texas Modern" period of 1880 to 1920, as the Mexican ranching industry declined, the increasingly subordinate status of Mexicans was naturalized through a selective remembrance of regional history. Cultural memory of the official and unofficial wars fought against Mexicans in the nineteenth century played a social role analogous to southern memory of Reconstruction and the Civil War during the Jim Crow era (Montejano, 223–24). The Texas War of Independence (1835–36) and the U.S.-Mexican War functioned in Texan memory in much the same way as did military and political conflict with the North in post-Reconstruction southern memory.[18] Commenting on this point in *With His Pistol in His Hand*, his study of border *corridos* (ballads), Américo Paredes identifies the comparable roles played by Mexicans and blacks in these mirror-image romantic narratives of southern history. In Texas in the late nineteenth century, "[t]he 'cattle barons' built up their fortunes at the expense of the Border Mexican by means which were far from ethical. One notes that the white Southerner took his slave women as concubines and then created an image of the Negro male as a sex fiend. In the same way he appears to have taken the Mexican's property [i.e., land] and then made him out a thief" (Paredes, 20). The memory of the Alamo and of later military conflicts with Mexicans, as Paredes explains, "provided a convenient justification for outrages committed on the Border by Texans of certain types, so convenient an excuse that it was artificially prolonged for almost a century" (19).

By the mid-1930s, anti-Mexican sentiment in Texas and elsewhere in the Southwest had become institutionalized in states' segregation discourses and laws regulating relations between whites and non-whites, particularly Mexican Americans and African Americans (Montejano, 78). Although this fact certainly suggests the two groups' shared historical condition under Jim Crow, in other ways their histories diverge, particularly in the striking patterns of affiliation between Mexican Texas and the *white* South, as illustrated in *Caballero*. Quite distinct from the war against the United States in which Texas participated, the region's semifeudal agrarian origins as a Spanish colonial territory and its nominal solidarity, as a part of Texas, with the Confederacy during the Civil War make the analogy perhaps more obvious than it might first appear. Cultural identification with a semifeudal agrarian social order—the hacienda and the plantation—which was eroded as a result of military defeat at the hands of "northerners," further binds these two regions, as *Caballero*'s southern affinities again demonstrate. In the late eighteenth century and for much of the nineteenth century this pre-modern seigneurial agrarian order dominated its region's cultural and socioeconomic landscape. Although the analogy can be extended to include much of the Mexican Southwest—and perhaps all of Greater Mexico—South Texas best illustrates the historical irony that to this day "unites" white southerners and Mexican Americans.[19]

This historical irony not only accounts for *Caballero*'s use of southern (plantation) literary and historical motifs but also helps explain how the novel semiallegorically resolves interethnic and regional rivalry. White southerners, of course, were the earliest and most populous group of U.S. settlers in Mexican Texas, arriving in large numbers in the 1820s. In *Caballero* a countervailing "southern" critique of Yankee values and motives identifies the marriage between Red and Angela as one based not on love but rather on a mutually beneficial convenience.[20] The narrator contrasts this marriage to the "true" love of the "southerners" Roberto and Susanita, an idealized romantic union embedded symbolically in the pastoral agrarian imagery that later reappears even as the Mendozas' hacienda world is displaced. Through the juxtaposition of these two marriages the novel makes a case for Mexican, masked as southern, culture as it pragmatically acknowledges the inevitability and benefits of integration under U.S. rule.

CONSTRUCTING THE NEW SOUTH(WEST)

In the interest of imagining this national consolidation, in chapter 19 of *Caballero* the narrator reproves Don Santiago for refusing to cooperate with Red McLane in his proposition to influence postwar South Texas politics. Had Don Santiago been shrewder, states the narrator, "he might have taken his visitor for an example of these *Americanos* swarming into Texas, and profited thereby; and seen the impotence of a handful of people who measured greatness by old traditions and old bloods, and the camouflage of pomp and ceremony and dress which only money can obtain" (J. González and Raleigh, 182). Had the don been more like his daughter Susanita he might have foreseen a future U.S. Texas in which Mexicans participated in a potentially beneficial relationship with arriving Anglo Americans like McLane. He also might have recognized that Mexicans could accept foreigners like Red without necessarily choosing to embrace them culturally.

Through other characters *Caballero* makes a similar statement for integration and conciliation based on pragmatism rather than love. When Don Santiago asks his friend Don Gabriel whether he too "loves" the Americans, Gabriel's response invokes the novel's central political premise: "Love them, Santiago? If I had the gift of prophesy [*sic*] I would say that there would never be love between us as a people. Yet a repulsing of those who would bring us at least understanding, like this Señor McLane, will bring us nothing of advantage" (J. González and Raleigh, 327). Padre Pierre echoes this view when he advises his parishioners, who have gathered to discuss their options in the face of the U.S. occupation, to "[s]eek the *Americano* officials who have influence and invite them to your homes and entertainments. Show them that we have much to give them in culture, that we are not the ignorant people they take us to be, that to remain as we are will neither harm them nor be a disgrace to their union of states" (54). Through passages such as these *Caballero* appears to place its hope in McLane's promise to Don Santiago that "you Mexicans are a conquered race, but what you are not as yet aware of is that the conquering boot of the *Americano* has no heel. . . . As a nation we do not confiscate. . . . What I am trying to tell you . . . is that you are no longer a colony of Mexico, and adjustment will have to be made to make you a part of the new Texas" (180).

Limón suggests that Red and Angela's romance more than

Roberto and Susanita's symbolizes the projected U.S. social order into which Mexicans shall be incorporated. But if Red's marriage to Angela is any indication, a future U.S. Texas will be marked as much by division and conflict as by mutual respect based on pragmatic self-interest. Without love, the novel intimates, this (national) marriage of convenience may prove to be unstable at best. Many characters who embrace Red do so with knowledge of the risks. Though Don Gabriel believes that "[i]t *is* men like [Red] who will really build Texas," he also fears "many will be harder than he" (J. González and Raleigh, 327). Angela, without openly expressing doubt, has no answer to her father's admonition that Red's "concern over the misery his countrymen are visiting upon the poor Mexicans is to further his personal ambitions." He bluntly tells Angela that she is "to be a lady of mercy so that he will have their allegiance for his schemes" (312). It is not simply that Red and Angela's marriage suggests that the "new social formation must, for the foreseeable future, admit the Mexican in a still-subordinate position" (Limón, "Mexicans," 246); through the contrast between its realistic portrait of Red and the idealized image of Roberto, *Caballero* makes a case—however repressed this argument may be by the novel's conciliatory premise—for southern (i.e., Mexican) culture in the context of a pragmatic recognition that Red represents the future. Despite Red's power and influence, the novel's southern affinities seem to declare, Red can never possess the seigneurial qualities that "southerners" like Roberto and Don Santiago have imbibed since childhood—the dignity, self-respect, pride, and morality identified with traditional Mexican agrarian society. Although the novel's attack on (Mexican) patriarchy throughout counters this southern analogy, *Caballero* does not renounce all aspects of traditional Mexican culture, just as it resists a blanket valorization of Red's modern capitalist perspective. If Anglo Americans do not respect and learn from their incorporated Mexican (southern) culture, the future may not be as harmonious as the novel's romances otherwise project.

The birth of Susanita and Roberto's child, the bicultural New South(west) personified, is to be the catalyst for a reunion between Susanita and her father. Susanita returns with her family to her hacienda home in the hope that the don's first grandchild will soften the patriarch's heart. When he fails to show up as expected, Susanita asks that they visit the bluff where he often went to view his ranch. Warrener discovers Don Santiago's body. The narrator underscores the irony "that an American, and the man who took his most beloved child, should be the one to close the lids over the eyes of Don Santiago de Mendoza y Soría" (J. González and Raleigh,

336). More ironic, though not unexpected given the novel's inter-section with plantation fiction, on the final page Robert—a slave-holder who will return with his new Mexican wife to his antebellum Virginia plantation—stands at the location where Don Santiago's Spanish colonist ancestors first looked out across the land that would become Rancho La Palma de Cristo.

The novel's socially symbolic project to depose Don Santiago, who is described at one point as the "monarch" of all he surveyed, in this way exists in precarious balance with its efforts at histori-cal recovery and cultural validation. *Caballero* must dethrone the don in order to pave the way for what it posits as the beneficial in-tegration—during and after the period in which the novel was written—of the Mexican border population into U.S. society.[21] But since cultural assimilation, whether in the nineteenth century or the modern period, was always problematic for Mexican Ameri-cans, the genteel history and culture that the don embodies must be preserved, a particularly important objective for middle-class Mexican Americans like González seeking inclusion in segregated Texas society.[22] This culture may also have had other inherent value and meaning for the authors of *Caballero*. The novel's histor-ical recovery project, which "[works] backward to establish the character of the Spanish Mexicans . . . and forward to record the Texas Ranger–led racist oppression and violence that descended on a seemingly tranquil, unified community," could have also served other political purposes (Limón, "Mexicans," 244). "Such a strategy," Limón believes, "might appeal to the guilt and anxiety of González's Anglo liberal audience and enlist its sympathy while affirming the historical primacy and moral rightness of the new Mexican middle-class elites in their efforts to lead their commu-nity" (244–45).

The final paragraphs direct the reader back to the Mendoza family's heritage and its hacienda mythology. A ranch hand says to Warrener, "See, there is the cross on the bluff. Don Santiago's father's father saw Rancho La Palma de Cristo in a dream from there, and when the dream came true he built the cross in thanks-giving to God. The family has been in Texas close to a hundred years, *señor*, if you did not know" (J. González and Raleigh, 336). In the final lines Warrener wonders what Don Santiago's last thoughts had been as he stood on the bluff just before his death: "[H]ad he held to the last to the staff of his traditions, speeding his soul with his head held high in the right of his convictions, to stand unafraid be-fore the God whom he had worshipped and, he believed, obeyed?" (337). If the U.S. nation, encompassing the border region, must be built, the (genteel) Spanish/Mexican history and culture embodied by Don Santiago, the novel suggests, must not be forgotten. In the same period that González and Raleigh sought to establish the historical (hacienda) pedigree of Mexican Texans in *Caballero*, the (Spanish) gentleman-rancher (*caballero*) emerged in the Southwest as one of the region's foundational historical figures. By virtue of the astonishing popularity of the narrative of Old (Spanish) California over a span of five decades, the Spanish gentleman-rancher served as a symbol for a romantic revival that reinvented California's Spanish/Mexican past as pastoral romance. The life of the film actor Leo Carrillo intersected seamlessly with the emergence of the pastoral myth. Drawing on his Californio rancher heritage, Carrillo constructed an autobiographical persona in *The California I Love*, an aristocratic Spanish/Californio *caballero*, to contradict his screen image as stereotypic Mexican "other." As chapter 4 argues, Carrillo's narrative project to restore his Spanish/Mexican heritage within the social constraints of Jim Crow–era Los Angeles reveals a series of negotiations with a dominant (popular) culture that simultaneously denigrated Carrillo's Mexican (*mestizo*) self while idealizing his Californio (Spanish) rancher ancestry.

Chapter

4

Ghosts of Old California
The Performances of Leo Carrillo

I N the opening passages of his autobiography *The California I Love* (1961), Leo Carrillo describes a vivid memory from childhood. Recalling a book that his parents cherished, Carrillo remembers "the awe I felt when, before I could read, it was pointed out to me that in the back of this beautiful book, in 'The Pioneer Registry,' there were four solid pages of material in small type dealing with the Carrillo family in California" (Carrillo, 15).[1] He recalls that the author of the work, the historian Hubert H. Bancroft, described his family as "'the leading one in [Mexican] California by reasons of the number and prominence of its members and of connections by marriage to so many of the best families'" (16). Born in Los Angeles in 1881, Carrillo was the great-grandson of Carlos Antonio de Jesús Carrillo (1783–1852), who as governor of California was one of the most notable political figures in the period just before the American occupation. Carlos Antonio wrote the first book on California by a native son, "Exposición dirigida a la Cámara de Diputados . . . sobre arreglo y administración del Fondo Piadoso" (Cleland, 17).[2] Carrillo's great-uncle, Carlos Antonio's brother José Antonio Ezequiel Carrillo (1796–1862), led the Californio military force that in 1847 defeated the U.S. army at the Battle of Dominguez and later signed the Treaty of Cahuenga ending the U.S.-Mexican War in California.

The "thick calf-bound book" that Carrillo's family treasured was volume 2 of Bancroft's *History of California* (1886). Published when Carrillo was five years old, Bancroft's work had drawn from autobiographical testimonials solicited from Californios, including Mariano Guadalupe Vallejo's "Historical and Personal Memoirs Relating to Alta California." As the two dominant rancher families in pre-U.S. conquest California, the Carrillos and Vallejos had been linked by a series of marriages since the early nineteenth century: Carrillo's grandfather, Pedro Catarino Carrillo, was a first cousin of Vallejo's wife, Francisca Benicia Carrillo. Though proud of his Californio heritage, Carrillo does not discuss at any point how his ancestors themselves may have viewed Bancroft's work. As Genaro Padilla remarks, because the collective Californio voice was "as much as gagged, if not altogether silenced" by Bancroft's project, many who had contributed saw the final work as an affront to the Californio community (Padilla, *My History, Not Yours,* 107). Carrillo's reference to his own family's eighty-year history in California, which was placed in "small type" in the work's appendixes, suggests the manner in which Bancroft's history wholly displaced the Mexican past. "One realizes this to be the case," explains Padilla, "upon seeing that the hundred or so personal narratives, comprising thousands of pages of [Californio] life history, are smothered by the weight of Bancroft's massive historical project, set into footnotes below the main narrative, revised and in many cases discounted by Bancroft" (107).

Rather than addressing Bancroft's absences and omissions, Carrillo seeks to restore what the *History of California* excludes. His own work contains a nostalgic remembrance of the Carrillo family's foundational role in the history of Alta California. It is a romantic, folkloristic account suffused with the pastoral aura of the myth of Old (Spanish) California.[3] In part because of its intersection with this myth, Carrillo's life-writing underscores the difficulty of any effort to reconstruct early Mexican American literary history, more so than the other Mexican American literary texts discussed in this study. In some of the scholarship emerging from the Recovering the U.S. Hispanic Literary Heritage project, for example, the historical, social, and cultural "truths" of the Mexican American community appear transparent, unproblematic, and easily accessible (Shohat and Stam, 178). Casting Carrillo as the personification of an ethnic version of false consciousness, Chicano/a studies critics have excluded Carrillo from scholarly discussion for more than thirty years.[4] Carrillo's exclusion has continued even as recent scholars have devoted full-length studies to the lives of the actor's Californio ancestors. That this rejection occurred during an era that has seen the rise of cultural studies, with its interdisciplinary sophistication and academic valorization of the "popular," only compounds the contradiction. Despite its own omissions and suppressions, *The California I Love* can no longer be dismissed, as it has in the past, as a work that unambiguously brands Carrillo as a southwestern surrogate for the U.S. "colonialist" regime.

Carrillo had his own reasons for embracing the mission mythology popularized in the late nineteenth and early twentieth centuries. These reasons derive from Carrillo's ethnic identity as a twentieth-century Californio and from his status as a Mexican

American entertainer seeking personal success and integration within U.S. society during the Jim Crow era. Echoing Padilla's theory of early Mexican American autobiography, F. Arturo Rosales points out that "a major reason why elite Californios adhered to what has appeared . . . as 'Fantasy Heritage' posturing was to resist the annihilation of their own community" (Rosales, 100). While not overtly adopting the Spanish myth, Californios such as Ruiz de Burton and Vallejo produced literary texts that reclaimed their families' seigneurial (hacienda) identities to oppose the new U.S. social order and the intrusion of modernity into their native region. In *Caballero* Jovita González and her coauthor Eve Raleigh similarly exploited the pre-modern Spanish agrarian past to interrogate contemporary cultural questions and negotiate a sociopolitical path for Mexican Americans in the modern era. Many early Mexican elites of the Southwest, moreover, were white, or passed for white, using Mexican, not Anglo, criteria passed down from the colonial era (Rosales, 100). As David J. Weber explains, "Whitening occurred throughout Spain's [colonial] empire, for a person's social status, or *calidad*, was never fixed solely by race, but rather defined by occupation and wealth as well as by parentage and skin color." In frontier or rural societies such as Alta California, continues Weber, "where institutions that maintained racial boundaries were relatively weak, it may be that social promotion occurred more rapidly than in urbanized, prosperous areas of New Spain. In [Alta] California, for example, racial distinctions at the official level nearly disappeared in some communities" (Weber, *Spanish Frontier*, 328). Carrillo's autobiographical incarnation as Spanish Californio rancher/aristocrat in *The California I Love* must be examined within this broader historical and cultural landscape—as well as within the pre-1960s era in which Carrillo lived. Adopting the persona of a Spanish Californian rancher/aristocrat was one facet of Carrillo's ambitious autobiographical project, which promoted an idealized image of California's Spanish/Mexican past as a way of dealing with the demons of race and class before the campaign for civil rights got under way in earnest. Published the year of his death, Carrillo's autobiography served as the capstone to his decades-long effort to project a countervailing romantic vision of his community's culture and heritage. The work in this manner imagined a space for Mexican American inclusion within segregated U.S. society.

Carrillo's autobiography spans a period of almost two hundred years. It begins with the story of the settlement of Alta California in the late eighteenth century by Carrillo's pioneer ancestors, one of whom, José Raimundo Carrillo, accompanied the first colonists to the region. It then recounts Carrillo's multigenerational family history in Southern California, his childhood in late-nineteenth-century Los Angeles, his career as an actor in New York and Hollywood, and his popular cultural incarnation during the 1950s as Pancho in the television western series *The Cisco Kid*. The work's narratives about Carrillo's youth and family heritage, which form the backdrop for a retelling of local Spanish and Mexican legends, are juxtaposed with chapters describing Carrillo's career as a comedian and actor and his friendships with such Hollywood film stars as Will Rogers, Clark Gable, Carole Lombard, and Wallace Beery. In Carrillo's Southwest version of the DuBoisian double-consciousness, the pre-modern agrarian (Spanish and Mexican) California of his youth exists in tension with the modern capitalist (Anglo American) Los Angeles of his adulthood. Before building his own rancho estate near Oceanside, California, Carrillo in the 1930s had begun to perform offscreen in the role of Spanish gentleman-rancher (*caballero*) at public events and celebrations.[5] He continued these appearances until the end of his life. When he died, Carrillo was as well known for his offscreen image as the flesh-and-blood embodiment—or picturesque relic—of "pastoral" (Spanish) California as for his roles in more than one hundred motion pictures.

Since Carrillo's image as genteel Spanish don permitted him to embrace an aspect of his (Mexican) ethnic self while simultaneously presenting him to the U.S. public as white (i.e., Spanish), it serves in *The California I Love*, as perhaps it did in Carrillo's life, as a symbolic resolution to the sparring identities of his Mexican American double self. This "resolution" involved a form of psychic repression whereby Carrillo's Mexican/*mestizo* self was displaced onto his (Spanish) Californio identity. Carrillo's repression of his ethnic self will be examined as a response to the aggrieved sociohistorical status of Mexican Americans and particularly the displaced Californio elite in the late nineteenth and early twentieth centuries. Since the condition of Mexicans in California in that epoch was one of degradation brought forth by the cultural, economic, and social reorganization of the region, Carrillo's restoration of Old (Spanish) California through his performance of the pastoral myth was all the more necessary (R. Flores, *Remembering the Alamo*, 91). This need to restore the image of a shattered past was especially acute given Carrillo's close identification with the dispossessed Mexican Californian oligarchy. Although written in the 1950s, Carrillo's autobiographical project was produced in a social setting reminiscent of the one that generated Adina De Zavala's *History and Legends of the Alamo and Other Missions in and around San Antonio* (1917), the sociohistorical context of which has been explicated by Richard Flores.[6] Much like De Zavala's positioning of the

Leo Carrillo and daughter Antoinette in parade regalia, ca. 1930s. Courtesy of the Leo Carrillo Ranch Historic Park, Carlsbad, California.

Alamo legend within the fractured contours of Mexican Texan social history, the historical frame Carrillo constructs for Old (Spanish) California in *The California I Love,* in which he embeds his autobiographical narrative, is the social displacement of Mexicans stemming from the forces of modernity (R. Flores, *Remembering the Alamo,* 91).

Though Carrillo's life narrative has yet to be embraced by literary scholars of the Southwest, the author's performances in various roles—as Californio, Mexican American, actor, celebrity, autobiographer, folklorist, and civic leader—merit closer examination, intersecting as they do with contemporary research in ethnic, cultural/media, and historical studies. A native son of California whose great-great-grandfather accompanied the first settlers to the region, a vaudeville comedian in his twenties and Broadway star in his thirties, Carrillo spent the last thirty years of his life struggling to reconcile his (Mexican) ethnic self with the celluloid images that both sustained his acting career and stigmatized his ethnic identity. Much as Ruiz de Burton, Vallejo, and González's identification with the Spanish colonial past serves to explode essentialistic conceptions of Mexican American cultural identity, Carrillo's performance of self overturns nation-based analytical models that too often continue to define Chicano/a ethnic discourse. Refuting such categorizations, Carrillo's career and life-writing reveal an existentially fraught historical figure whose cultural identity necessarily became interwoven with his public performance as ethnic "other." Carrillo's multiform identities may in this sense be said to evoke the ethnic identity of the Mexican American generation, that group of intellectuals, writers, and leaders who came of age professionally during the 1920–50 period.

LOCATING CARRILLO AS ACTOR AND CELEBRITY

In an era when few Latinos had careers in the film industry, Carrillo's was established during the 1930s, a decade in which he performed in thirty-six movies. Though he sometimes appeared in starring roles, by the late 1930s Carrillo had settled into a career as a supporting actor. As Gary D. Keller notes, because Carrillo was highly adept at accents, he was one of the busiest character actors of the 1930s and 1940s (Keller, *Hispanics*, 78). "It was the use of [Chinese, Mexican, Italian, and Japanese] dialects in my stories," states Carrillo in chapter 31, that had earlier "launched me on my career [as a comedian] in vaudeville" (Carrillo, 190). Though the film roles that followed his vaudeville career were diverse, Carrillo became known for his ethnic characters, roles in which he typically played the evil or outcast counterpart to an Anglo American protagonist. Carrillo's most notable motion pictures—encompassing both ethnic and non-ethnic roles—include *Girl of the Rio* (1932), *Viva Villa!* (1933), *Love Me Forever* (1935), *The Gay Desperado* (1936), *Twenty-Mule Team* (1940), *Crazy House* (1943), *Follow the Band* (1943), *Frontier Badmen* (1943), *Phantom of the Opera* (1943), *Bowery to Broadway* (1944), *Gypsy Wildcat* (1944), *Moonlight and Cactus* (1944), *Crime, Inc.* (1945), *The Girl from San Lorenzo* (1950), and *Pancho Villa Returns* (1950) (Reyes and Rubie, 440). These and dozens of other Metro-Goldwyn-Mayer films in which Carrillo starred, which have yet to be critically assessed by ethnic and film studies scholars, constitute a cultural record of the actor's mediated performances of (Mexican American) identity during the Jim Crow era. They provide insight into a life and career that at some level are emblematic of the cultural and existential condition of all Mexican Americans during that period. Though already an established star, Carrillo's fame increased during the 1950s, when he was in his seventies, because of his role as Pancho in television's *The Cisco Kid*. One hundred fifty-six episodes of this show appeared between 1950 and 1956. Because of the series and earlier motion pictures and radio programs based on the same character, from the late 1920s through the 1950s the Cisco Kid became one of the more familiar figures in U.S. popular culture.[7] To this day, he remains, along with Zorro, one of its rare Hispanic heroes.

Despite a diverse body of work that included starring roles on Broadway, today Carrillo remains for many virtually indistinguishable from his screen persona as stereotypic (Mexican) ethnic "other." As early as the mid-1930s, it was an image irrevocably fixed in the popular imagination. As Keller comments, in his early films Carrillo "lived down to the stereotype faithfully, as a gambling, murdering, extorting, pimping . . . border bandido" (Keller, "Image of the Chicano," 30). According to Allen Woll, "Even if Carrillo [in his movie roles] had a legitimate source of money, as in *Girl of the Rio* or *In Caliente*, he still was depicted as bearing an uncontrollable urge to engage in illegal acts" (Woll, 37). The characters that he portrayed were not only prone to criminality and violence but they also were typically "treacherous cowards . . . with no loyalty even to [their] criminal peers." Carrillo's physical aspect in these roles was "oily, ugly, [and] crude" (Keller, "Image of the Chicano," 30). Though sometimes sinister, sometimes comic, his characters, moreover, were always inept (Pettit, 143). In dozens of MGM movies produced during the 1930s and 1940s, Carrillo thus entered the U.S. popular imagination as greaser, bandit, gangster, or simply the "bad Mexican" (Keller, *Hispanics*, 48). Though Carrillo does not address his typecast screen image in *The California I Love*, he does speak of feeling "aggravated" by the "synthetic cowboys" featured in his westerns. "Most of these," he states, "were incubated on Madison Avenue in New York" (Carrillo, 212). Yet, as this chapter argues, Carrillo's performance of identity as Spanish gentleman-rancher in *The California I Love*, and at his many public appearances, served implicitly to contradict his film image as Mexican (ethnic) "other."

Carrillo's movie performances as Mexican (ethnic) "other" may be measured by the public response to one of his films—an episode that does not find a place in his autobiography. 1932's *Girl of the Rio*, which cast Carrillo as a corrupt Mexican official, created a furor in

Leo Carrillo on movie set, ca. 1930s. Courtesy of the Leo Carrillo Ranch Historic Park, Carlsbad, California.

Mexico, prompting a formal protest from the Mexican government. The protest noted that the film portrayed Mexican justice to be a matter of who could pay the most for the verdict of their liking (Keller, *Hispanics*, 118). The theater that showed the film in Mexico City received threats of violence, and a special delegation visited Pres. Ortiz Rubio to request an immediate ban on showing the movie (Woll, 33). Despite these actions, the film's success led to a sequel, *In Caliente,* in which Carrillo again appeared, a movie that, as Arthur G. Pettit states, "features the same assortment of cabaret dancers, corrupt gamblers, excitable domestics, and brown buffoons who speak broken English" (Pettit, 144).

Although Carrillo perfected such film roles, critics of his work show little appreciation for the circumstances that the actor faced as an ethnic performer in early Hollywood.[8] Nor have they examined Carrillo's film image in light of contemporary scholarship on racial and ethnic stereotyping. As a Latino performer, Carrillo had limited career options available to him. Like early African American actors such as Hattie McDaniel and Butterfly McQueen, whose contributions to film have been recognized, Carrillo, whose *mestizo* phenotype made him identifiably "ethnic," faced a paradoxical professional dilemma in Hollywood. Given the circumstances of the studio star system, as Keller explains, "Hispanic film actors and actresses had the option of either being typecast negatively if they retained their Hispanic identity, or denying that very identity, by what the industry euphemistically called 'repositioning' themselves" (Keller, *Hispanics*, 113). "Repositioning" meant to anglicize one's image by taking a nonethnic screen name, as Rita Hayworth did by changing her name from Margarita Carmen Cansino. Because of the popularity of the formula plot in movies of that era, moreover, "the ethnic *other* almost invariably played the outcast and the evildoer" (113–14; emphasis in original). Compelled by his *mestizo* phenotype to retain his ethnic identity, Carrillo built a successful career performing stereotypical characterizations of Mexicans and other "ethnics" in dozens of films, roles that other Latino actors of that era, such as Anthony Quinn, also performed.

Though he appeared in many roles not deemed stereotypical, once Carrillo had been typecast as "ethnic," even if he had wished to play nonstereotypical roles, as a contracted studio player he was obligated to perform roles dictated by MGM. Just as McDaniel's career in Hollywood was limited to supporting roles as maids and servants, Carrillo had little power to influence the path that his screen career would take. And much like McDaniel's success in films such as *Gone with the Wind*—for which she won the Academy Award for best supporting actress—Carrillo's screen fame reflected his capacity to mirror and mimic—while masking his own sense of ethnic cultural identity—the racial fantasies of the European American "colonialist" psyche. What Donald Bogle has argued in relation to performances by early African American film actors is therefore equally true of Carrillo. In some of his film roles as Mexican bandit or revolutionary Carrillo appears to be "signifying" on, or subverting, the roles forced on him, revealing an imagination that could potentially turn these demeaning roles into resistant or parodic performance.[9] Like early black film performers, Carrillo was criticized for accepting such demeaning roles. But these roles should be viewed no differently than those of black performers of the same era as analyzed by Bogle. As he observes, "[T]hrough their black characters, the actors accomplished the almost impossible: they proved single-handedly that the mythic [negative] types could be individualized and made, if not into things of beauty, then at least into things of joy. Almost every black actor of the period approached his role with a *joie de vivre* the movies were never to see again. Indeed, the enthusiasm the actors poured into their characters seemed often to parallel their own gratitude that at long last blacks were working in films" (Bogle, 36–37). At the very minimum, as an actor Carrillo was conscious of the characterizations that he created on film and derived some of them from his early work as a vaudeville comedian. Describing his talent for mimicking the dialects of various racial groups for comedic effect, Carrillo suggests this very process in chapter 31: "A great deal depended . . . in the case of a mimic like myself, in catching the gestures and phraseology of the particular racial group with which we were dealing. If we did that and told the stories good naturedly and with proper timing and punch lines we could have 'em rolling in the aisles" (Carrillo, 191).

Carrillo does not deny that the high salaries offered by Hollywood film studios lured him away from the Broadway stage. Though his film image belied his reputation as a dramatic actor, having achieved fame on Broadway in his early thirties Carrillo was reluctant to work in a new medium deemed inferior by theater performers. "All of us legitimate actors turned up our noses a bit at the new entertainment medium—the motion picture—which seemed to be associated with player pianos and little hole-in-the-wall film houses where the 'flickers' were shown," he writes. Even the addition of sound tracks to movies "failed to impress us greatly," Carrillo notes, "except in one respect . . . [and] that was the money" (Carrillo, 209). According to *The California I Love,* when he arrived in Hollywood at the height of the Great Depression Carrillo's contract paid him $3,500 per week, a salary that Broadway could not match. As a contracted MGM actor, Carrillo's income was soon comparable to that of the Hollywood elite. Though always a supporting actor, his annual income was $30,333 in 1935 and $57,832 in 1936 (Aaker, 121). As Carrillo remarks in chapter 35, "[T]here was one great reward for me in the early portion of my film career besides my association with [actors like Wallace Beery]. . . . This was the monetary return" (Carrillo, 212).

Although as a Latino actor Carrillo achieved a level of financial success in Hollywood equaled only by major stars such as Ramon Novarro, Dolores del Rio, and later by Anthony Quinn, after being typecast in the 1930s he would never again play the dramatic roles that had made him famous early in the century on Broadway. As Carrillo describes in chapters 31 through 35, after his theatrical fame launched his film career he returned in 1929 to the city of his birth. Earlier, in chapter 3 of his book, which relates the downfall of his family's nineteenth-century ranch empire, Carrillo reflects on the irony that MGM Studios was built on land in Culver City that had been a part of his Uncle Andrés Machado's Los Angeles ranch. In what can only be deemed a final indignity for an elderly actor who three decades earlier had left the theater to act in movies, at the end of his life Carrillo would reprise the stock figure of the stereotypic Mexican companion in *The Cisco Kid* for a television audience.

Carrillo's role as Pancho, the Cisco Kid's inept but loyal cohort known for his Spanish-inflected malapropisms, did not represent an intrinsic shift in his screen image. Though seemingly antithetical to Carrillo's movie roles as bandit or criminal, Pancho conformed to another stereotype from early westerns, that of the "good or faithful Mexican," a figure usually portrayed as a "bumbling, buffoon-like sidekick . . . commonly from the lower class" (Keller, *Hispanics*, 63). In his childlike and clownish aspect the "good or faithful Mexican" approximated the black "tom" and "sambo" in movies of the same era.[10] And yet a number of factors complicate any contemporary effort to analyze Carrillo's performance of this stereotypic role. First, although patterned after the stereotype from early westerns, Carrillo's character appeared alongside a "Spanish" hero of the West, a rarity for that era or today. Secondly, Carrillo initially rejected the role of Pancho for its demeaning characterization, suggesting that he hoped late in his career to break away from the ethnic caricatures that had established him as a film actor. Thirdly, Carrillo's initial reticence suggests that the role of Pancho must be placed within the same context of institutional racism in Hollywood that had constrained Carrillo's big-screen career. Yet, despite his initial doubts about the role, Carrillo played Pancho in precisely the manner that he had first criticized (Aaker, 122). As his co-star, Duncan Renaldo, recalled of Carrillo's performance, "'He overdid it, but everyone liked him. His accent was so exaggerated that when we finished a picture, no one in the cast or crew could talk normal English'" (122). Six years on national television as Pancho made Carrillo a household name, and after the series went into syndication the character became recognizable throughout the world. "Everywhere I have gone on my trips," Carrillo notes in chapter 35, "I have been greeted with welcoming cries of 'Hey, Pancho' in whatever language happened to be spoken in that particular country" (Carrillo, 212).

Carrillo's film and television roles have yet to be examined through the lens of cultural theory on racial stereotyping, particularly Homi Bhabha's reformulation of early models that framed analysis narrowly upon negative and positive imagery. Bhabha's theory of ambivalence problematizes early criticism of Carrillo's onscreen and offscreen personae. It also elucidates the complexity of Carrillo's bifurcated public image/identity as Mexican "greaser" and Spanish aristocrat, shedding light on Carrillo's own conflicted consciousness as an ethnic subject. Bhabha argues that the stereotype characterizes the ways in which colonial discourse relates to the colonized subject, which may be both derisive and desiring at the same time. The stereotype, Bhabha believes, enacts a simultaneous attraction/recognition and repulsion/disavowal of the "difference," or "otherness," of the colonized subject. As Bhabha phrases it, the stereotype "gives access to an 'identity' which is predicated as much on mastery and pleasure as it is on anxiety and defense, for it is a form of multiple and contradictory belief in its recognition of difference and disavowal of it" (Bhabha, 75). For example, in U.S. western literature and motion pictures the Mexican has been portrayed as both savage bandit (e.g., Alfonso Bedoya as the memorable antagonist in *The Treasure of the Sierra Madre*) and the most faithful and obedient of servants (e.g., Carrillo himself as Pancho in *The Cisco Kid*); he embodies the threat of rampant sexuality and yet he is the proverbial docile peasant; he is the swarthy "greaser" and yet he is also the aristocratic Spanish *caballero;* he is a person for whom treachery and manipulation seem second nature and yet he is the primitive and simple-minded Mexican/Indian peon; he is the hypersexual "macho," or "Latin lover," and yet he is the impassive and asexual "wetback." Cultural discourse and iconography similarly portray the Mexican and "Latin" female as both bawdy trollop and demure *señorita;* she is the unpredictable "spitfire" and yet she is also the submissive wife; she is the lower-class femme fatale and also the aristocratic Spanish "belle." Bhabha suggests that such examples demonstrate that stereotyping is not simply "the setting up of a false image which becomes the scapegoat of discriminatory practices" but rather a more complex enactment of ambivalence (Bhabha, 81). Rather than being antithetical figures, argues Bhabha, the "colonized" and "colonizer" are entangled as subjects who together live out the social and psychic conditions of colonialism.[11] The varied and contradictory manifestations of stereotyping, as illustrated by Carrillo's own public image as both (despised) Mexican "greaser" and (idealized) Spanish aristocrat, capture this sense of entanglement.

Bhabha therefore asks that the point of critical intervention "shift from the ready recognition of images as positive or negative, to an understanding of the *processes of subjectification* made possible (and plausible) through stereotypical discourse" (Bhabha, 67; emphasis in original). Rather than setting out to identify and debunk stereotypes, critics must excavate the psychic and sociohistorical processes that constitute "colonized" and "colonizer" as subjects. Displacement or subversion, states Bhabha, "is only possible by engaging with the *effectivity* [of colonial discourse]; with the repertoire of positions of power and resistance, domination and dependence that constructs colonial identification (both colonizer and colonized)" (67; emphasis in original). In constructing the "positionalities and oppositionalities of racist discourse," stereotypes may involve, for example, "projection and introjection, metaphoric and metonymic strategies, displacement, overdetermination, guilt, aggressivity; the masking and splitting of 'official' and phantasmatic knowledges" (81–82). By opening up stereotypes to a recognition of such submerged convolutions in the relationship between "colonized" and "colonizer," Bhabha's theory has profoundly reshaped discussion of ethnic representation.[12] These processes cast new light on Carrillo's performances of (ethnic) identity, a point to be further explicated in the next section.

In light of Bhabha's reconceptualization of racial stereotyping, earlier criticism of Carrillo's life and career appears reductive. Yet to a generation of Mexican American activists and scholars who came of age during the Chicano movement, Carrillo's performance of identity, whether as Mexican "greaser" or Spanish aristocrat, could perhaps not have represented anything but the height of ethnic betrayal. Unlike Anthony Quinn, whose film career had by the early 1950s moved beyond stereotypical roles, Carrillo has been remembered by "movement" critics for his stereotypical big-screen characters or for his equally dubious television performance as Pancho.[13] Unfortunately, this early view of Carrillo continues to shape discussion of his autobiography. Writing in 1993, Francisco Lomelí voices a representative response. Presuming that the genre of autobiography adheres to an aesthetic of verisimilitude, Lomelí criticizes Carrillo's book for its convergences with romance/fiction and divergences from objective history. For him, *The California I Love* represents little more than a "fish out of historical waters." Carrillo's autobiographical persona as Californio appears to be "a glossy Hollywood stunt to hide the real facts of social friction." And yet for Lomelí, Carrillo's "false" account possesses enough "truth" to reveal Carrillo's betrayal of his (ethnic) community. By misrepresenting California's "turbulent past," the critic notes, *The California I Love* demonstrates the author's loyalty to the "conquering forces: first the Spanish *conquistadores* and [then] the Anglo Ameri-

can invasion and takeover of California." Lomelí also conflates Carrillo's autobiography with his film image, using the latter to dismiss
the former: when *The California I Love* "is combined with the character [that Carrillo] portrayed in . . . *The Cisco Kid* . . . who typifies
an inarticulate but faithful Mexican companion, the result is a
double-edged stereotype denigrating [to] Mexicans" (Lomelí, 89).

Aside from Carrillo's image as actor and celebrity, his reputation among scholars of Chicano and ethnic studies can be traced
to two sources: the writings of Carey McWilliams and the Chicano
movement. Twenty years before the advent of the Chicano movement, in *Southern California: An Island on the Land* (1946) and *North
from Mexico: The Spanish-Speaking People of the United States* (1948),
McWilliams fixed Carrillo's image as the personification of the
Southwest's Spanish myth.[14] Citing Carrillo in both works to illustrate his indictment of this myth, McWilliams portrays the actor
as a hopelessly compromised (ethnic) surrogate for the white establishment, a figure who could at best masquerade as a Mexican
for an uninitiated white, or misguided Mexican American, audience. Reporting on a "Spanish Days" celebration in *Southern California,* McWilliams observes that a "careful scrutiny of the names
of [the] fancily dressed ranchers" participating "reveals that Leo
Carrillo is about the only rider whose name carries a faint echo of
the past and he is about as Mexican as the ceremony is Spanish."
For McWilliams, such "Spanish" celebrations approximate a southwestern version of a minstrel show: "Ostensibly a gay affair, the
annual ride represents a rather grim and desperate effort to escape
from the bonds of an American culture that neither satisfies nor
pleases. Actually there is something rather pathetic about the spectacle of these frustrated business men cantering forth in search of
ersatz weekend romance, evoking a past that never existed to cast
some glamour on an equally unreal today" (McWilliams, *Southern
California,* 82).

Two years later, McWilliams returns to the same subject in *North
from Mexico,* with Carrillo once again serving as the symbol par ex-
cellence of the Southwest's "fantasy heritage." In a section satiri-
cally titled "The Man on the White Horse" McWilliams describes
Carrillo in *caballero* regalia at a Cinco de Mayo parade, noting that
the actor, "a *Californio* three hundred and sixty-four days of the
year," becomes a "Mexicano" on Cinco de Mayo. Here McWilliams
once again portrays Carrillo's performance as Spanish don as a
type of (ethnic) parody: "Elegantly attired in a ranchero costume,
he sits proudly astride his silver-mounted saddle and jingles his
silver spurs as he rides along. The moment he comes into sight, the
crowds begin to applaud for he is well known to them through the

unvaryingly stereotypic Mexican roles which he plays in the films. Moreover, they have seen him in exactly this same role, at the head of this or some similar parade, for fifteen years. Of late the applause is pretty thin and it may be that the audience is becoming a little weary of the old routine" (McWilliams, *North from Mexico*, 38).

McWilliams cites Carrillo to rebuke "native Californians" as a group not only for promoting a myth whose function "is to deprive . . . Mexicans of their heritage" but also for embracing the political status quo of the era (McWilliams, *North from Mexico*, 39). Though "[h]armless in many ways," he states, the "attempts to prettify the legend contrast most harshly with the actual behavior of the community toward persons of Mexican descent." Among the younger generation of Mexican Americans, he notes, "the fantasy heritage, and the institutions which keep it alive, are resented as still additional affronts to their dignity and sense of pride" (40). Within the context of interethnic strife that characterized the era, "native Californians" such as Carrillo, according to McWilliams, serve as convenient surrogates for the (white) political establishment. In appointing figures such as Carrillo to civic committees, white officials "realize that they have achieved the dual purpose, first, of having a Mexican name on the roster for the sake of appearances, and, second, that the person chosen will invariably act in the same manner as Anglo-Americans of equal social status" (39). Carrillo did in fact serve on a number of such committees. He was a member for fourteen years of the California State Beaches and Parks Commission, which he joined to promote the preservation of Southern California's Spanish and Mexican historical sites. He considered his role in designating the Placita or Plaza of Los Angeles—the original downtown district—a state park his most important accomplishment as a member of the commission. As Carrillo recalls in chapter 46, "It solaced my soul to see that the birthplace of the Pueblo was to be preserved forever as a memorial to the brave souls who had come there . . . and taken part, amid many hardships, in the establishment of El Pueblo de Nuestra Señora La Reina de Los Angeles de Porciúncula" (Carrillo, 272). Among other civic positions in which he served, Carrillo was appointed to the city commission that investigated the status of race relations in Los Angeles after the Zoot Suit Riots in June 1943.

McWilliams's view of Carrillo contrasts dramatically with Leonard Pitt's laudatory 1966 appraisal in *The Decline of the Californios*. Rather than dismissing the Old (Spanish) California myth—and Carrillo's rendering of it—as reactionary, Pitt places Carrillo squarely within the Californio folk tradition. Carrillo's autobiographical performances, Pitt believes, "masterfully" captured the

Mexican Californian oral tradition as passed down from his ancestors. Against the modern-day dismantling of the Spanish myth,
Carrillo was the last historical figure who could legitimately speak
for the Californios:

> The romantic heritage gives every indication of continuing
> indefinitely, despite an unprecedented debunking from sociol-
> ogists, school teachers, and historians and a decimation in the
> ranks of the romantics. Leo Carrillo personified the romantic
> tradition until a few years ago, and with valid license, having
> been born into a venerable local family at the Los Angeles
> Plaza . . . He spoke Spanish well, played the guitar, rode
> horseback, took part in fiestas and rodeos, listened carefully to
> the conversation of his elders and transmitted their oral tradi-
> tion masterfully, read a good deal of local history, and wrote
> his autobiography with a deep sense of ancestral pride. The
> smiling, waving Carrillo perched on a lavishly bridled horse
> was an inevitable part of any southern California parade for
> two decades. But Carrillo was the last figure who could legiti-
> mately personify the Spanish past—although many consid-
> ered him a mere creation of Hollywood—and his death in
> 1961 left a gap in the front ranks of many Los Angeles parades.
> (Pitt, 293)

More recent critics have similarly noted that McWilliams's critique of California's "fantasy heritage" failed to recognize that the
Old California myth was appropriated differently by Californios
and white Americans. As James A. Sandos, for example, observes,
"While Mexicans as Californios preserved and celebrated their culture, whites needed to use the ambiguous construct of 'Californio'
to avoid the logic of their own racial preferences." Whites, more
than Mexicans, according to Sandos, "constructed this Californio
heritage as white European, and then celebrated its accomplishments." They did so "to curtail the damage to their interests that
unbridled racism, with its attendant rejection of the Californios,
would have brought them" (Sandos, "Because He Is a Liar," 108).

Also contradicting McWilliams's portrait of Carrillo as ethnic
surrogate are several passages in *The California I Love* that position
Carrillo politically as one who did in fact support desegregation
and civil rights for Mexican Americans. In chapter 46 Carrillo announces his support for Earl Warren, whom he had endorsed in
the California gubernatorial race in 1942. Kevin Starr notes that
after campaigning for Warren in that year, Carrillo "became the
closest thing to a pal Warren seems to have had in public life: Pancho to Warren's Cisco Kid, a combination factotum, court jester,

master of ceremonies, and sometimes hatchet man of the sort most politicians, even Warren, seem to find necessary" (Starr, *Embattled Dreams*, 262). As Carrillo worked on his autobiography in the late 1950s, his friend Earl, now chief justice of the United States, had become the target of right-wing criticism for his court's rulings broadening civil rights, including the historic 1954 *Brown vs. Board of Education* decision, which ended segregation in public schools. Whether or not Carrillo endorsed all of the Warren court's decisions, he did not withdraw his support for Warren when the former governor faced heated criticism. Warren's friendship with Carrillo, strengthened by his exposure to Mexican American culture as a child, may even have influenced Warren's stance on segregation. Starr continues on this point: "Within the limits of the Old California myth ... Warren had excellent relations with Mexican-Californians." This statement is true, in part, because, "[a]s a boy in Los Angeles, [Warren] had attended Mexican festivities in the Plaza and been enchanted by the dancing and singing, the gaily colored horses, of these gatherings. Like so many Protestant Californians, Warren revered the myth of Old California as a Spanish Arcadia of white-walled, red-tiled haciendas and a colorful, pastoral way of life. Whenever possible, he attended the annual Old Spanish Days Fiesta in Santa Barbara" (Starr, *Embattled Dreams*, 263).

Given Carrillo's friendship with Warren, what Starr concludes about Warren's political identity may have been equally true of Carrillo's (repressed) ethnic identity: "There is much in Warren's career to suggest sincere albeit submerged liberal instincts running alongside the hard-boiled stance of the [conservative former] prosecutor" (Starr, *Embattled Dreams*, 262).

Despite such "submerged" sympathies, Carrillo's anti-communism was the hallmark of his public political identity, a perspective that distanced him from the views of the more progressive branches of the Mexican American civil rights movement of the 1960s. According to Carlos M. Larralde and Richard Griswold del Castillo, after World War II Carrillo served as one of the figureheads for the Hispanic nationalist political organization known as the Loyal Democrats. This group's anti-communist views led it to ignore anti-Mexican Ku Klux Klan activities in San Diego and to side with the California legislature's Un-American Activities Committee, which "conducted a witch hunt for Communists and militant labor organizers like Luisa Moreno" (Larralde and Griswold del Castillo, 8). The Loyal Democrats summarized their views in a leaflet: "'Leave us Mexicans out of your Communistic sneaky underhanded [activities]. . . . Any Mexican with a religious background would grind you . . . into meat'" (quoted in Larralde and Griswold del Castillo, 8). Carrillo refers briefly to cold war politics in chapter 45, which recounts his "unofficial" appointment as goodwill "ambassador to the world" by the governor of California, Goodwin J. Knight. During the last years of his life, Carrillo traveled throughout Latin America in this missionary capacity, "trying to spread the spirit of American idealism and decency as opposed to the brute force and cruelty of . . . dictatorships" (Carrillo, 266). Through this work Carrillo hoped to help "overcome the insidious efforts of world Communism to dominate the two American Continents and to undermine the United States" (267). The message he delivered as goodwill ambassador, he believed, would "help mankind in its struggle against the evil forces of Communism and dictatorship" (268).

The California I Love therefore also functioned at one level as the actor's rejoinder to the cold war politics of the 1950s (R. Flores, Remembering the Alamo, 127). Carrillo's Mexican American (ethnic) identity certainly bore a complex relation to a cold war political atmosphere that branded any dissenting Americans as unpatriotic or treasonous. Carrillo constructs his identity as Californio aristocrat, in part, in response to the ideological struggles that defined the cold war era (119). Because Carrillo's film image had stigmatized him as Mexican (ethnic) "other," the actor uses The California I Love to reaffirm and textualize his patriotism and "whiteness." He does so in the work not only by performing the identity of Spanish Californio caballero, which he had been doing offscreen since the 1930s, but also by openly proclaiming his anti-communist beliefs.

Carrillo's anti-communism must also be located in relation to his career as an actor during the McCarthy era. From 1947 to 1961, a person's ability to work in Hollywood's motion picture industry depended on whether or not his or her name appeared on a list of suspected communist activists or sympathizers—the blacklist. Larralde and Griswold del Castillo indicate that as an ethnic actor Carrillo faced a greater possibility of being blacklisted than non-ethnic actors if he did not support the work of the Joint Fact-Finding Committee on Un-American Activities of the California legislature, the regional committee of the House Un-American Activities Committee (HUAC). The chairman of the California committee, Sen. John Tenney, whom Carrillo befriended, "destroyed the careers of many people in the film industry, both Anglos and Mexicans" (Larralde and Griswold del Castillo, 16n. 57). Tenney "played on [the] sympathies of [his supporters] to promote his career and destroyed those who questioned him" (16n. 58). Major ethnic performers such as Dolores del Rio were victims of Tenney's abuse. After returning to work in Mexico, Del Rio was banned from reentering the United States because she had expressed support for leftist exiles from the Spanish Civil War. Another Mexican-born actress, Rosaura Revueltas (the sister of the novelist José Revueltas), who starred in *Salt of the Earth*, an independent film made by a group of blacklisted Hollywood producers, was deported and had her visa permanently revoked. During that era even major mainstream stars, such as Charlie Chaplin, were persecuted as a result of anti-communist hysteria. Carrillo's own response to HUAC is captured in a 1947 telegram. Rather than joining actors such as Humphrey Bogart and Lauren Bacall in support of Hollywood figures called before the first HUAC hearings, Carrillo instead sent the following message to the committee: "'Congratulations on your splendid courage. Communist rattlesnakes are bent on inoculating the mind of our American youth. Clean out the rats. You are not injuring our industry. You are helping to keep them American. Bless you. Leo Carrillo'" (quoted in Kanfer, 68–69). Despite his misguided faith (if one interprets this message at face value) in the committee's red-baiting of Hollywood figures, Carrillo's anti-communism conformed to mainstream political ideology in the cold war era. This ideology was embraced by politicians such as Earl Warren as well as by Hispanic political organizations such as the League of United Latin American Citizens (LULAC) and the G.I. Forum. As Larralde and Griswold del Castillo explain, the umbrella group with which Carrillo's nationalist political organization Loyal Democrats was affiliated—Free Clean American Mexicans—comprised members of the G.I. Forum, LULAC associates, and people from several religious groups, such as the Knights of Columbus (Larralde and Griswold del Castillo,16n. 58).

NOSTALGIA, MEMORY, HISTORY

Carrillo's acting career depended on the image of the Mexican that he, a dark-complected *mestizo*, sought to repress and displace through his autobiographical persona as a genteel Spanish Californio rancher. Carrillo rehearsed this identity for decades in his appearances at parades and other celebrations, and he textualized it at the end of his life by writing *The California I Love*. Through his performance of California's mythic Spanish past, Carrillo consciously embraced his Mexican ancestors' pre-modern agrarian world. No longer the lowborn "greaser" bandit of the movies, in his book the "real" Carrillo could be glimpsed. Quite distinct from his many screen characters, this autobiographical incarnation was Carrillo's reenactment of his oft-seen public role as the living emblem of California's "halcyon" Hispanic past. Earlier Carrillo had reclaimed a portion of the land that his Californio ancestors once owned.

Bought with the fortune he earned in Hollywood, Rancho de los Kiotes north of San Diego was where Carrillo entertained his motion picture friends in the seigneurial tradition of Mexican hacienda culture.[15] Completed in 1937, with its architecture designed by Carrillo, this ranch is today a California State Historical Landmark.[16]

Given its romantic cast, *The California I Love* may be placed within the context of post-U.S. conquest life-writings by Mexican Californians, many of whom portrayed the pre-1848 Spanish/Mexican era either in pastoral terms similar to the mis-

Leo Carrillo's studio portrait, 1940s. Courtesy of the Leo Carrillo Ranch Historic Park, Carlsbad, California.

sion myth or as a period in which seigneurial (i.e., pre-capitalist) values provided a sustaining moral framework as well as (Mexican) sociocultural coherence. Padilla's theory of early Mexican American autobiography, as explicated in chapter 2, elucidates the profound nostalgia that imbues many of these texts. For Padilla, nostalgia for an idealized pre-1848 Mexican community in such works represents less an elitist attachment to the old (seigneurial) ranching order than an oppositional response to dispossession, subjugation, and disillusionment. Rather than judging the nostalgic tendency in early Mexican American autobiographies as a "self-deluding compensation" Padilla sees it as a "strategic narrative activity—conscious of its general social implications—for restoring order, sanity, social purpose in the face of political, social, and economic dispossession." The theme of dispossession in such works "was often articulated in an autobiographical sigh of deep sadness and [nostalgic] longing for another sociocultural life." But in these texts, Padilla continues, there is always "a barely suppressed rage": "Throughout the Southwest, nostalgia mixed with anger functioned to mediate the manifold social forces that infringed upon the spirit of those people who resided in the vast territory that became the western United States in 1848 but that geospiritually became a kind of floating island upon which Mexican (American)s were left to work out their historic destinies" (Padilla, *My History, Not Yours*, 11).

Padilla's model helps illuminate both the recurring nostalgia in *The California I Love* and the repressed memories that disrupt the work's romantic rendering of Californio history. In his youth Car-

Leo Carrillo at Rancho de los Kiotes, ca. 1940s, in Leo Carrillo Ranch Historic Park poster. Courtesy of the Leo Carrillo Ranch Historic Park, Carlsbad, California.

rillo witnessed the aftermath of the Californio elite's dispossession, which for his own family meant a fall to wage laborer status from its former position as ranchers and *hacendados*. In chapter 10 Carrillo recalls that during the Mexican era "[m]y own people . . . were given the vast Rancho Alisal, then the Sespe Rancho, and other relatives received comparable tracts all over Southern California" (Carrillo, 60). As Carrillo suggests, in 1850 his family's landholdings made it among the most powerful families in California, with ranches in San Diego, Los Angeles, Ventura, Santa Barbara, and San Luis Obispo Counties. Because of the family's many branches, it is difficult to estimate the total acreage of all of the Carrillo ranchos; in 1850 their holdings certainly encompassed more than 100,000 acres and probably substantially more. Carrillo describes what the loss of this land meant for his family. In chapter 8, "The Sad Legacy of Tío Andrés," Carrillo presents a portrait of his uncle, Don Andrés Machado, who, when Carrillo was a child, lost the "thousands of acres" of land owned by the Machado family in Los Angeles.[17] Carrillo notes that the family's ranch in Culver City was eventually "reduced to a small area hardly enough for the casa" (48). Don Andrés died shortly after the loss of that land. Carrillo's haunting childhood memory of his uncle's funeral serves as a eulogy not only for his own family's loss but also for the passing of the Mexican agrarian social order in Southern California: "I remember going to the funeral: I was four years old. It was spectral: the horse-drawn hearse with black curtains on the windows which afforded a view of the simple coffin, the black-robed priests, the women with rebozos wrapped around their faces, the great concourse of buggies wending their way to the sacred burial ground. In those days they had what are called today 'professional mourners,' who screamed and mourned with great emotion, and frightened me" (48–49).

Decades later, while touring with a Broadway show as a young actor, Carrillo visited Los Angeles. In describing a chance meeting with members of the Machado family, Carrillo juxtaposes his own privileged status as a prosperous entertainer with that of the dispossessed descendants of the Machados. As he recounts, "[O]ne evening, as I started for the theater in the shiny new sports car I had just purchased, the thought came to me that my supply of clean silk shirts was low." Driving down a Hollywood side street, he sees a "little shack" with a "crude hand-lettered sign" identifying it as a laundry. Inside the shack, Carrillo is astonished to meet the proprietors: his cousin, Don Andrés's daughter, Felicita, and her mother, Carrillo's Aunt Gracia, now ninety-eight years old. "Quietly we talked of the family, of the destruction of their home, of the troubles which had been visited upon them, of their faith through it all" (Carrillo, 50). An earthquake had destroyed the "old casa," and afterward the "remaining [Machado] land was all taken over" (49). The next morning, Carrillo is "so overcome with emotion at the seemingly miraculous reunion that I got in my car and, instinctively, drove towards Ballona Creek and the old Machado rancho." As he arrives, he reflects on the changes that have taken place in the rural space of his childhood.[18] "Street cars and busses [sic] and automobiles clattered and roared through what had been open fields or country lanes. Ballona Creek had become a flood channel. The bending, lacy willows were only a memory" (50–51). Finally, "amid businesses . . . and homes," he finds "the site of the gracious old adobe dwelling." But "where proud horses once had champed at the long hitching rack . . . only a trace of one wall . . . was to be seen" (51). Moved by his memory of the Machados, Carrillo vividly recalls "my early days at the rancho, a flash back to my boyhood, the sight and sound of the bailes and fiestas" (49). He observes that exactly where "Tío Andrés' house had stood a giant oil derrick [now] upreared against the sky." This drilling activity was, he explains, the "beginning of the Great Baldwin Hills oil discovery! The Machados, proud and impoverished, had been sleeping on millions" (51).

The nostalgia-mediated bond between past and present, between the pre-modern agrarian (Spanish/Mexican) California of Carrillo's childhood and the modern capitalist (Anglo American) California of his adulthood, forms a central trope throughout *The California I Love*. The weight of the romantic Californio past permeates Carrillo's consciousness from childhood. As he explains in chapter 2, "It was difficult sometimes to separate the present from the past. Spirits seemed to dwell with us as well as living people. . . . Legends were interwoven in our daily lives. We played games which utilized the feats of our ancestors and our kinsmen. . . . [T]he stories I tell [therefore] are not mine alone. They are filled with the spirits of those who have gone before" (Carrillo, 20). Carrillo often explores the interplay between past and present by recalling forgotten Spanish place-names, symbolically recovering the region's Spanish/Mexican heritage for a contemporary nonnative audience. For example, Carrillo recounts that Beverly Hills was once the Rancho Rodeo de las Aguas (also known as San Antonio); Glendale was the Verdugo Rancho; and Irvine was originally a part of the Sepulveda family's Rancho San Joaquín. Almost every place-name in *The California I Love* is similarly juxtaposed with its Spanish antecedent.

The most memorable of these place-name references concerns the region in Los Angeles where the motion picture industry was established. In 1930 Carrillo began his career at MGM Studios in Culver City. On his first day of work, Carrillo walked into his third-story dressing room and looked out the window. "[N]oting the Baldwin Hills, the distant sweep of the Santa Monica Mountains, the vista toward the sea, the vast expanse of the film lot itself," Carrillo suddenly realizes that "this location was not new to me." He continues, "Just outside there beyond the window where I now stood . . . I saw the exact spot where, beneath the willows so many years before, I had caught my first minnow." As noted previously, Culver City had been a part of his Uncle Andrés's Rancho La Ballona. In a symbolic moment imbued with nostalgia for the Mexican agrarian world of his childhood, Carrillo realizes that he had "come home" (Carrillo, 23).

Carrillo also reclaims other aspects of Hollywood history for the Mexican community, including the derivation of the name, which Carrillo explains in chapter 10. "According to legend," the name derives from a Mexican boy's Spanish translation of the English name of a plant that grew in the mountains above present-day Hollywood. A real estate developer who was looking over his property in the foothills asked the boy if he knew the name of a plant with red berries that grew in abundance on his land. The boy answered, "In Spanish it is toyon, but in English it is holly-wood." Carrillo spells out the reason for this usage: "This was a common expression in the Spanish mind because the identification of a tree or shrub usually was coupled with the word 'madera' meaning wood, so it was quite natural for the Mexican boy to answer holly-wood." "And so," Carrillo concludes, "Hollywood with a capital 'H' was born" (Carrillo, 61). By retelling this folk story, Carrillo reclaims for the Mexican American community in California one of the most recognizable place-names in the world. This passage also represents one of the few in *The California I Love* in which Carrillo acknowledges a Mexican—as opposed to "Spanish" Californian—ethnic identification. Though he consistently uses the term "Spanish" or "Californian" to denote his own cultural identity, here Carrillo labels the boy's ethnicity as "Mexican," a figure who clearly stands symbolically for the historical Spanish/Mexican presence in Los Angeles.

Through the discourse of nostalgia Carrillo not only dramatizes the trajectory of his own life, from rural Mexican California to cosmopolitan New York and Hollywood, but also affirms that California possesses a hidden Spanish and Mexican past that few acknowledge, thereby expressing skepticism toward hegemonic narratives that excluded this history. Carrillo's efforts in artifactual preservation as a member of the California State Beaches and Parks Commission, moreover, offer evidence of a more traditional involvement in historiographic work. Carrillo considered one of the most meaningful accomplishments of his life to have been his role in designating the Placita, the original downtown district next to Olvera Street, a state park. His description of the political process by which he achieved this goal includes a moving passage indicative of the manner in which Carrillo's family narrative in *The California I Love* embodies early California history. The plaza project "was something dear to my heart," he notes, "because the old Pico House Hotel was on the site of my Great Uncle José Antonio Carrillo's home across from the little Mission Church" (Carrillo, 271). Later Carrillo points out that "this memorial to the birthplace of the pueblo became consecrated to posterity . . . only a block or two from the spot where I had been born." The *kiosko,* or bandstand, "was erected in the Plaza exactly on the spot where," according to family legend, "the musicians on the day of my birth had been playing during the fiesta." Carrillo confesses that the Plaza restoration project was therefore "a sentimental triumph for me" because "around this area there clustered for me many tender memories" (272).

Through such passages Carrillo's autobiographical persona as Californio *caballero* takes on a new meaning. They suggest that while *The California I Love*'s nostalgic rendering of early California history at one level conforms to the mission myth, this fact should not discredit it as a text embedded in (Mexican) California's past and present. Since many of the Californio testimonials collected by Bancroft similarly depict the pre-U.S. conquest era through an aura of wistful longing for the old Spanish/Mexican agrarian social order, this quality may in fact be said to enhance the work's authenticity as a Californio text.[19] At a minimum, one can no longer attribute *The California I Love*'s allegiance to a romanticized Old (Spanish) California exclusively to the mission myth—as McWilliams, for example, had believed. (McWilliams's criticism, of course, predated Carrillo's autobiography.) Much as the Californio testimonials equate land dispossession with the loss of Mexican history, by recovering the tales of a family whose history is woven into the fabric of California's past, Carrillo's autobiography similarly represents a textual intervention in the dominant historical discourse about California and the larger Southwest. Following in the tradition of such Californio testimonials as Vallejo's "Historical and Personal Memoirs Relating to Alta California," *The California I Love* seeks to restore a Spanish/Mexican heritage that has traditionally been excluded from hegemonic constructs.

Locating Carrillo as Colonial Subject

While Padilla's theory elucidates passages in *The California I Love* in which memories of dispossession or displacement disrupt nostalgic reflection, it proves insufficient for interpreting the work at the level of psychic perception. Though Padilla's model intimates how nostalgia gives rise to various forms of repression within the Mexican American autobiographical consciousness, it does not fully investigate the range and depth of these repressions. The psychic dissension that characterizes Carrillo's simultaneous performances as Californio aristocrat and Mexican "other" suggests the psychological processes involved in the construction of colonial subjects described by Bhabha. Repression, sublimation, projection, displacement, guilt, masking, splitting—these are some of the psychic processes that Carrillo's performances of (ethnic) identity evoke. Carrillo's negotiation of (ethnic) identity through his autobiographical performance of the myth of Old (Spanish) California offers a means of tracing three of these processes—repression, sublimation, and displacement. Carrillo's offscreen and literary performances of the Spanish myth may also be read as a form of personal repression whereby one "face" of his ethnic self was displaced onto another level of practice. As Flores postulates in relation to Adina De Zavala's construction of a Texan subjectivity in her *History and Legends of the Alamo,* Carrillo, through his performance of the myth of Old (Spanish) California, enacted his abandonment of his Mexican (ethnic) identity and "reattachment" to his Californio/Spanish (white) identity (R. Flores, *Remembering the Alamo,* 88).

Rather than restoring the Mexican/*mestizo* heritage of the California that he loves, Carrillo, with few exceptions, reconstructs the region's past in Hispanocentric terms akin to the Old California myth. Carrillo in this manner (re)assures his reading and viewing public that his family genealogy is irrefutably Spanish and upper class, the antithesis of his screen image as Mexican (ethnic) "other." His multiethnic homeland, "California del Norte," is described, not surprisingly, as "granddaughter of imperial Spain, born of the union of Conquistadores with the new land on the Pacific shore . . . [the product] of a [Spanish] inheritance [that] was very strong" (Carrillo, 8). The book's epigraph, a poem by Carrillo entitled "The Footprints of the Padres," introduces this motif with references to the "days of the old missions" and "the days of Spanish fame . . . when those dear old Spanish families ruled the Golden State." "What a different California at that very early date," Carrillo reflects, "the black-eyed señorita and the caballero too" (5). Capitalizing on the enduring popularity of the Southwest's Spanish "fantasy heritage," Carrillo's publisher, Prentice-Hall, provided a book design and format appropriate to the work's romantic western motif. The first edition of *The California I Love* is adorned with medieval Spanish symbols in the form of coats of arms, ranching brands, and Catholic iconography. The work went through three printings within just fourth months after its publication. Along with Carrillo's celebrity as a film and television actor and his storytelling skills, other factors may have contributed to the work's popularity as a western text.

Though not listed as a coauthor, Carrillo's "collaborator" in the writing of *The California I Love* was Ed Ainsworth, a columnist for the *Los Angeles Times* and author of several books about the American West. In the work's foreword, entitled "Amigos," Carrillo indicates that *The California I Love* was written with the "sympathetic guidance" of his friend, who helped "arrange my material, balance it and pace it" (Carrillo, vi). One can only speculate on the role that Ainsworth played in shaping the style and content of Carrillo's work. Though his name does not appear on the book's dust jacket or title page, Ainsworth's participation as an editor or "collaborator" who clearly served, at some level, as mediating authorial consciousness obviously complicates any analysis of Carrillo's text as either autobiography or history. As a journalist, Ainsworth spent many years writing feature articles on California history (May, 244n. 1). His writings suggest striking affinities with books by early romantic folkloristic regionalist ethnographers such as J. Frank Dobie and Charles Fletcher Lummis. Such southwestern ethnographers, as José E. Limón explains, sought to "translate" folklore for a popular audience, collecting folk tales from a community and then representing them in publication. This representation was "done in an embellished, stylized form usually translated into a standard literary language . . . so as to make the original text sound more like 'high' literature, fit for a dominant literate reading public." Through such a translation of regional culture, "the romantic regionalist [believed], a better appreciation [could] be had of the 'authentic' genius and spirit of the 'folk'" (Limón, *Dancing with the Devil*, 51). Carrillo himself may also have been influenced by Dobie, Lummis, and other like-minded "popular" ethnographers of his era. But if Ainsworth did in fact contribute significantly to *The California I Love*'s romantic folkloristic style, this influence would not have contradicted Carrillo's own predilection for romance as demonstrated by his offscreen performances as Spanish gentleman-rancher.

Though the Spanish gentleman-rancher self-construct appears more prominently in the work's opening and closing chapters, Carrillo acknowledges no contradiction in his repeated claim throughout the book to a pure Castilian racial lineage. In chapter 1, for example, he takes pride in noting that the Carrillos were among those "of Spanish blood whose veins carry the red fire pumped from the hot foundations of medieval Castile" (Carrillo, 8). Providing justification for this claim, chapter 2 relates Carrillo's journeys in Spain, where the actor traced his family name to the thirteenth century. "We were known as the 'Carrillos of Albornoz,'" he explains, "and I have one document dating back hundreds of years showing the family crest" (15). Though regarded by many as a voice of the Mexican American community, Carrillo does not refer to himself as a Mexican at any point in *The California I Love*. Carrillo, in his Spanish rancher persona, asserts throughout the book that he was an American who was demonstrably proud of his (Spanish) Californian ancestry. And as if to allay any fears that this Spanish incarnation might itself be misconstrued as inordinately "ethnic," Carrillo explains in chapter 2 that his family "were violently American by birth and inclination." Though "[w]e had no vestige of ancestor worship . . . the example of our immediate forbears [sic] . . . was always held up before us . . . [and] we were taught to be proud of the accomplishments of those whose name we bore and to try to live up to the great example which they had set in the history of California" (16). Since Carrillo's fetishistic allegiance to his Spanish ancestral identity represses his Mexican (ethnic) self by constructing him as a "white" descendant of Europeans, such passages in *The California I Love* cry out for interrogation. But, as previously noted, this theme must also be understood as both a statement of Carrillo's deep sense of pride in the Californio past and as a reflection of the differing racial categorizations passed down to him by his Mexican Californian culture.

Flores's research on the Texan historian and folklorist Adina De Zavala's *History and Legends of the Alamo* has informed my understanding of Carrillo's repressions in *The California I Love*. Several striking autobiographical parallels between the Californio actor and the Texan historian/folklorist stand out. Both were descended from the Mexican elite and lived during an era when the socioeconomic processes identified with modernity brought about the decline of the Southwest's Mexican agrarian social order.[20] At the same pivotal historical juncture, moreover, Carrillo and De Zavala shared a remarkably similar obsession. Both were possessed by a passion to recover a Spanish/Mexican narrative of origins as a means of expanding the dominant historical discourse. For both, the obsession took the form of artifactual preservation of Spanish and Mexican historical sites as well as the recovery, through writing, of the Southwest's early Spanish/Mexican past. And both pursued these objectives during a period of interethnic strife that made overt statements of Mexican American (ethnic) solidarity highly problematical for these authors. In wider terms, Carrillo and De Zavala's parallel recovery projects constituted a critical response to the racially stigmatizing and psychologically debilitating effects experienced by Mexicans following this population's social and economic displacement in the Southwest in the late nineteenth and early twentieth centuries.

Of mixed Mexican and Irish ancestry, De Zavala dedicated her life to the preservation of the Alamo as a historical site. A collection of myriad narratives about this site, *History and Legends of the Alamo* was the "distillation of more than twenty years of collating, collecting, writing and research . . . compiled from . . . historical documents, previously published sources, folklore and legends concerning the Alamo and missions in other areas of Texas" (R. Flores, "Introduction: Adina De Zavala," vi). In contrast to the romantic myth and its idealized hegemonic renderings, De Zavala's study "weaves a clear and putatively accurate narrative that chronicles the Indian, Spanish, Mexican, Texan, and U.S. presence at the Alamo" (R. Flores, *Remembering the Alamo,* 77). As its historical breadth suggests, De Zavala's collection of texts and tales countered hegemonic constructs by construing history "as a summation of the past, influenced by social actors from both sides of the border." Though she celebrates all things Texan, explains Flores, De Zavala "is equally adamant about the Mexican and Spanish roots of Texas" (84).

Flores unravels the paradox that led De Zavala "to empathize with Mexicans while celebrating Americanism, to work unceasingly for the historical preservation of Spain and Mexico's artifactual past while simultaneously holding little value for her partial Mexican heritage" (R. Flores, *Remembering the Alamo,* 89). Why, during a period of intense interethnic turmoil in Texas, did De Zavala fixate on the Alamo, "a shrine of Texas liberty and bastion of anti-Mexican sentiment," to the exclusion of other issues that more directly concerned Mexican Americans? (84). In Flores's analysis, De Zavala's celebration of a Texan identity through her manifest passion for the Alamo serves as a disguise effected by the process of sublimation. Drawing upon Peter Stallybrass and Allon White's model, Flores observes that "sublimation—the displacement of energy that leads to various shades of disguising and disclosing—is a response to certain forms of social and cultural hegemonic practices" (89). Given the anti-Mexican atmosphere in Texas during the era in which she lived, De Zavala could not openly validate the Mexican side of her identity. "Unable to confront directly the sources that socially and economically displaced Mexicans," argues Flores, De Zavala "emplotted them as the historical rationale of the Alamo; stymied by the racial hierarchies of the period, she displaced her ethnic self onto a Texan identity and a passion for the material past" (90). De Zavala's "disguise" as Texan resulted from her deeply felt need to repress "the depth of the social, cultural and economic domination experienced by Mexicans." Flores concludes, "In place of validating her own mestizoness . . . [De Zavala] forges a unified Texan subjectivity and displaces her 'cultural otherness' onto historical places. Her life is spent in search of the 'lost realms' of Spanish and Mexican Texas precisely because her ethnic sense of self has been displaced by a Texan subjectivity" (89).

Carrillo's autobiographical performance of the legendary Spanish Californian *caballero* suggests a process of psychic sublimation and displacement strikingly similar to De Zavala's. At one level, Carrillo's self-construct certainly reflects his deep sense of pride in the Californio past. In the pre-1960s era it also constituted a personal response to the forces of anti-Mexican racial exclusion of which Carrillo's stereotypic film characters were an obvious product. However, Carrillo's "reattachment" to his Spanish Californio identity must be further understood in relation to his popular cultural incarnation on film as Mexican (ethnic) "other." Carrillo's film image indicates that the actor could not readily suppress the existential fact of his Mexican/*mestizo* (ethnic) alterity. His offscreen and literary performance of the genteel Spanish *caballero* captures the urgency of Carrillo's need, owing to this popular screen incarnation, to displace his Mexican/*mestizo* (ethnic) self onto another level of cultural practice.[21] Just as the racially defined constraints that limited Carrillo's film career have been overlooked by the actor's critics, so too have the inimical circumstances of Southern California's Jim Crow sociocultural context in which Carrillo, a descendant of the Californio *rancheros*, lived for most of his life.

Historians Richard Griswold del Castillo, Albert Camarillo, Carey McWilliams, and, more recently, David G. Gutiérrez, Douglas Monroy, and Martha Menchaca, among others, have examined the pre-1960s history of California's Mexican (American) population. Given the interethnic conflict that characterized much of this era, Carrillo, despite his wealth, could not have remained untouched by anti-Mexican discrimination as it became institutionalized in the state through Jim Crow covenants and other racial barriers. Though Carrillo does not cite any instance of such discrimination in his autobiography, his *mestizo* phenotype would have made him indistinguishable in appearance from members of the large Mexican immigrant and Mexican American population that resided in Los Angeles when the actor lived there after 1930. Carrillo had left Los Angeles thirty years earlier to pursue his acting career. After residing for seventeen years in New York, he returned to his city of birth in 1929 as a contract performer for MGM Studios. Events that occurred soon after his return would define for decades the dominant perception of Mexican Americans as a racial minority in Southern California.

After the stock market crash of late 1929, many unemployed whites in California blamed Mexicans for their suffering. As Monroy explains, this sentiment prompted government leaders to call for the repatriation of Mexicans in the state. In 1931 "the state of California passed legislation forbidding contractors from employing Mexicans and other 'aliens' on public jobs, although such . . . work had long been their acknowledged domain" (Monroy, *Rebirth*, 148–49). This legislation was followed by "[municipal] ordinances restricting work on public improvements to citizens" and other "nativist pressures encouraging preferential hiring for 'Americans.'" Together these factors "persuaded or convinced or forced many Mexicans to repatriate." In the same year, "local and federal authorities initiated a coordinated effort to round up and deport 'illegals.'" According to Monroy, "[T]he racial thinking that motivated the dragnets meant that anyone who looked Mexican to the authorities could be snared, regardless of his or her rootedness in the north or affinity for old Mexico" (149). Carrillo's wealth no doubt shielded him from the most virulent aspects of the era's anti-Mexican xenophobia. It seems inconceivable, however, that such egregious injustices targeting Mexicans did not touch Carrillo's life and therefore at some level influence his construction of (ethnic) self-identity.

Independent of the widespread Mexican (American) labor unrest between 1920 and the 1950s in Southern California's agriculture industry, events in urban Los Angeles during the early 1940s led to a new wave of anti-Mexican hysteria. During World War II—when Carrillo was at the pinnacle of his fame as a film actor—"[a]mong the most important causes of the deteriorating interethnic relationships in the region was Anglo reaction to the emergence of a 'pachuco gang' subculture among 'second generation' youth" (D. Gutiérrez, 123). After the Zoot Suit Riots of 1943 underscored "the increasing volatility of ethnic and race relations in wartime Los Angeles," the press and local officials responded with racist tirades against the Mexican (American) community. Official discourse "[painted] zoot-suiters, pachucos, and Latin gangs as the predictable results of the primitive and backward culture of the 'Mexican colony'" living in Los Angeles. In the aftermath of the riots, an infamous report issued by the Foreign Relations Bureau of the Los Angeles County Sheriff's Department "developed an elaborate sociobiological description of Mexicans' innate proclivities." It contended, among other things, "that Mexicans were naturally disposed to violence, with biological urges 'to kill, or at least to let blood'" (125).

Carrillo's enactment of his Spanish Californio identity and repression of his Mexican (ethnic) self resulted from his experience of ethnic alterity as a Mexican American film actor who performed the racialized movie roles that both reflected and provoked such anti-Mexican hostility. Just as De Zavala, obsessed with a historical site whose legend stigmatized Mexicans, was driven to repress her Mexican (ethnic) self and displace it onto a Texan subjectivity, Carrillo fixates on his Spanish Californian self because of his pressing need to sublimate his Mexican/*mestizo* (ethnic) identity during an era in which anti-Mexican bigotry pervaded social institutions, such as the law, and cultural institutions, such as the film industry. Carrillo's autobiographical performances as aristocratic Spanish don thus result not necessarily from the pretense and chauvinism that his claim to a Spanish (Californio) lineage might imply. They also follow from Carrillo's felt need, as a Mexican American professional struggling to negotiate the parameters of race and class in the pre-1960s Jim Crow era, to repress his Mexican/*mestizo* self and displace it onto a Spanish/Californio identity that would, in racial terms, serve to confer "whiteness" upon the actor.

Flores argues that De Zavala's utopian vision, as expressed in the legends collected in *History and Legends of the Alamo*, seeks to "'fix' the problem of [Mexican] socioeconomic displacement by pointing to various forms of restoration and recalling the 'enchanted city of Tejas' where social and racial cleavage are unknown" (R. Flores, *Remembering the Alamo*, 82–83). The utopian project for social restoration "semantically keyed in De Zavala's legends," he explains, "serves as the muted and displaced social voice of [her] subjective speech" (90). In Carrillo's work this sublimated "social voice" finds expression in the author's self-construction as the living incarnation of the pastoral myth of Spanish California. After returning to Los Angeles to begin his film career, Carrillo was confronted daily by his stigmatized Mexican (ethnic) self through his typecast film performances as Mexican "other." At the same time, he observed in the sensationally popular Old (Spanish) California myth that the genteel (Spanish) Californio rancher had become a figure that attracted near cultural reverence among a majority white population seeking to plant historical roots in the region. Compelled to repress his Mexican/*mestizo* self, Carrillo displaced his cultural otherness onto his Spanish Californio identity. He sustained this offscreen identity even as he struggled to reconcile the self-evident *mestizo*-ness of his screen image with his offscreen performance of identity as Spanish Californian rancher/*caballero*. And yet, though Carrillo's complex performance of identity may appear to be a distinctively modern process, the actor's Californio ancestors performed a similar type of self-fashioning act in the late nineteenth century as they sought inclusion within white American society. As Weber observes, though "race did not stand as a barrier to upward mobility" in Mexican California, the frontier population "denigrated others of darker hue, and tended to 'whiten' themselves as they moved up the social ladder by denying their Indian and black ancestry." In the post-conquest period "the racial biases of the nouveau riche [landed] Californios actually increased . . . in part because they sought to put themselves on an equal footing with the race-conscious Anglo-American newcomers" (Weber, *Mexican Frontier*, 215).

While Carrillo's life in "disguise" may for some suggest a southwestern version of the colonized subject as "mimic man," Carrillo's negotiation of his public and private (ethnic) identities, and particularly his performances of recognition and disavowal of his ethnic alterity, make his life and career a compelling illustration of Bhabha's model. Emerging from his concept of ambivalence, mimicry, according to Bhabha, is an inevitable process "of counter-domination produced by a miming of the very operation of domination" (R. Young, 148). Because mimicry is never entirely indistinct from mockery, the mimic man is by definition "a contradictory figure who simultaneously reinforces colonial authority and disturbs it" (Sharpe, 99). The "*menace* of mimicry" is precisely "its *double* vision which in disclosing the ambivalence of colonial discourse also disrupts its authority" (Bhabha, 88; emphasis in original). Mimicry, in Bhabha's model, is therefore more aptly understood as "camouflage" than "disguise," "not a harmonization of repression of difference, but a form of resemblance, that differs from or defends presence by displaying it in part, metonymically" (90). "[A]s a trope of partial presence," it "masks a threatening racial difference only to reveal the excesses and slippages of colonial power and knowledge" (R. Young, 100). Bhabha's model suggests the circuitous psychological, cultural, and historical convolutions of Carrillo's *The California I Love*. Carrillo's career as a performer, actor, and comedian, moreover, opens up multiple levels of imbricated meanings in *The California I Love*'s intricate psychic repression and displacement of the author's Mexican/*mestizo* (ethnic) self. The chapter that follows identifies a similar self-fashioning process in a Mexican (American) autobiography otherwise strikingly antithetical to Carrillo's. It turns away from the actor's privileged Hollywood world to examine the hacienda as cultural icon as it emerges in the construction of Mexican (American) ethnic subjectivity within my own family's contested narrative of origins.

5

Heroes and Orphans of the Hacienda
Testimonial Memory as Resistance and Repression in Francisco Róbles Pérez's "Memorias"

Chicano/a literary and historical studies have increasingly focused attention on Mexican American autobiography. Since 1988, when a special issue of *The Americas Review* entitled "U.S. Hispanic Autobiography" appeared, commentators have examined its status as a distinct genre and explored the socioideological and cultural dimensions of its nineteenth- and twentieth-century texts.[1] Since many of Chicano/a literature's foundational narratives are autobiographies, or fictions that are in large measure autobiographical, critics of Mexican American writing have consistently wrestled with the nature of autobiographical texts.[2] At the same time, Luis Leal's pathbreaking studies have directed his successors toward the archaeological endeavor of recovering that vast catalog of Mexican American autobiographical narratives that have remained unpublished or unavailable to a wide audience. Padilla's *My History, Not Yours*, discussed in chapters 2 and 4, follows both critical paths. Not only does he proclaim the need for "the archival recovery, editing, translation, and publication of this body of foundational literary discourse," which in his own case revolves around that set of Mexican American texts, most still unpublished, collected during the 1870s by the historian Hubert H. Bancroft, but Padilla also demands, from himself and others, "critical and interpretive activity that shall establish the discursive genealogy (its continuities as well as discontinuities) of our literary traditions" (Padilla, *My History, Not Yours*, 7).[3]

Drawing on the work of Padilla and other scholars of historical and autobiographical narrative, I would like to examine Francisco Róbles Pérez's "Memorias," an unpublished journal of personal reminiscences, written between 1990 and 1992, by a Mexican (American) immigrant.[4] Born in 1908 in the state of Zacatecas, Mexico, Pérez is a former farm laborer. He is also my paternal grandfather.[5] The 250-page manuscript, 70 pages of which have been transcribed from the original handwriting and translated from the Spanish, recounts his childhood on a hacienda in Mexico, his immigration at the age of thirteen to the United States, and his youth as a farm worker in Southern California. I would like to amplify Padilla's work by examining not only the nostalgic cast of my grandfather's account but also a second family narrative that "Memorias" suppresses—a narrative that foregrounds gender and class contradictions in late-nineteenth- and early-twentieth-century Mexican hacienda society.

My interest in this research project developed in an accidental fashion. While transcribing my grandfather's manuscript, quite by chance I became involved in a clash between two branches of my family that took place at the funeral of my "aunt," Isabel "Chavela" Róbles.[6] The source of the conflict was a second version of Pérez history offered by the Róbleses, a group of relatives whose genealogy from the later nineteenth century to the present is closely interwoven with the Pérez family line. Largely suppressed in my family until comments at Chavela's funeral brought it to light, the Róbles narrative led me to interrogate the rhetorical strategies, ideological currents, and sociohistorical particularities of "Memorias." In this chapter I will first show how certain counter-discursive socio-ideological articulations embedded in nostalgic memory make "Memorias" a perfect example of Padilla's model. My second and broader objective, however, is to show that as Padilla carries out his project to restore the writings of early Mexican American autobiographers, and to extend the Chicano/a literary canon into the nineteenth century, he almost inevitably resuppresses underlying social contradictions within California (Mexican) hacienda society—a suppression, as I have elaborated in chapter 2, most notable in his account of the Mexican American politician, rancher, and author Mariano Guadalupe Vallejo.

I attend first to my grandfather's nostalgic idealization of hacienda life in pre-revolutionary Mexico. Rather than mark this aspect of the text with an ideological label, however, I will, as Padilla's nuanced readings of Mexican American autobiographies propose, measure the utopian aspects of my grandfather's account against (1) his dislocation and dispossession as a child buffeted by the social upheaval of the Mexican Revolution and (2) his aggrieved economic and sociocultural status as a Mexican immigrant laborer in the United States. As in many Mexican immigrant narratives and nineteenth-century Mexican American autobiographies, nostalgia for an "idealized and unobtainable" past serves a fundamental oppositional function in "Memorias," certainly enacting an imaginative communion with the narrator's lost family and community but also articulating "resistance to cultural evisceration" in

The Pérez Family Tree

Santa Ana Pérez
m. Leandra Lira

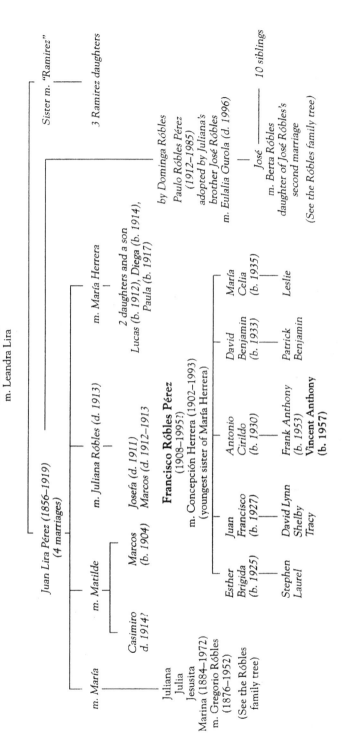

The Pérez family tree.

The Róbles Family Tree

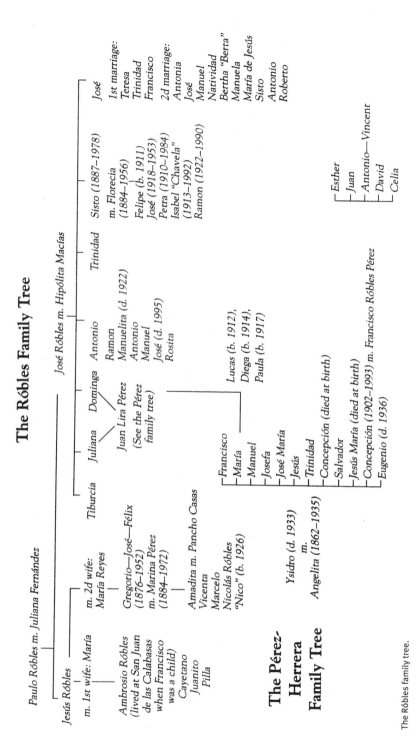

The Róbles family tree.

the United States. As Padilla puts it, nostalgia serves "the reintegrative psychic and social need for sustaining an idea of the past and for fixing a version of history within a cultural text that would mark historical presence in the face of erasure" (Padilla, 16).

My next level of analysis responds to my accidental encounter with the Róbles narrative in order to demonstrate that, while correct in defending early Mexican American autobiographies from the charge of indulging in the "hacienda syndrome," Padilla's model obscures social contradictions in those foundational life stories emerging from within pre-U.S. conquest Mexican agrarian (ranch) society.[7] Within my own family, the Róbles family's oral narrative turned my grandfather's text into a terrain of intense contestation, challenging his nostalgic memory in ways that cannot be contained or elaborated by Padilla's theoretical paradigm. As I evaluate Padilla's usefulness in analyzing my grandfather's employment of nostalgia, the recovered Róbles counter-history, which foregrounds women's narratives and declares my great-grandfather's role as a hacienda manager in the repressive Porfirian hacienda social economy, inevitably moves to the foreground. Recovering the suppressed, anti-nostalgic counter-narrative of Dominga Róbles—who, according to her family narrative, was raped by her brother-in-law (my grandfather's father), Juan Lira Pérez, in 1912—not only (re)historicizes my grandfather's representation of his father's life but also further challenges Padilla's reading of Californio autobiographical testimonials.[8] As it highlights the random, even accidental, nature of historical investigative processes in my own family narrative, the Róbles counter-narrative identifies the constructed nature of all literary and historical recovery projects—whether familial, group, or national.

My interest in these foundational narratives obviously constitutes part of a larger genealogical project to uncover an unclear family and community history. Though my own family's narrative is no more representative of the Mexican American past than any other Chicano's or Chicana's family, I have found that investigating my own background has helped me better negotiate the history of Mexican American society as a whole. My project in this way seeks to bridge Mexican American autobiographical narrative and historical literary scholarship, underscoring the constructed nature of both. Peeling back the layers of my family's Chicano/a and Mexicano/a history demonstrates that whether narrated by my grandfather, by other Mexican American grandparents and families, by Chicano and Chicana fiction writers, or by Mexican American historians, the recovery of our past remains incomplete, often suppressed, and untranscribed. Like members of the Buendía clan, who struggle for more than a century to read and translate Melquíades's encoded parchments in Gabriel García Márquez's *One Hundred Years of Solitude* (1967), we have only begun to decipher our history and escape the labyrinthine "city of mirrors." Though a number of contemporary works stand as exceptions, too often writers and scholars of the Mexican American past seem unengaged by our not so distant early social history.[9] As we have struggled to recover our historical origins—a Mexican cultural heritage that has been excluded or denigrated by hegemonic culture—too often we have read our *abuelos'* (grandparents') stories uncritically or failed to pursue these histories wherever they may lead. Just as so many autobiographies by our nineteenth-century ancestors reify a Mexican agrarian religiocultural inheritance in the face of cultural rupture and dispossession, so too, in the interest of recovering our history, have some of our most informed writers and critics placed their faith in a utopian vision of a unitary and collective Mexican cultural space imagined in the distant past.[10] Even Padilla, though he foregrounds the constructed, even fictional, character of all Mexican American life-writing, himself evades but cannot help but evoke the profound contradictions, arising from nostalgic desire, in early autobiographical texts.

Nostalgia and Resistance

I began to delve into my family's history when, as an undergraduate, I went to Mexico for two years to study Latin American literature. Prior to my visit, I felt reluctant to reveal certain legends about my Mexican ancestors to my Chicano and Chicana friends. I often secretly questioned their genealogical lore, not the humble origins of their *antepasados* (ancestors) or their families' suffering as immigrants and laborers in the United States, but their representation of the Mexican Revolution. I understood that many of my friends were, like my own family, descended from *los de abajo* (people of the lower classes)—to use the title of Mariano Azuela's novel of the Mexican Revolution. But after I began to read modern Mexican literature and to develop a clearer understanding of the hacienda—the foundational socioeconomic institution in Mexican history—I felt that we had, as a group, become alienated from our history.[11] When speaking with my Chicano and Chicana friends or family members, I either held my peace about my grandfather's obscure past or revised my history. Rather than acknowledge my grandparents' unspoken pain and profound ambivalence about the revolution and its aftermath, I portrayed my paternal grandfather, who emigrated from Mexico in 1921, as an impoverished *campesino* (farm worker) whose family had sympathized with Pancho Villa's revolutionary insurrectionists.[12]

This narrative of origins was not entirely a fabrication; like most Mexicans of his generation, my grandfather embraced the Villa legend and idolized Francisco Madero, the liberal Constitutionalist political leader who in 1911 helped topple the Díaz regime. But my omissions marked the unconscious content of my family history, omissions also found in some of the Mexican American literary and historical texts I had read up to that time. These texts, like many recent works, designate the inception of Mexican American history as either the great migration to the United States in the early twentieth century or the military defeat of Mexico in 1848.[13] Privileging the modern Mexican American social experience, they rarely delve into the Southwest's Spanish and Mexican eras—when a seigneurial ranching system dominated the region—or the pre-revolutionary hacienda era in Mexico. Rather than imagining links between Mexican history and the Mexican American experience by applying the borderlands paradigm to the realm of history, many instead construct boundaries between the early period and the modern. This contradiction became more apparent when I visited Mexico in the early 1980s to attend classes at UNAM (Autonomous National University of Mexico). While studying there, I first read the fictions of such modern Mexican authors as Juan Rulfo (*Pedro Páramo*, 1955) and José Revueltas (*El luto humano* [Human Mourning], 1943). Long before the writers, poets, and scholars of the Chicano movement began their project to recover and revitalize a Mexican American cultural and historical patrimony, these earlier writers had interrogated the Mexican national mythologies and ideologies surrounding both the revolution and the pre-revolutionary (hacienda) period. The Mexican American narratives and myths I had sought out as a Chicano college student participating in the struggle to contest and expand U.S. history had been critically scrutinized by Mexican writers, artists, and scholars. Rulfo carried out a definitive critique of the Mexican myth of origins, demonstrating how the hacienda and its identification with a tradition of *caciquismo* determined the direction and outcome of the Mexican Revolution. Revueltas's earlier novel debunked the mythology of the revolution itself, portraying it as a peasant movement betrayed by state bureaucrats in thrall to conservative political interests. Rather than discovering a stable originary "homeland," which, when I was in my twenties, I still believed was possible, I found in Mexico a society marked by profound contradictions and almost unfathomable complexity—one still struggling to come to terms with its own history. Speaking of the development of Latin American history, Carlos Fuentes remarked that "[t]he Utopia of foundation was exploited, degraded, and finally assassinated by the epic of history, activity, commerce, and crime," a sentiment that my readings of that time underscored.[14] The engagement with the past by Mexican and other Latin American writers achieved its apotheosis in Rulfo's fiction and García Márquez's *One Hundred Years of Solitude*, the latter work indebted to both Rulfo and Revueltas, and thus one that speaks to Mexican and Chicano/a history as well as to the more general Spanish American past.

Though authors such as García Márquez, Rulfo, Revueltas, or, in the U.S. context, Faulkner, do not refrain from delving into the labyrinthine convolutions of historical memory—where Rulfo and Faulkner felt the most at home—I have encountered in some Mexican American literary and historical texts a reluctance to embark upon critical inquiry into the early Mexican (American) past. Our sociohistorical condition as an aggrieved ethnic minority requires that we document and analyze the contemporary period, yet these circumstances can also limit our historical vision. Even in my own research I have in the past found myself drawing back from certain investigative paths, denying myself the critical freedom needed to approach the "truths" about our early history. In an earlier version of this very research project I unintentionally (re)suppressed the story of the rape of Dominga Róbles and thus downplayed my great-grandfather's role in the hacienda economy. And as "Memorias" demonstrates, members of my family, and particularly my grandparents, were displeased to find me using the skills acquired from my university education to retrieve and expose long-buried family secrets.

My genealogical research attempts just such an expansive recuperative project, and in fact, my grandfather's memoirs are themselves the result of the investigation into my family's history I began twenty years ago while studying in Mexico. While a graduate student in the late 1980s, I began a series of taped interviews with my grandfather, which over the course of six years developed into a full-length written autobiography. These interviews were my opportunity to explore my family's Mexican past as well as to establish a closer relationship with my grandfather in the language of his forebears. I could not have known how the conflicted genealogy they would bring to light would continue to weigh on the lives and consciences of family members.

A critic of Faulkner once remarked that all of the author's major characters "enter the fiction trailing behind them clouds of familial and regional qualifiers . . . the grandparents, parents, and siblings, the hill country or bottom land or tidewater, whose cumulative significance is the indispensable background of identity" (Karl, 133–34). Similarly, I found that certain (over)determining historical qualifiers—which in *Absalom, Absalom!* reach back into distant family and community memory rooted in the southern plantation landscape—also shape contemporary Mexican American subjectivity. Juan Preciado, the Mexican *campesino* in Rulfo's *Pedro Páramo*, returns to the rural village where his mother grew up to search for his origins; in Faulkner's novel Quentin Compson, tormented and obsessed with the past, attempts to recover the history of the U.S. South. In the same fashion, Mexican Americans today carry on our shoulders and in our consciences the sum of the combined memories of our families and communities. For the same holds true within Mexican American society as Faulkner observed in the South: "[T]here is no such thing as *was* . . . time [history] is not a fixed condition, time [history] is in a way the sum of the combined intelligences of all men who breathe at that moment" (Faulkner, *Light in August*, 179). Yet Mexican American collective memory is rooted not only in the twentieth-century urban or rural United States but also inevitably in the hacienda and rancho social landscape of prerevolutionary Mexico and the nineteenth-century Southwest.

Since I could visit my grandfather only twice a year, on one occasion I asked him to begin writing down the stories of his life in Mexico and as an immigrant. Thirty-five notebooks, filled with Spanish prose written in the style of a child and carefully numbered to avoid chronological confusion, have been the result. Noting that his education "was only three years in primary school," my grandfather repeatedly apologizes for his "poor orthography and grammar" (F. Pérez, 3). And yet he is proud of his acquired knowledge, drawn from his lifelong experience in the real world in Mexico and the United States. "My philosophy is my own—I didn't go to any university," he states early in the narrative. "What I'm saying I've compiled from a long and bumpy journey over the face of our mother Earth" (26). Although I have estimated that the edited manuscript will be 250 pages, the final version may be longer. I have not transcribed many of the notebooks covering the post-1936 era, nor have I determined precisely how the hours of tape-recorded interviews—which complement the written account—will be integrated into the text.

I also recorded hours of interviews (which I am incorporating into a written family narrative) with my grandmother, Concepción Herrera Pérez, who, in keeping with her reputation for shrewd family diplomacy, measured each word that she spoke with the painstaking care of a politician, unlike my grandfather. (I later learned the reasons for her reticence.) In what initially struck me as a deliberate refusal to grant me entry into the vaults of family history, she skirted events that I suspected were crucial to our family's narrative of origins. I felt like an ethnographer trying to wrest critical information from an unwilling or suspicious inter-locutor. The analogy of an ethnographer may seem an odd one to apply to my relationship with my grandmother, but it illustrates my ignorance at that time of my family's history and particularly the women's stories within this history. By retrieving one woman's account from a longstanding patriarchal tradition of family legend and lore, I hope in this chapter to begin filling in some of the tradition's gaps and omissions. For all of my grandfather's candor in narrating his childhood experience of hacienda society, it displaced more effectively than my grandmother's reticence a side of our early history that Chavela's funeral would only coincidentally bring to light. Since the patriarchal myth is rooted in sociohistorical reality, it must be examined for what it can tell us about not only Mexican American cultural memory as a whole but also the role of the hacienda in the evolution of this memory.

Though I first encouraged my grandfather to write his story, and I now serve as its translator and editor, the journal itself is entirely my grandfather's work.[15] It begins with his childhood in the pre-revolutionary period, which he portrays as a pastoral and idyllic life in the hacienda communities outside of Jerez, where his father worked. Though born in 1908, my grandfather nostalgically recalls the Porfirian (hacienda) period of the late nineteenth century. The text ends with the account of his attempt to rear five young children on farm-worker wages in the United States during the depression. "Memorias" thus spans roughly thirty years of Mexican and Mexican American history.

My grandfather, Francisco—who we believe passed away in 1994 or 1995—was the son of a bookkeeper named Juan Lira Pérez, a business associate from the 1880s to 1913 of a group of landed *hacendados* near the city of Zacatecas in central Mexico.[16] Though born into relative privilege in an era of socioeconomic polarization that set the *hacendado* elite apart from *campesinos*, my grandfather's comfortable early circumstances were short-lived. Orphaned at eleven, he was forced to fend for himself during a time of social and economic upheaval.[17] Immigrating to Southern California in 1921, he worked for more than fifty years as a ranch laborer. Thirty-six of those years he spent at Rancho Sespe, a six-thousand-acre citrus farm in the Santa Clara Valley owned by the Spalding sports equipment manufacturing family. (As noted in chapter 4, Rancho Sespe had once been owned by the Californio *ranchero* Don Carlos Antonio Carrillo, Leo Carrillo's great-grandfather.) My own grand-father had a number of occupations at this ranch: "I picked fruit for twenty years, then, as a gardener, planted vegetables and flowers and trees. . . . I once helped dynamite a mountain on which the owner built a cabin; and for two years I worked with an agronomy engineer to build a nine-hole golf course, which Mister Keith Spalding had ordered" (F. Pérez, 40).

My grandfather and his wife reared a family in the workers' camp, Sespe Village (also called the Mexican Village), where 150 Mexican families lived. Unable to return to Mexico and reclaim his father's land and status because of the civil war and its aftermath, my grandfather remained within the ranks of agricultural laborers in a country where Mexicans were not only cultural outsiders but also exploited as laborers and excluded as racial inferiors. His family's fall from the Mexican upper class due to the war's disruption of the hacienda economy left my grandfather with a dual class identity. He could sing the praises of the revolutionary leader Villa, yet also revile him as a bandit who had disenfranchised his father and forced young Francisco to leave his homeland for good. Similarly, he could nostalgically recount the heroics of the martyred Constitutionalist leader Madero, yet with pride list the modernizing achievements of the dictator Díaz, whom Madero had replaced.

In the early sections of "Memorias," my grandfather reconstructs the life of that fifty-seven-year-old established businessman and accountant who was his father. In these early passages, my grand-father harks back to life in a "harmonious" rural community in a pre-revolutionary and "colonial" Mexico.[18] He was born on the eve of the civil war, to "Don Juan Lira Pérez and Doña Juliana Róbles de Pérez," in the "beautiful small town of Jerez [de García Salinas], in the state of Zacatecas" (F. Pérez, 1). "Direct descendants of the seventeenth-century Spanish pioneers and founders of Jerez," both his parents had deep roots in that region. My grandfather remembers his father saying once that his own "father, Santa Ana Pérez, and uncles were descended from the original founders and settlers of the town" (2). "Memorias" thus forges a genealogical link between Lira Pérez and the Spanish colonial settlers of Mexico. Assuming that the locality's first settlers had been "conquistadors," my grandfather concludes, despite a chronological discrepancy, that his own grandfather must have come from Spain. He points out that the town's name may have been "inspired by the town of Jerez de la Frontera in southern Spain" (2).[19] This Spanish link reappears at the time of my uncles' and my father's births, for these light-haired infants are cited as proof that the blood "from my Mexican ancestors, descendants of the [Spanish] *gachupines*, continues" (32).

Francisco Róbles Pérez at age twenty-three with his two eldest children, Esther and Juan, at Long Beach, California, 1931.

These passages appear to reflect little more than those racial and class contradictions rooted in the Spanish conquest and colonial domination of Mexico's indigenous peoples that have been previously explicated in chapters 1 and 2. Rather than acknowledging his *mestizo* (Spanish/Indian) cultural lineage, my grandfather, steeped in his father's nineteenth-century mores, claims his descent from the Spanish conquerors.[20] Yet, as Jesús Flores Olague and his coauthors point out, although in the sixteenth century "[t]he presence of diverse racial groups was one characteristic of the [Zacatecan] mining centers . . . the permanent relationship established between these groups . . . exhibited the presence of one dominant group: the *mestizo*" (J. Flores Olague et al., 83). Even without taking into account the various groups of Chichimeca Indians in that region conquered by the Spanish, "numerous groups of indigenous Mexicans, Tarascans, and Tlaxcaltecans—which accompanied the Spaniards in their expeditions and participated in the pacification of the Indians who inhabited the region—formed part of the new settler population around the Zacatecan mines" (89–90). However indirectly, my grandfather acknowledges this Indian and *mestizo* lineage through his use of the word *gachupin,* a term for Spaniard that can be used pejoratively. Its use in the above quote suggests the narrator's (un)conscious desire for distinction from the Spanish conquerors as well as his identification with the region's Indian and *mestizo* population.

Other sociocultural motivations, however, contribute to this seemingly contradictory aspect of my grandfather's autobiography. His nostalgia for a legendary Mexican (Spanish) world, and more specifically his construction through memory of a childhood and youth spent within the "mythic" (Spanish) hacienda past, are examples of what Padilla calls the author's "epistemological ground of subjectivity" (Padilla, 158). Like other early Mexican American autobiographers, my grandfather views his originary, pre-migration cultural and social "ground of being" against the nightmare backdrop of his experience as a Mexican immigrant living within the Anglo American sociocultural regime.

Let me briefly explain how my grandfather's effort to narrate the story of his origins conforms to Padilla's theoretical model. Coming six years after the death of his mother, Juliana Róbles Pérez, and marking the end of his hacienda childhood and the start of his hardscrabble existence as a *descalzo* (barefoot waif), the death of his father is the defining moment of my grandfather's life. Nostalgic desire is thus interwoven with retrospective longing. As a boy orphaned at an early age and forced to fend for himself at various jobs before making his way to the United States, my grandfather wished to embrace a father and a community that he knew only in childhood. By retrieving his father's myth from the sociohistorical ruins of the revolutionary era, my grandfather's testimonial remembrance reenacts the short-lived relationship that his father's unexpected death in 1919 abruptly ended. But if we accept orphanhood as a figuration embodying deeper sociohistorical and cultural currents, the death of Lira Pérez can also stand as that traumatic moment of sociocultural rupture that Padilla identifies as key to understanding the Mexican American autobiographical consciousness. In the figure of the *descalzo*, my grandfather alludes to his suddenly precarious socioeconomic status: "The person writing this [account] was a *descalzo*, because the first shoes that I owned were bought sometime in 1910. Since my feet grew fast, I couldn't use them for very long. I didn't own another pair until I crossed the U.S. border in 1921. Someone bought me a secondhand pair there for twenty-five cents, but they were too big for me. When I put them on without socks and walked, my feet sweat and slipped. The noise they made when I crossed the border at Juárez made me think that someone was following me. When I recall this event, it now seems both curious and fitting to me that I write it down, so that you know where Don Francisco came from" (F. Pérez, 15).

My grandfather uses the word *descalzo* to capture not only his desperate circumstances when he crosses the border at El Paso but also the many sociocultural and class-bound transitions he was forced to make before and after he crossed the border.[21] The first was from membership in the "high" society of the Mexican rancher class to the status of a homeless orphan at the height of the revolution. The second took him from his life as a servant for a wealthy Mexican family in the city of Torreón to that of an impoverished, displaced immigrant laborer in a foreign country.

But, as the above passage suggests, for my grandfather *descalzo* also possesses a tragicomic and picaresque quality, for unlike most Mexican immigrant autobiographies, my grandfather shared with nineteenth-century Mexican American writers the distant, fond remembrance of an "upper-class" hacienda past. According to family history, Lira Pérez had by the late nineteenth century become a successful accountant, managing the affairs and finances of several local haciendas—livestock ranches owned by the landed elite of central Zacatecas. Though not a *hacendado* himself, by the turn of the century he had become closely associated with this privileged class. Orphanhood thus functions in my grandfather's account at two levels. At one level, it represents his abrupt separation from his father's secure world and, soon after, from the Mexican culture of his ancestors. The *descalzo* is, therefore, a prince in disguise. Though he had only a third-grade education, my grandfather sometimes set his "high" cultural status against the lower-class background of the farm laborers with whom he worked at Rancho Sespe. The community in turn acknowledged this background respectfully, electing him to several local public positions. At another level, "Memorias" is obviously an immigrant narrative as well, which charts the narrator's struggles as a destitute Mexican laborer in what he increasingly comes to view as a money-obsessed society overtly hostile to Mexicans. At this level, orphanhood signifies his cultural and socioeconomic estrangement as an exploited immigrant in the United States. He will thus always be a *descalzo*.

The contestatory Róbles narrative will expose certain sociohistorical deceptions in this notion of orphanhood as well as in the representation of Porfirian hacienda society in "Memorias." For the moment, though, let us consider the usefulness of Padilla's paradigm for understanding this figure, and "Memorias," in total. Padilla has established that early Mexican American autobiographies exhibit a "consciousness split by contending sociocultural regimes" (Padilla, 51). Much like W. E. B. Du Bois's concept of the "double self," this "double-consciousness" originates in that moment when the author's Mexican religiocultural identity comes under the dominating influence of an Anglo American sociocultural regime. For the nineteenth-century Mexicans living in what was once northern Mexico and is now the southwestern United States, this moment came with the 1848 U.S. military victory over Mexico and the annexation of its northern region. As my grandfather's memoir and other narratives of Mexican emigration show, an equally sharp cultural break has taken place among twentieth-century Mexican immigrants. Symbolized by the border crossing, this rupture results from both the forced emigration from the Mexican homeland and the inevitable accommodations that Mexican immigrants have to make in a country with fundamentally different sociocultural traditions.

All of the many studies examining Mexican immigration to the United States agree that a huge number of immigrants arrived during the twentieth century's first three decades. Mario Barrera, for example, cites an estimate that by 1928 more than one-tenth of Mexico's population had moved to the United States (Barrera, 68). More recently, David G. Gutiérrez writes that "[a]lthough immigration and demographic statistics for [the] era are notoriously inaccurate, most scholars concur that at least one million, and possibly as many as a million and a half Mexican immigrants entered the United States between 1890 and 1929" (D. Gutiérrez, 40). In accounting for this migration, Barrera notes that while the political upheavals created by the Mexican Revolution caused a great many to emigrate—particularly "those who happened to be on the losing side at a given moment"—economic and social factors were perhaps more significant, for "[a] large number of agricultural workers during this time were displaced from the land as the process of [Porfirian] modernization was ruthlessly pursued" (Barrera, 68). Furthermore, between 1875 and 1910, the Mexican population increased by approximately 50 percent. As Friedrich Katz explains, "[T]he number of laborers available to central Mexican haciendas greatly increased . . . as the massive expropriations . . . created a new landless proletariat, which the limited industry in most parts of central Mexico could not absorb" (Katz, 28, quoted in Barrera, 68).

In *My History, Not Yours,* Padilla examines the dramatic break in sociocultural self-consciousness portrayed in late-nineteenth- and early-twentieth-century Mexican American autobiographies—one typically represented in Mexican immigrant autobiographical narratives by the border crossing. Refusing to dismiss early autobiographical texts as ideologically self-deceiving, he views their nostalgic impulse as a complex rhetorical strategy with a hidden counter-discursive objective. As we shall see in my grandfather's narrative, though admittedly shot through with contradictions, this strategy sustains the Mexican American autobiographer's pre-U.S. (Mexican) cultural identity in the face of threats from Anglo American social institutions. Viewed in this light, my grandfather's efforts to link himself to Spanish colonial forebears invokes the powerful historical presence of his Mexican ancestors. Such a legacy grants my grandfather, and his Mexican American children, grandchildren, and great-grandchildren, an (ethnic) cultural memory in the face of "orphanhood" in Mexico and the United States.

Like the nineteenth-century Mexican Californian autobiographers who measure the past according to their "present" aggrieved socioeconomic and cultural condition, my grandfather foregrounds his struggles with poverty, displacement, and "slavelike" experiences as an immigrant farm worker. In an understated tone, he relates the brutal, inhuman work and his own felt status in the United States as a commodity, a deracinated and alienated figure apparently without hope or future. "Memorias" identifies three forces of rigid exclusion and severe abuse during the 1930s: the exploitation of Mexican agricultural laborers by American landowners, the suppression of Mexican efforts to organize a union, and the racial segregation that Mexican (American) farm workers were forced to endure.[22] Taken together, these forces constitute my grandfather's depression-era plight.

My grandfather's account of his participation in a 1936 labor strike in Placentia epitomizes this precarious status, as well as his efforts to lift himself and those around him above their desperate condition: "I joined a society of united Mexican workers and started to work on its behalf. We fought to defend the human, civic, and economic rights of Mexican agricultural workers. But we were a small group, perhaps forty in number, and none of us was educated nor had funds to sustain the organization. We asked ten cents in dues from each worker's paycheck. We eventually called a strike to try to improve our lives, but it was in vain. We lost after two months. Many of the strikers were thrown in jail and others were physically abused on the picket line. In one confrontation, the police used tear gas against us. In this struggle, [the ranchers] had no respect for women or children. Our only recourse was the Mexican Consulate in Los Angeles, but [the ranchers] later blocked our communication with this office" (F. Pérez, 33).

Gilbert G. González devotes a chapter to the broader strike of which my grandfather's group was a part in his study of Mexican citrus worker villages in Orange County, calling it the "largest . . . ever to affect the [citrus] industry" and "one of the most violently suppressed in California's intense labor-capital relations of the 1930s" (G. González, 135). González's detailed description throws added light on my grandfather's sociocultural status as an immigrant farm worker. The strike by nearly three thousand citrus pickers was more than a workers' revolt against employers:

> The organization of work and society dictated that the employees and their communities as well should take up the workers' cause. Union locals originated from within the community's culture and organization so that many of the union leaders were prominent patriotic committee members as well. . . . The strike, like the cultural life of the village, was a community affair thereby accentuating existing sharp social divisions and submerged hostilities separating the villagers from the dominant community. The grim social reality in the citrus belt—the tragic poverty of life in the villages, and moreover, the political dominion over the villagers—appeared in bold relief. Inevitably, the strike assumed ethnic, economic, and cultural dimensions. Class warfare and ethnic rivalry shattered the industrial peace that had long rested on the myth of contented Mexican labor. (135)

Lisbeth Haas also provides an account of this 1936 strike in her history of the Southern California communities of San Juan Capistrano and Santa Ana. Haas's reconstruction of the violent response by ranchers and police echoes my grandfather's description. As she explains, "Attacks on the barrio . . . [reflected] the way in which race politics fortified coercive labor structures. Vigilantes attacked participants in the nightly strike meetings in each barrio, sometimes using tear gas. On July 7 during a meeting of 115 Mexican men, women, and children in Placentia, 'one hundred ranchers drove up . . . each . . . armed with a new axe handle'" (Haas, 208). My grandfather's oral story of his narrow escape from armed attackers who broke up a union meeting in Placentia—which, when I first heard it, appeared to have been filtered through, and distorted by, decades of cultural remembrance—in fact mirrors the following description in Haas's book: "On the single evening of July 10, vigilantes smashed the windows of a meeting place in Anaheim while the meeting was in progress, disrupted a large meeting in La Habra, and broke up a smaller one in Placentia, where they hurled twenty tear gas bombs into the room and wielded clubs against those who ran out. Barrio residents said they could not sleep because the tear gas filled their homes. The sheriff had already issued a 'shoot to kill' order against the strikers, thus implicitly giving license to vigilante activity" (208).

My grandfather's activism reflects the widespread labor unrest among California's farm workers during the 1930s. During that time a series of strikes and labor-related protests by Mexican and Mexican American laborers ravaged the state's agriculture industry (D. Gutiérrez, 106); "well over 160 major strikes occurred between 1933 and 1937 alone" (101). As Rodolfo Acuña affirms, "Given the industrialization of agriculture, the exploitation of Mexican labor, and the abuses of the contract labor system, conflict would have occurred without the depression; the events of 1929 merely intensified the struggle" (Acuña, 209). My grandfather's account, as told to me in part in an interview, endorses the view that Mexican and Mexican American labor strife during this period "often took the form of organized race conflict" (D. Gutiérrez, 100).

Recriminations followed in the wake of the 1936 strike. As Gilbert G. González explains, "Many radicals or suspected radicals were denied jobs even years later" (G. González, 158). My grandfather and other farm workers were among those blacklisted because of their participation in the strike.[23] Forced to move, my grandfather took his family to Ventura County, fifty-five miles away, where he was soon hired to pick grapefruit, for twenty-eight cents an hour, at Rancho Sespe, outside the town of Fillmore. (He contacted Gregorio Róbles, his brother-in-law, who, along with other Róbles family members, had made his way to Fillmore several years earlier.) My grandfather recalled that the foreman at Rancho Sespe asked him where he had lived most recently. When he said Orange County, the foreman asked if he was a striker. My grandfather, of course, said no: "If I had said yes, they wouldn't have given me work . . . and at that time I had four children to support and feed, all of school age with the exception of the youngest, who was three" (F. Pérez, 42). My grandfather evokes the Mexican farm workers' defiance toward the growers by citing a remark that he overheard at Rancho Sespe: "In the dining hall of the workers' camp at Rancho Sespe, I heard a [Mexican] 'bracero,' a plebeian, make the following comment while he ate: 'One must eat the gringo's food, but should throw the plate in his face.' I leave this statement to your critical judgment. In difficult times, all things are acceptable" (48).

During the 1960s, when the United Farm Workers union began organizing workers at Rancho Sespe, my grandfather voiced support but refused to join the union. Not only had his earlier experience made him cautious but in 1941 he had narrowly managed to keep his job and (company) home during another strike and subsequent mass firing of farm workers, this time at Rancho Sespe. In that strike, according to my father and grandfather, at least 80 percent of the Mexican and Mexican American families in the village were left homeless; the landowners removed their possessions and left them on the side of the highway half a mile away. My father, Tony, who was eleven at the time, recalled seeing these displaced families, with children who were his friends, waiting with their possessions on the road as it rained. The strike occurred throughout Ventura County, and eventually more than six thousand workers and their families were evicted from company housing (Menchaca, 87).

Martha Menchaca describes this 1941 event in her study of Mexican Americans in Santa Paula, a town situated five miles from Rancho Sespe. As she explains, "[T]he coalition of [Ventura County agricultural] unions . . . crippled the county's lemon industry because the walkout prevented the harvesting, packing, and distribution of all citrus. In essence, there was a complete work stoppage because the harvesters, packers, and canners were all on strike" (Menchaca, 84). The growers carried out their threat to evict the strikers, "a devastating experience for the workers especially since many of them had resided on the ranches for two or three generations" (87). As my father recalled, although some of the strikers eventually made their way back to Sespe, the mass eviction transformed the small Mexican Village at Rancho Sespe—particularly with the hiring of many migrants from Oklahoma to replace the Mexican strikers.

A second encounter just after my grandfather's arrival in Sespe in 1936 underscored for him that, although the location had changed, his social position as a Mexican farm worker remained the same: "After we settled into our little house in the workers' camp at Rancho Sespe—the last great hacienda in Califonia—I met an American rancher and foreman whose property bordered the camp. He introduced himself, then said to me, 'I hope that your family, especially your children, respect my property and don't trespass beyond that wire fence.' He added these humiliating words: 'Any individual who doesn't own a piece of land, or at least, a home in which to live, is not worthy of being a citizen of any country.' We were thus eating the bitter bread of the exiled" (F. Pérez, 35).

For my grandfather, these two exchanges with American landowners captured something crucial about his life. "Why was man born?" he asked. "To struggle, just as birds were born to fly." To remain steadfast in the face of unjust suffering formed a defining trait of Francisco's life as a young farm worker during the 1930s. His description of himself at twenty-seven as "ambitious, genial, self-confident, humorous, and above all, hardworking" makes it clear that my grandfather felt more than up to that struggle (F. Pérez, 34). Reflecting on the arc of his life, he similarly concludes that the stories he tells are "a part of a past that is filled with memories and not a few sufferings, but today I am proud for having surmounted them. . . . I was a child in Mexico, then a youth in the United States, a man, a mature man, and now I am an old man. . . . I am so old I already have one foot in the 'other world.' And what more than this is the inheritance of mankind? Today I am content that the maker of the infinite universe has granted me and my family the divine grace of living for so many years" (46).

And yet, as Esther Pérez Doran, Francisco's daughter and eldest child, and my aunt, wrote in a 1965 college essay entitled "A Story of Death in Mexican American Culture," life in Sespe Village continually tested the Pérez family's strength and spirit. According to Esther, the village community lived under a "feudal system" completely dominated by the landowner, Keith Spalding. Esther juxtaposes this North American *hacendado* and, first, her own family's tenuous status and meager living conditions in the farm worker camp, then her father's brutal work as a laborer:

> Once a month the lord and master, the owner of Rancho Sespe, would make his rounds on horseback and look down at his "peasants." An "edict" would first go out to the village stating when Mr. Spalding would arrive so that we could prepare by watering our beautiful yards and by putting on our best Sunday clothes. But I made it a point never to appear to show any interest in this event, in this wealthy man who was the

giver of all things in Sespe. I already knew better; I had seen my father, black with dust and soaked with perspiration, come home from picking lemons and oranges after a hot day. For this backbreaking work he was paid the great sum of a couple of dollars a day and allowed to rent a three room house without heat, without indoor water, and without indoor plumbing (the homes were very cold and damp; in fact, I am still trying to get warm after all those cold years). My mother worked in the ranch's packing house at Sespe, where the pay was worse; later, my brothers also worked picking fruit. At Sespe, the Mexican community had a life without any hope for the future. I hated the people who were responsible for this, who made my father and mother work so hard for a crust of bread and a dried tortilla. But my father showed that while a man's body may be economically bound, his spirit is not; although he had only a third grade education, he read avidly and passed this habit along to his children.[24]

González's description of housing in the Mexican Village at Rancho Sespe mirrors my Aunt Esther's account: "Photographs appearing in the *California Citrograph* indicate that the 'Mexican Village,' in comparison to 'white' housing, was vastly inferior, reflecting a rough and undesirable location and at best the housing resembled rural shacktowns. The rooms of even those houses built for single Anglo-Americans were larger than the rooms of family housing for Mexicans. For example, the eight-by-thirteen-foot rooms for a single man were larger than the ten-by-ten-foot house furnished for a Mexican family . . . and more than one-quarter the size of a family house provided by the [nearby] Limoniera Ranch, which measured eighteen by twenty-two feet" (G. González, 41).

The racialized space of Rancho Sespe embraced other local social institutions as well. For the white community of Fillmore, education translated into opportunity and hope. For Mexican Americans from the "village," however, a high school education did little to change one's status and circumstances. Aunt Esther relates in her essay her own efforts, after finishing high school, to obtain employment at Rancho Sespe's payroll office:

> I had gotten straight A's as a student, which helped me realize my dream of going to nursing school. In high school I had also taken courses in typing, bookkeeping, and shorthand. I did very well in these classes, and my bookkeeping teacher recommended me to work in Rancho Sespe's payroll office. I interviewed and was not accepted. Later, I learned that a white girl who had not finished high school was given the job. My family

was very upset by this rejection. . . . Several years later, I was visiting my family in Sespe after graduating from nursing school. The same man who had refused me the job came by to see my father. He saw me carrying my new uniforms. He was surprised, and congratulated me on graduating. He remarked, "Now you can take care of me when I get sick." Although I said it to myself, my response was, "You can drop dead!"

My grandfather's idealization of a mythic Mexican homeland founded on the imagined pastoral landscape of rural Zacatecas must be understood in relation to Esther's descriptions, the ranchers' comments mentioned earlier, and the varying historical accounts of his community's struggles. His imaginative return to the Mexican pastoral landscape of his *abuelos* and his ancestor's hacienda society not only represents a spiritual solidarity with the immigrant and farm worker communities sharing his origins but also stands as a defense against the perpetual "threat of social erasure" by colonizing U.S. sociocultural and economic institutions (Padilla, 6). This nostalgic recuperation reaffirms a cultural and genealogical presence in the face of my grandfather's forced separation from that world as a child and his continued separation from both Mexican and American society as an adult. It thus forms the foundation of his, and his children's, Mexican (American) subjectivity within the racially hostile spaces described above.

Just as his orphanhood may be read as a figuration for the cultural fragmentation of Mexican immigrants and farm workers in the United States, the reconstituted topography of rural Zacatecas stands as the originary epistemological ground of his cultural subjectivity. Situated "exactly in the center of the Mexican Republic" (F. Pérez, 2), the Zacatecas region where he was born is for my grandfather the geographic and cultural "heartland" of the nation. As descendants of its Spanish settlers, he and his father are thus "native sons" of a region that, according to popular sentiment in Mexico, embodies the Mexican national character. When recalling his visit to the city of Zacatecas shortly after his family was forced to leave Jerez in early 1914, my grandfather asks the reader's patience as he not only "describes the topography of that great capital" but also strategically conflates this topography with Mexico's Spanish colonial history. "The city was founded in 1600 after the Spaniards discovered silver there," he explains. "It is situated in a small valley surrounded by mountains. The most prominent is the Bufa mountain, which contains the richest silver mine ever discovered on the American continent" (5).

What my grandfather cannot acknowledge in his remembrance

is the actual status of these great mines—symbolized by the Bufa mountain in the center of the city of Zacatecas—at the end of the Porfirian era. In their study of economic dependency, Fernando Henrique Cardoso and Enzo Faletto explain that the Mexican mining industry exemplified late-nineteenth-century underdevelopment throughout Latin America. While observing that during the thirty-five-year Díaz reign, "Mexico recovered much of its economic dynamism thanks chiefly to renewed exploitation of its silver wealth," Cardoso and Faletto also note that by 1914, when my grandfather saw the Bufa for the first time, three-quarters of Mexico's mines "belonged to foreigners" (Cardoso and Faletto, 105). My grandfather's mythic, pastoral, and communal vision of Zacatecas shows no sign of the enormous concentration of property in the hands of politicians, foreign speculators, and surveying companies, which Cardoso and Faletto find characteristic of the time (106).[25] Nor does the deeply conflicted nature of the earlier colonial (hacienda) period, as I have discussed in chapter 1, find a place in my grandfather's account.

For my grandfather, his Spanish ancestors, the Mexican "heartland," and the outlying landscape of his mining and hacienda society together establish a heroic, legendary, and prosperous Mexican past, rather than a photograph of disjuncture and exploitation. Other references to pre-revolutionary Jerez add to his portrait of a land populated by descendants of Spanish founders. Especially powerful are his memories of his father, the principal inhabitant of that "colonial" and late-nineteenth-century world. Since my grandfather left the hacienda community at age six, stopped regularly attending school at seven, and became orphaned at eleven, his memories of the pre-revolutionary period probably derived from stories he heard as a child from his father. My interviews with my grandfather and the text of "Memorias" suggest that his knowledge of early Mexican history came primarily, though not exclusively, from the same source. Not surprisingly, then, his memories of his father are inseparable in the text from his romantic representation of the outlying hacienda landscape of Jerez—a town situated forty miles from the capital.

Nor did his father simply embody familial origins; in fact, as Pérez patriarch his overshadowing presence participates in that genealogical and sociocultural rootedness in Mexico that my grandfather traces back to its Mexican (Spanish) colonial "founders." Though my grandfather enjoyed reading fiction, I do not think he had ever read Juan Rulfo or other modern Latin American novelists. And though detective fiction as well as science fiction delighted him, he did not seem fond of sweeping historical narrative (he once told me that Don Quixote had not impressed him because he considered it "fantasy"). Nevertheless, in "Memorias" my grandfather often describes hacienda society in a manner reminiscent of Rulfo's mythic rendering. At the opening of Rulfo's novel *Pedro Páramo*, for example, when asked which lands near a central Mexican rural town belong to a local *hacendado*, a peasant answers with a series of admonitory questions: "See that mountain, the one that looks like a pig's bladder? Good, now look over there. See the ridge of that mountain? Now look over here. See that mountain way off there? Well, all that's the Media Luna, everything you see. And it all belongs to Pedro Páramo" (Rulfo, 4). The mountain described is Cerro de la Bufa itself, which is situated near Rulfo's native community in the bordering state of Jalisco. In much the same way as Rulfo's novel, my grandfather notes in "Memorias" that in "colonial" times "people of property didn't measure their property in hectares, parcels, or plots, but rather by how far their vision reached; once these men began to dedicate themselves to the raising of sheep and other livestock, within the course of years, they counted herds in the thousands, if not millions" (F. Pérez, 2). Here, and in many other places as well, my grandfather grants a larger-than-life quality to that Mexican colonial history refracted by Rulfo. And yet, both of these renderings of the founding Zacatecan haciendas find support in historical accounts. Enrique Semo cites a report written in 1579 by the *alcalde* (mayor) of Zacatecas, Hernando Vargas, which states that in the Valley of Aguascalientes, the granary of the Zacatecan mining industry, "more than 100,000 cows and 200,000 sheep and 10,000 mares grazed between the town of San Juan [del Río] and Querétaro, which are seven leagues apart" (Semo, 73). In keeping with this portrait of a bountiful hacienda landscape, San Juan de las Calabasas, the hacienda where my grandfather spent much of his childhood, is his "beloved native village," a place where "everything was the color of roses and all of the food was sweet" (F. Pérez, 14). The cultural landscape of central Mexico stands in sharp contrast to my grandfather's later cultural uprootedness, permanent forced exile, and "slavelike" experience as a farm laborer. Hacienda life in Jerez was a carefree "vacation" or "adventure," the rural landscape symbolizing the innocence and freedom of childhood.

And in the center of this pastoral landscape stand the boy and his father, whose close relationship, rooted irrevocably in the nineteenth-century hacienda social space, is conveyed through brief and poignant remembrances of childhood. Early in "Memorias" my grandfather shares this recollection: "[I remember] asking my father, when I was four or five, the following question: 'Tell me how many tortillas I have eaten in my entire life.' My father answered, 'I'd say about a hundred.' Wouldn't you agree that such childish questions, though silly, are at the same time philosophical?" (F. Pérez, 5).

In this way, the hacienda landscape contains within it not only communitarian rootedness but also familial intimacy between father and son. Of course, other relatives inhabit this world as well, providing background on the maternal side of my grandfather's family and complementing the emphasis in "Memorias" on patriarchal lineage. Francisco's maternal grandparents, ghostly presences in the narrative, lived in a hacienda village near Jerez and took care of him while his father worked. By providing the names and titles of these *abuelos*—Don Ambrosio Róbles (who in fact was his grandfather Don José Róbles's nephew) and Doña Hipólita Macías Róbles (his grandmother)—my grandfather reasserts cultural continuity and familial pride in the face of their total erasure from the historical ledger of the United States. He insists on carrying such a title forward himself, often referring to himself in "Memorias" as "Don" Francisco, the name his father always affectionately used and thus a constant reminder of his father's love and perhaps even of Francisco's hacienda ancestors.

As for his own mother, Juliana (daughter of Don José Róbles and Doña Hipólita), my grandfather says that he does not remember her at all. She died in 1913, soon after giving birth to her third child; thus the only "mother" my grandfather knew was Doña Hipólita. (In the following section I address the central roles Juliana and her older sister Dominga play in "Memorias.") As if to claim for his mother and her parents the same noble ancestry he posited for his father's ancestors, my grandfather asserts that Doña Hipólita and the Róbleses "were from a proud family with deep roots in Zacatecas, and though I never knew my mother, I use her family name as a part of my own" (F. Pérez, 30). As my Aunt Esther told me in a telephone call, my grandfather did, in fact, always sign his name as "Francisco Róbles Pérez." In the same conversation, Esther also told me that, although my grandfather only briefly mentions his Róbles forebears in "Memorias," she believes he was as proud of his Róbles ancestors as of the Pérez line. Nonetheless, the emphasis throughout the early part of "Memorias," the only section in which my grandfather delineates his family's origins, is on the nobility of the Pérez ancestors. As might be expected, my grandfather's remembrances of the Róbles grandparents—conveyed in "Memorias" as well as in conversations with me and with Esther—are completely removed from the Róbles-Pérez clash apparently initiated by Lira Pérez and rekindled in 1992 by Berta Róbles.

Mexican customs, traditions, and events such as weddings and funerals are also set within the hacienda's retrospective space. Like the landscape itself, these practices affirm as well the communitarian and familial qualities of my grandfather's Mexican world. Hacienda weddings, for instance, were "grand events" in which "all families and friends in the community cooperated." The food preparations were highly communal. Some families "would prepare a cow for the celebration's meal, others two lambs, three pigs, and a few goats—this, of course, doesn't include the dozens of chickens. As for tortillas, no fewer than ten women were grinding corn and making tortillas before and during the celebration. Not only family members came, but the whole community, without any need for invitations. A second party took place the day after, a *tornaboda,* with music and more music and dancing" (F. Pérez, 28).

This communal vision of Mexican hacienda society is closely linked to that self-contradictory "rupture" of crossing the U.S.-Mexican border. In a telling passage about listening to a record by his favorite opera singer, Mario Lanza, my grandfather reflects further on his ancestral Mexican hacienda community and its Spanish colonial past: "I feel content in my journey through this life that I did something for my family and that I continue being the trunk of the future family tree, [following] those Spanish pioneers who one day gave us a language and a religion—even though, as Bernal Díaz del Castillo said [in his account of the Spanish conquest of Mexico], they came with the cross and the sword" (F. Pérez, 37).

Although the last line acknowledges a buried Mexican (Spanish) colonial mythos, which the Róbles counter-narrative will foreground and interrogate, "Memorias" elsewhere elides pre-revolutionary social conflict. Dwelling on the work's projection of an almost Edenic past, however, is rather useless. It is more instructive to view "Memorias" within the context of my grandfather's life as an uprooted Mexican who, even after seventy years in the "belly of the monster" (to use José Martí's description of life as a Hispanic in the United States), still views himself and his U.S.-born descendants as displaced migrants and orphans alienated from their Mexican culture and history. Recording his Mexican (Spanish) colonial heritage is his way of bequeathing to his immediate family and Chicano and Chicana descendants a connection to an ennobling past.

Not simply aristocratic pretense or genealogical self-invention, then, my grandfather's nostalgic restoration of a mythic Spanish colonial world is a socially empowering reassertion of cultural continuity and pride, in the face of deeply felt cultural displacement and fragmentation. "With my hand on my chest, Don Francisco is writing this history," he announces early in the narrative, "the *descalzo* who one day crossed the Río Grande somewhere near El Paso with his rags on his head—and I am not at all ashamed to say this, because it is the truth" (F. Pérez, 3). Rejecting the stigma that U.S. cultural and economic formations seek to force upon his Mexican American descendants and community, he implicitly urges his Mexican American readers to follow him in shedding their internalized "American" habits. More important, by juxtaposing his status as an orphaned *descalzo* with his action as Don Francisco, writing the "history" of the family, my grandfather suggests that his "nostalgic" narrative be read in the light of his later experiences in the United States.

While specific memories of his father are interwoven throughout my grandfather's description of hacienda society, other passages place his father within the more mundane world of day-to-day affairs. Though described throughout the narrative as a businessman who worked most of his life as an accountant for *hacendados*, Lira Pérez in fact operated several other businesses after his departure from Jerez. At one point he bought and sold animal bones, a product he acquired from the livestock haciendas of central Mexico. (Wool, hides, tallow, horsehair, and bones—along with meat—were standard products of livestock haciendas.) My grandfather remembered accompanying his father to examine train cars filled with bones, which his father was selling or purchasing. After leaving Jerez, for a time Lira Pérez also owned a butcher shop.

As "the only trained business administrator in that region," before his displacement from Jerez, Lira Pérez had apparently prospered in the hacienda economy: "He was educated at the university in the state capital in business administration, [and] since he was fifty-two-years old when I was born, I imagine that he must have already practiced his profession for more than thirty years by then" (F. Pérez, 6). Following this chronology, Lira Pérez would therefore have begun his career in 1878, two years after the political takeover by Díaz, the dictator whose name is synonymous with the period of the modern hacienda and with the widespread injustices and repressions this hacienda economy brought about. Although Díaz met opposition throughout the 1880s in Zacatecas, "[t]he consolidation of the Porfirista regime, which was initiated with the assassination [in 1886] of the last dissident [Gen. Trinidad García de la Cadena] . . . culminated [in the state] in 1888, when Jesús Aréchiga became governor" (J. Flores Olague et al., 139). As reviewed in chapter 1, Díaz's thirty-five-year reign has generated a substantial body of scholarship. He has been credited with "industrializing" the hacienda system and thus bringing modern capitalism to a predominantly rural society. In his analysis of early-twentieth-century Mexican immigration to the United States, Acuña explains that Díaz's policies "encouraged the industrialization of agriculture, mining, and transportation, which led to the uprooting of the Mexican peasants, many of whom moved northward" (Acuña, 147). Modernization under Díaz, in short, led to the demise of the communal village and commercialization of the hacienda. And yet, as Cardoso and Faletto point out, for Díaz "the old hacienda system remained the most effective means of keeping the peasants submissive," and therefore he "needed its support" (Cardoso and Faletto, 107). Lira Pérez's career spanned the Díaz period of hacienda dominance from 1880 to 1911.[26] Or as my grandfather proudly announces, in his father's youth "the great haciendas and latifundios [large landed estates] began to be formed . . . and that was exactly where my father first began to practice his profession" (F. Pérez, 11).[27]

The single extant photograph of Lira Pérez was probably taken in September 1912, during Independence Day celebrations in Jerez. He was fifty-six, a tall, well-dressed, gaunt man who stands in front of a group of townsfolk surrounding him and another man. While the aged *campesino* at the extreme left, and most of the others in the photograph, wear *sombreros* made of straw, my great-grandfather's *sombrero* appears to be made of felt and displays embroidery on its brim. He stands in front of what appears to be a patriotic parade, grasping the reins of a wagon drawn by three white horses and decorated with Mexican banners and flags. Perhaps reflecting his position as a hacienda manager, Lira Pérez stands to the right of the man in the center of the photograph, who, I remember being told, was the son or relative (or perhaps another foreman) of Don Jacinto Carlos, a *hacendado* who employed Lira Pérez. (Don Jacinto Carlos, I also remember being told, was captured and executed by the revolutionaries.) The lower-class folk in the audience behind these two men seem to squeeze into the photograph's frame. At the extreme right of the picture, next to Lira Pérez, stand his two young sons. My grandfather Francisco, at age four or five and dressed in the white clothes of Mexican *campesinos*, holds his hand before his face. Marcos, his older half-brother, stares like his father directly into the camera.

I have often imagined how this photograph survived the events of the ten years that followed—not only the chaos of the revolution itself but also the family's forced departure from Jerez in early 1914, their journey during the civil war, Lira Pérez's death in 1919, and Francisco's subsequent orphanhood and emigration. It is unlikely my grandfather carried the photograph with him when he

Juan Lira Pérez (standing at right in dark sombrero) with two of his sons, Marcos and Francisco (far right), in Jerez on Independence Day, September 1912.

emigrated in 1921. My Aunt Esther believes my grandmother Concepción's mother, Angelita Herrera, transported it to Placentia when she emigrated with her sons in 1920. Esther's theory about the photograph's origins, however, serves to illustrate the random nature of any effort to trace one's family history to the Mexican Revolution and earlier—or, for that matter, of any historical or literary recovery project in any era or setting. My grandfather, it turns out, never acquired the photograph of his father; in fact, he had nothing to do with the Herreras' decision to transport it to the United States. Lira Pérez married his fourth wife, María Herrera, in 1912 or 1913. She was the elder sister of Francisco's future wife, Concepción. Had Lira Pérez lived to see Francisco marry, he would have discovered that he and his son were also in-laws (see family trees). Esther believes that María sent the photograph of her husband to her mother, Angelita, not long after her marriage. When my grandfather, two years after his father's 1919 death, immigrated to the United States with several of the Herrera sons, the photograph was probably already in Angelita's possession at her home in Placentia, where my grandfather probably saw it for the first time. When Angelita died in 1935, my grandmother Concepción acquired the family photo album where the photograph was kept. I remember being fascinated as a child by this, and other, images of the Mexican past collected in this album.

By writing his memoirs my grandfather tried to grant "textual permanence" to his father's life and his own (Padilla, 4), thus bequeathing to his Mexican American descendants the foundational narrative of their familial and cultural origins. At another level, though, he struggled with the need to resist those sociocultural and economic forces that defined his aggrieved status as a Mexican immigrant laborer in the United States. Though often eliding the social conflicts of the early Mexican/Spanish past, "Memorias" therefore participates, however mediated by a language of nostalgic reflection, in that critical discourse that Ramón Saldívar has identified in modern Chicano/a narratives. Notwithstanding its suppressions, if judged first as an immigrant narrative, my grandfather's autobiography joins with other life-writings, such as Ernesto Galarza's *Barrio Boy*, to explore what Saldívar terms the "imaginary ways in which historical men and women live out their lives in a class society, and how the values, concepts, and ideas purveyed by the mainstream, American culture that tie them to their social functions seek to prevent them from a true knowledge of society as a whole" (R. Saldívar, *Chicano Narrative*, 6). But another layer of the palimpsest of history in "Memorias" remains to be peeled back. As the Róbles family narrative will reveal, my grandfather's representation of Mexican hacienda society both records and obscures its underlying socioeconomic and cultural formations.

CHAVELA'S FUNERAL

An incident that caused an unexpected shift in my perspective as I was recuperating and interpreting "Memorias" offers a cautionary reminder of what critics of autobiographical narrative have termed the "impulse to self-invention" (Couser, 19).[28] Certainly, what happened at a relative's funeral underscores Padilla's emphasis on the "centrality of thick socio-historicized readings of formative Mexican American (autobiographical) narratives and the historical particularities of their production" (Padilla, xi). One could even see this event as an example of what Padilla calls "discontinuity" in the discursive genealogy of Chicano/a literary traditions (7). More important, though, the funeral encounter I will now discuss strongly suggests that readings—including Padilla's—of early Mexican American autobiographies must be self-critically aware of their own omissions and suppressions. As the Róbles family helped to reveal, my grandfather's nostalgic desire worked to conceal social contradictions buried deep in his father's hacienda past. To ensure that such powerful shaping forces do not remain unexamined, scholars who recover and interpret autobiographical narratives by individuals whose "voices have not merely been forgotten . . . but suppressed" (xi) must be constantly aware of the issue of fictionality in these texts and must also delve critically into representations of early Mexican history. The nostalgic impulse in Mexican American autobiographies is certainly the product of sociocultural rupture and fragmentation, but as Padilla himself suggests, this impulse constructs a "master" narrative that works to suppress or exclude much of what does not conform to the author's projection of the past. Nor does recognizing and retrieving such textual sublimations undermine the obvious need to restore the integrity of these early autobiographers' lives. In fact, this restoration can be enhanced by foregrounding those submerged relations so often inherent in the social manifestations of these lives.

At a time when I was beginning to transcribe my grandfather's manuscript, a strange occurrence at a cemetery revealed more about my grandfather's relation to his past and his sense of self-identity than I had to that point been prepared to grasp. When Aunt Chavela was laid to rest in July 1992, the myth of my grandfather's father was figuratively exhumed. The funeral was held in Santa Paula, a rural community north of Los Angeles and five miles from Rancho Sespe. Descendants of both sides of my grandfather's family, the Pérezes and Róbleses, were present. At the small cemetery a priest read a prayer over Chavela's grave, and my parents and I passed by her casket. We greeted members of both sides of my grandfather's family. My father stopped to speak with Nicolás "Nico" Róbles, always a mysterious figure in my family. Though he too was raised in Rancho Sespe and attended Pérez family events, his relation to the Pérezes had never been entirely clear to me. Some of the other Róbleses in attendance, my father later admitted, he had not seen in twenty years. A younger couple, Berta and José Róbles, introduced themselves as my father's cousins, though my father had never met them before.

When I returned a few minutes later, I was startled to find myself in the midst of an argument, one made all the more improbable by the locale. My parents later told me that, after introducing herself, Berta launched into a tirade against the Pérezes and particularly against the family patriarch Juan Lira Pérez. That my father and his siblings, all American-born, neither knew their grandfather nor, with the exception of Aunt Esther, took any interest in their dead ancestors, made this confrontation all the more baffling. Hearing the commotion, others gathered nearby, watching in astonishment and dread: here was a person without shame or self-respect, their countenances seemed to say. Face-to-face with my father, Berta attacked the character of the Pérez patriarch and, by association, that of his four succeeding generations. The spitefulness of Berta's colloquial Spanish cannot be captured in a literal translation. In effect, she called our long-deceased patriarch a philandering criminal who in Zacatecas had left a trail of hate and misery in his wake. This scandalous legacy, she claimed, was Lira Pérez's answer to what had once been a trusting friendship between the two families, one that, as I would learn, went back to the nineteenth century. Concluding with a string of curses, she informed her stunned audience that the Pérez family's grandfather had raped Dominga Róbles, his wife's older sister, who for a short period in 1912 had come to live with the couple while my great-grandmother Juliana was recovering from childbirth. Her accusations left us speechless. Later, I discovered that the product of that alleged crime, Paulo Róbles Pérez—half-brother and cousin to my grandfather—was adopted and reared by Dominga's brother, José.

My grandfather, whose heartfelt memory of his father had created Lira Pérez's ancestral presence in my family but whose stories make only passing reference to the Róbles complaint, had apparently been wary of just such a clash. Immediately after the cemetery service, he quietly left without speaking to any of the Róbleses. Though not likely to take insults without responding in kind, in deference to Chavela and others in attendance my father listened to Berta's grievance without answering. But like many others, he was dumbfounded by the curious spectacle, which, as I later learned, centered on events that occurred in the 1912–13 period in Jerez.

The forty-five-year-old woman before us was José Róbles's daughter—but she was also a Róbles by *marriage*, having wed Paulo's son José Pérez (her second cousin).[29] Eighty-plus years after Lira Pérez's alleged transgression, on the occasion of a gathering of the two family branches, she now sought retribution. According to the Róbles account, as divulged by Berta and later supported by some of the other Róbles relatives, the Róbles family believed that the illegitimate Paulo would be legally recognized by his father. But the boy was spurned, and he and his mother were barred from claiming any inheritance upon Lira Pérez's death.[30] Growing up in the family of his mother, the child suffered the stigma of a confused identity as the bastard child of a man detested by those who reared the boy. My grandfather never acknowledged the kinship. As if keenly aware of the Róbles family's "dispossession," in "Memorias" my grandfather proclaims his privileged status as "primogenitor," the legitimate firstborn son with inheritance rights to his father's property in Jerez (F. Pérez, 2). (In fact, Lira Pérez had two sons before Francisco, Casimiro and Marcos, my grandfather's half-brothers, whom Lira Pérez also included in his will.[31]) My grandfather had even gone to a funeral in Santa Paula, California (where many Róbleses settled), that his half-brother Paulo also attended, but as one of my aunts later recalled, when asked to meet the elderly gentleman, my grandfather answered, "I don't have any brother."

The figure of Don Juan Lira Pérez, embodying an honorable historical and cultural patrimony in my own family's tales, served quite a different function in the Róbles family narrative. The legend of the alleged rape and the father's repudiation of his child, passed down through several generations and carried to the United States when the Róbleses also emigrated, became, in at least one family branch, a central trope in the mythos of the Róbleses' historical origins. To this day, in this family narrative Lira Pérez signifies not honorable origins and ancestry, but rather those intangible sociohistorical and cultural currents, bound to the semifeudal hacienda landscape, that contributed to the Róbles family's status in Mexico and later exodus to the United States.

Leaving us to gather ourselves, Berta and her husband then departed, but the story was not yet finished. Nico, another Róbles "cousin" and my grandfather's godson, who in the fifty years that he had lived and worked alongside the Pérez family to my knowledge had never spoken a word to any of us about our founding patriarch, then pulled my father aside. As if dispelling any misplaced belief that Berta's remarks might simply be the unfounded "hysterics" of an angry *mujer*, he calmly told my father that the Róbles family had shown great self-restraint in dealing with the matter of the "rape" at that time. Though more discreet than Berta, Nico's final message was all the more startling for its brevity. Underscoring the historical injustice that Lira Pérez had, for some of the Róbleses, clearly come to personify, he said, "Your grandfather did something awful . . . y lo hubieran podido matar . . . they [the Róbleses] could have killed him for what he did . . . they could have killed your grandfather for what he did to that girl"—words all the more chilling because Lira Pérez was also Nico's grandfather (see family trees).

Before I propose an answer to the questions that arose from this incident, I should first briefly reconstruct those events occurring between 1912 and 1914 that my grandfather and Berta have so differently described. I begin with the obvious: that at least one branch of the Róbles family has remained aggrieved now for almost a century, as a result of events involving my grandfather's father two years prior to his departure from the town of his birth. In a manner different from my grandfather's usual nostalgic bent, his account of this time in "Memorias" stresses Lira Pérez's precarious political position. Though the local sociopolitical circumstances of the forced flight are not intimated, my grandfather indicates that as an associate of the hacienda elite his father was viewed as an enemy of the insurgents and that he left his ancestral home because soldiers were planning to execute him. (As I will explain in the next section, Lira Pérez paid protection money to the insurrectionists for a time, but in early 1914, perhaps a few months before the Battle of Torreón on April 2 , his agreement with the rebels was broken.)

The legend of his 1914 flight, which had fascinated and disturbed me as a child, as well as the reasons for the exodus, I can now see are plainly inscribed in the margins of my grandfather's memoirs. My earlier desire to reconstruct an acceptable version of my family's past had led me to dismiss these passages as youthful "adventures," largely extraneous to my grandfather's narrative of origins. In his account of events in early 1914, my grandfather describes how his father hid in a well for three days without food while the soldiers searching for him sacked and burned his property at San Juan de las Calabasas. Several of Lira Pérez's employers—including Don Jacinto Carlos, whose son or employee may be the other man in the 1912 photograph—had been executed by the insurrectionists. The haciendas where his father had been employed for more than three decades were raided. Stories by members of my grandmother's family, the Herreras—who lived on the nearby Tesorero and Víboras haciendas—recount battles between federal troops and rebel soldiers on the hacienda grounds. Salvador Herrera—my grandmother Concepción's eldest brother and a man who lived to be ninety-seven—described these engagements in a tape-recorded interview with Aunt Esther. He recalled soldiers from opposing sides screaming epithets at each other in the midst of a battle at Tesorero. His wife, Jesusita, remembered one battle that occurred in and around the hacienda chapel. My father told me that Jesusita had once told him a bullet shot during a local battle landed between her feet as she was cooking one day in her kitchen. (Salvador and Concepción's sister, María, as previously noted, became Lira Pérez's fourth wife and bore a child by him in 1912. Though Concepción was six years older than her husband Francisco, and therefore likely to be more familiar with her brother-in-law Lira Pérez's life in Jerez, my grandmother rarely mentioned his name. When I asked her for information about him during an interview, she said she knew nothing.)

Before escaping from the town, my great-grandfather, according to the narrative written by his son, only narrowly evaded his pursuers. When the fallen patriarch emerged from his last hiding place, he escaped with his six-year-old son under the cover of night. What now strikes me in this section of my grandfather's otherwise nostalgic remembrance of his childhood is his lasting resentment that "when the disturbers of the peace, those blood brothers of ours, arrived in Jerez, they executed people and they forced many others to flee. . . . They wanted to kill my father, too. Many times he escaped by the skin of his teeth. . . . [A] week later we all escaped through the mountains by burro, one for each of us" (F. Pérez, 4).

This and other stories from my grandfather's past recall Rulfo's portrait of the revolution in his foundational fiction *Pedro Páramo.*[32] The image of his father escaping in the dark is my grandfather's sharpest memory of this journey through the mountains, and although Lira Pérez lived for another five years and my grandfather remained in Mexico for two more after his death, this childhood trauma—the originary moment of separation from his ancestral Mexican community—serves in "Memorias" as what Padilla names the point of sociocultural rupture in the Mexican American autobiographical consciousness. By fixating on the image of his father on that night, my grandfather cannot but push aside the humiliating details of the previous days. Approximately eighty years after his father's inglorious retreat, my grandfather remembers the tall figure in front of him on that night, restored imaginatively to an honored position within the idealized cultural geography of his settler ancestors. "There, fleeing from his ancestral home," my grandfather writes, "went an honorable and productive citizen . . . who at one time was a descendant of the most prosperous and propertied *hacendados* in the entire valley of Jerez" (F. Pérez, 4). Neither his father's exile nor his own permanent displacement can be viewed by my grandfather except in the light of the mythic (hacienda) past. His is the elite class perspective of a child whose secure and comfortable world was overturned by a ragtag group of peons. The peasant soldiers who sought his father, he suggests, were actually using their newfound power for short-term gain. As my grandfather sarcastically remarks, "[W]e left at night so that our loyal Mexican 'brethren,' people who one day were our employees and we the employers, couldn't detect us" (4).

We have come a long way from the family narratives of some Chicanos whose *antepasados* were said to have ridden a raid or two with Pancho Villa—but we must go further. As I would later learn through my research, at the time that my grandfather's mother Juliana was pregnant in 1912–13 with her third child, her older sister Dominga had come to the Pérez household to care for her. At least one branch of the Róbles family charges that Lira Pérez raped his sister-in-law, only to then renounce his illegitimate son Paulo. Aunt Esther, however, believes that the relationship may have been consensual and that it lasted longer than the Róbleses' charge suggests. Astute accountant that he was, Lira Pérez may have realized that legally recognizing the male child would create a web of financial difficulties for his other sons and family in Jerez. If Esther is right, it was then that he broke off relations with the Róbleses. According to this interpretation, if Lira Pérez had only supported and acknowledged the boy, the accusations of rape would never have been made. Obviously he did not foresee his forced departure from the town a year or so later. He may even have been forced to leave before the child was born.

But this extramarital relationship was not the end of the tale that Lira Pérez, while in Jerez, had written for himself. The fierce nostalgia that imbues my grandfather's account of the escape from town also obscures yet another side of his father's life during the 1912–14 period: an apparently secret relationship with María Herrera, who would later become his fourth wife but who at the time lived with her family twenty miles from Jerez at the Víboras hacienda. (After Francisco's father's death in 1919, his stepmother María and her siblings were extremely important to Francisco; her family took care of him, and, as mentioned earlier, he eventually married María's youngest sister Concepción.) As my grandfather perhaps unintentionally acknowledged in a tape-recorded interview in 1987, when his father left Jerez in early 1914 on short notice, he took Francisco, his mistress/wife María, and their two children—a boy named Lucas, born in 1912, and a baby girl named Diega, born a few months before the family's flight. Although "Memorias" does not mention María as being a part of Lira Pérez's life in Jerez, in this interview María appears in my grandfather's description of their 1914 journey. After they left the mountains, they boarded a train but were forced to ride on its roof because it was filled with soldiers on their way to battle. This episode recalls the train rides described in Galarza's *Barrio Boy*, the early chapters of which are also set at the height of the revolution. My grandfather remembers María sitting on the curved roof at night, holding Diega, struggling to keep herself and the baby from falling off the shaking train. Clearly contradicting this taped recollection, "Memorias" instead states vaguely that it was "during his father's stay" in Torreón, where he lived on and off between early 1914 and his death, that both Lucas and Diega were born. By suggesting that Lira Pérez met María after leaving Jerez, the text erases the secret affair with María. Since this third relationship means that between 1912 and 1914 Lira Pérez had four children by three women—Paulo by Dominga Róbles; Lucas and Diega by María Herrera; and Marcos II, who died in infancy in 1913, by his wife Juliana (see Pérez family tree)—Berta's impassioned complaint at the funeral becomes more compelling. These relationships may also explain why my grandmother chose not to speak of Lira Pérez when I interviewed her: her eldest sister María was one of the three women with whom Lira Pérez had children over this three-year span. If the family chronology I have collected is correct, Lira Pérez's first child (Lucas) with his mistress María was born in 1912, either just before Lira Pérez's wife Juliana died or very soon afterward. This would mean that both María and Juliana were pregnant at approximately the same time. And yet, although María could presumably have been blamed for Dominga's abandonment by Lira Pérez, the Róbles family narrative does not mention her at all, suggesting that the Róbles accusation centers upon Lira Pérez's abuse of Dominga, rather than his decision, if this is in fact what occurred, to take María, rather than Dominga, with him.

The Róbles narrative instead draws other conclusions from the events of this time. Both Dominga and Juliana died at a young age, Juliana in 1913 and Dominga, who was at least fifteen years older than her sister, in 1922. My Aunt Esther, who for a time mistakenly believed that Dominga had died in 1916, once joked that the aging patriarch may have poisoned these sisters to extricate himself from the legal and personal morass he had created. While this theory is chronologically impossible in the case of Dominga, I obviously have no way of determining the complete truth of Lira Pérez's complex relationship with the Róbleses. Rather, for this family, as Galarza, quoting Henry Adams, cites in the epigraph of *Barrio Boy*, "the memory was all that mattered." Similarly, as the scholar Guillermo E. Hernández reminded me after reading an earlier version of this chapter, my family narrative raises many more questions regarding what actually happened between my great-grandfather, Juliana, Dominga, and the Róbles family. Although I once validated as truthful Berta's account by concluding that the rape did occur, Hernández, a literature scholar at UCLA, argued that many other questions have to be raised before accepting this interpretation. Generalized preconceptions about what constitutes Mexican culture, he observed, become moot when one encounters real people and real families—as opposed to either formal studies or narratives passed down through multigenerational family history. As scholars, he asserted, we know little about traditional Mexican culture and its labyrinths of desire, sexuality, moral tolerance, or about interactions among genders, ages, and classes at the rural and regional levels. Following Hernández's admonition—which mirrored my initial skepticism toward Berta's narrative in the first draft of this project—I have drawn back from my earlier published conclusion.[33]

Since Berta's account presents a plausible interpretation of what may have occurred, it possesses as much "truth" as my grandfather's "Memorias" on the question of Lira Pérez. But I have no way of determining that what it posits regarding Lira Pérez's motivation and actions almost a century ago is the "truth." Other recent evidence also supports my decision to retract my earlier conclusion.

When my Aunt Esther met with Dominga Pérez, Paulo's daughter (who is named after her mother), she dismissed her cousin Berta as the family gossip—as have other Róbleses at various times.[34] Esther even spoke with Berta herself by telephone, but after agreeing to meet my aunt at her home, Berta did not show up. Along with my grandfather's "Memorias" and the other stories I have collected and continue to trace, Berta's narrative, I now see, forms one of the many tales that collectively constitute my family's cultural memory. Though these tales provide insight into my family's past, they are just as partial and speculative as those of any other family's. And since they have been passed down from earlier decades and centuries, they will always be missing the pieces needed to fully clarify such stories as Juliana and Dominga's. Faulkner explores this very point through the character of Quentin Compson in *Absalom, Absalom!* Through this character's frustrated efforts to uncover his bewildering familial and community history, he learns the limits of historical "truth": "We have a few old mouth-to-mouth tales; we exhume from old trunks and boxes and drawers letters without salutation or signature, in which men and women who once lived and breathed are now merely initials or nicknames. . . . [The people] are there, yet something is missing . . . they are like a chemical formula exhumed along with the letters from that forgotten chest, carefully, the paper old and faded and falling to pieces, the writing faded, almost indecipherable, yet meaningful, familiar in shape and sense, the name and presence of volatile and sentient forces" (Faulkner, *Absalom, Absalom!*, 37).

Yet my Aunt Esther's passing remarks on the cause of Juliana's and Dominga's deaths do perhaps throw added light on the origins of the Róbles narrative, for as Berta's and Nico's comments insinuate, the Róbles family excoriated Lira Pérez not only for "raping" Dominga and repudiating Paulo but also for the deaths of both sisters at an early age. Juliana apparently died of natural causes while recovering from childbirth. After losing their second daughter, Dominga, nine years later in 1922, however, the Róbles family may have concluded that any of their daughters who came in contact with Lira Pérez would meet a tragic end—or perhaps that the Pérezes simply brought tragedy to the family. I have not yet determined with any certainty the class status or political sympathies of the Róbleses when they lived near Jerez. Though they were not identified with the *hacendado* elite, it is not clear that they were impoverished *campesinos*. Some members of the ancestral Róbles family did not leave Mexico until the 1950s.

By preventing further contact between the Pérez and Róbles families, the revolution settled the issue of the illegitimate child—

or so it seemed. For my purposes, the appearance of the insurrectionists in Jerez in 1913 serves two functions. First, by destroying Lira Pérez's career, dispossessing him of his property, and forcing him into permanent exile, it gave him the comeuppance the Róbles family believes he deserved for his treatment of their daughters and perhaps for his decades-long role in the repressive hacienda social economy. This financial ruin explains my grandfather's socioeconomic and cultural orphanhood. Had his father neither left Jerez nor lost his property, my grandfather probably would not have needed to immigrate to the United States. Second, the civil war ensured that the mystery of Lira Pérez's relationship to the Róbles family would probably never be fully revealed except as a set of highly contradictory and deeply self-interested family narratives. The Róbleses never had the opportunity to confront the despised founding father of one line of their family or—because some of them remained in Mexico until after World War II and others had only brief contact with the Pérezes—his immediate heirs. Though eighty years had passed, Chavela's funeral offered those Róbleses who identified with Berta an occasion to meet the descendants of Don Juan Lira Pérez, who, owing to their unique construction of the past, knew almost nothing of the "other" side of their patriarch's life.

I have only recently learned from Aunt Esther of another irony in my family narrative. My grandfather always blamed his mother's death in 1913 on her sister Dominga! Refusing to imagine his father in any other light, he came to view this older sister as a wily temptress and seducer of a distinguished and reluctant patriarch. According to this twist, my grandfather's bedridden mother died of a "broken heart" brought on by the shock of her own sister's betrayal. Not only does this turn of plot make for a dramatic denouement but in this way my grandfather transferred the blame for Lira Pérez's alleged crime onto the Róbles family, thus allowing him to embrace a long-dead father and mother by salvaging untarnished memories of them from the chaos of Mexican (family) history—his most ambitious narrative sleight of hand.

Yet by acknowledging a "consensual" relationship between Lira Pérez and Dominga, this story could well have been my grandfather's answer to the Róbleses' rape accusation. Esther's own recollection of her father's castigation of Dominga, my grandfather's refusal to acknowledge Paulo at the 1984 funeral, and the subsequent revelations brought to light by the Róbles narrative have led me to conclude that my grandfather viewed his half-brother Paulo as a bastard and interloper—and a legitimate member of *neither* side of Francisco's family. Though Paulo was in fact a closer relative than half-brother, since their mothers, Juliana and Dominga, were sisters, from my grandfather's perspective, as he expressed it to Esther, Paulo's mother Dominga was to blame for a great many of his father's troubles, most significantly the death of Francisco's mother Juliana of a "broken heart"; this may explain why the Róbleses as a group can be set apart in "Memorias" from my grandfather's cherished memories of the Róbles "matriarch" Doña Hipólita, who was the only mother my grandfather ever knew.

THE MADERISTA REBELLIONS

After Chavela's funeral, what struck me about my grandfather's narrative was not only its evasion of the Róbles perspective and nostalgic aggrandizement of Lira Pérez but also the multitude of absences, silences, and suppressions that seemed to determine its representation of Pérez family history. The tales through which my family remembered its historical origins were built on the buried ruins of the anti-nostalgic Róbles counter-narrative, and this "other" history might be said to signify more than the forgotten grievance of a single family. It symbolized as well the displaced histories of groups marginalized within Mexican society itself—such as women, Indians, and *campesinos*—who lived within the semifeudal hacienda social order. By focusing narrowly on the modern period without acknowledging the "trailing" historical qualifiers such as those found in my own family's past, some Mexican American literary and historical studies approach nineteenth-century history much like my grandfather did. In the interest of recovering our early Mexican (American) past, they overlook those suppressions, silences, and anomalies in this distant historical experience, thereby erasing our sociocultural links to the hacienda. Berta's complaint, which transgressed the traditional Mexican codes of respect and honor paid to elders and ancestors, provoked key questions about Chicano and Chicana origins and history that my earlier readings of historical narratives had raised but not yet fully resolved.

The Róbles family narrative illuminates some of the class-based social contradictions and gender-defined conflicts within hacienda society that formed the originary social landscape of the revolution but which my grandfather's nostalgic idealization of his father's life effectively suppressed. My grandfather alludes to his father's local political predicament and forced exile, but his single reference to the events leading up to the 1913 "well" episode is tellingly brief— a brevity that elides the painfully sublimated reality of the family's exodus: the Constitutionalist forces who gained ascendancy in rural Zacatecas in 1913 wished to put Lira Pérez to death because of his association with the *patrónes* (landed bosses) in the region.

The rebellions recounted in "Memorias" occurred in the summer of 1913. Since my grandfather was only five years old at the time, his interpretation of the sociopolitical landscape within which these violent clashes took place must have come from stories told to him by his father until his death in 1919. Over the years since then, these stories, like all of the others in "Memorias" and in my family's collective memory, were subject to the vagaries of memory. Echoing earlier novelists such as Faulkner and Proust, as well as Freudian theory, Gore Vidal (*Palimpsest*) employs the palimpsest as a metaphor for human memory: one never remembers an actual event but rather one's earlier remembrance of the event, until late in life one has only memories of earlier remembrances of earlier recollections, and so forth. Many other contemporary writers of historical fiction, both in the United States and Latin America, also reject the notion that imagination and memory are ever independent of each other.

By drawing from the historical scholarship on the period, however, one may sketch a picture of the political events that shaped the lives of my grandfather and his father. The violence in Jerez was one of a multitude of lesser uprisings throughout the rural region around the capital during mid-1913. These skirmishes preceded by a year the major battles between federal troops and northern (Villista) and local revolutionary forces in the cities of Torreón and Zacatecas. The actions were carried out by groups that were a part of the early Madero movement—the first phase of the Madero Revolution in Zacatecas—a movement that had come to prominence in the state two years earlier. The Maderistas opposed the Díaz dictatorship and began armed activities to end the regime in the border region of Zacatecas and Durango in February 1911. Led by José Luis Moya, Pánfilo Natera, Martín Triana, and Trinidad Cervantes, the Maderistas sought a transformation of the political system and a role in the governmental decision-making process. According to historians, "The immediate effects of the Madero Revolution in the [region] were limited: the removal from office of the governor and his substitution by one who fully represented the cause of Maderismo . . . and the substitution of various functionaries in the occupied regions by revolutionary officers" (J. Flores Olague et al., 157). Although Zacatecan Maderistas claimed that the 1911 Ciudad Juárez agreement, which ended the Díaz regime, did not change the political structure of the Mexican government, up to the summer of 1911 none of the Maderista groups in Zacatecas espoused any ideas other than those set forth by Maderismo (157).

Even before the February 1913 coup that ended the Madero presidency, the Zacatecan Maderistas were disappointed with his leadership. By the time the president was assassinated, opposition to the government was widespread throughout the region and was being expressed in the form of rebellions and banditry. And while the official state political apparatus recognized the new administration of Victoriano Huerta, local functionaries with Maderista ties, who held either civil posts or positions in the rural forces, immediately rebelled (J. Flores Olague et al., 158). Led by Natera— the great Zacatecan hero of the revolution whose bronze statue today stands atop the Bufa alongside that of Villa—the Maderista militants began armed actions to carry out the Constitutionalist revolution. Their forces quickly took control of most of the state. At this point, Lira Pérez's status as an associate of the *hacendados* must have marked him as an opponent of local, perhaps newly recruited rebels in Jerez. Some of the insurrectionists he faced could well have been former peons recruited from the very haciendas where he had worked for more than three decades.

The objective of the second phase of the Madero revolution in Zacatecas was the end of *cacicazgo*. Porfirian modernization and industrialization had amplified the social contradictions within hacienda society, as discussed in chapter 1. The hacienda social economy was controlled for generations by *caciques* (local landed bosses), who wielded absolute power over peons, servants, and tenants. Even before the worst depredations of the hacienda system under the Díaz dictatorship, in its mid-nineteenth-century manifestation *cacicazgo* meant serfdom for the great majority of Mexicans. Speaking at the Mexican constitutional convention of 1856, the same year that Lira Pérez was born, reformer Ponciano Arriaga denounced the injustices of the hacienda social order:

"[T]he rich Mexican landowner . . . or the majordomo who represents him, may be compared to a feudal lord of the Middle Ages. On his domain, with more or less formalities, he makes laws and executes them, administers justice and exercises civil powers, imposes taxes and fines, has jails, chains, and jailors, inflicts punishments and tortures, monopolizes trade and forbids any other business than that of his estate to be carried on without his consent. As a rule the judges and other public officials on these estates are the landowner's servants or tenants; they are henchmen incapable of acting freely, impartially, or justly, or of enforcing any law other than the absolute will of the master" (Arriaga, 97).

The second phase of the Madero movement constituted a social revolution with more radical goals than those of the first phase. Not only did diverse sectors of the Zacatecan population participate in the movement but also, in seeking an end to *cacicazgo*, they "radicalized the substance of [earlier] demands, which now included substantial changes in rural and mining work conditions, higher living standards, a redefinition of the structure of private property . . . and a desire for more effective, honest, and respectful government administrations" (J. Flores Olague et al., 156).

In the summer of 1913, Zacatecan Constitutionalist forces responded to Huerta's coup by carrying out reprisals and other military actions against groups identified with the hacienda system—"landlords, *caciques*, Federals, sometimes clerics, and Spaniards (though rarely Americans)" (Knight, 42). Accounts of these revolts in northern Zacatecas capture what probably happened in nearby Jerez, where Lira Pérez was a hacienda employee: "[Justo] Ávila, a small rancher at odds with the Lobatos hacienda, raised the latter's peons in revolt, recruiting 500 men. . . . Lobatos was an hacienda with an absentee owner and, more important, a notoriously harsh *administrador*. Other properties suffered: the huge, Spanish-owned El Saucillo, near Rincón de Ramos, was sacked; peons were reported to have taken over estates at Pinos, to the east, where the *rurales* had mutinied. Soon, towns became targets. At the mines of Los Tocayos the entreaties of the miners' wives prevented the triumphant rebels from dynamiting the company building; at Sombrerete the *jefe* and his men held off the rebels for a while, but finally the town was taken and sacked" (43).

Rural grievances and recruitment were all-important in these uprisings (Knight, 43). Since landowners and *caciques* had exploited their peons, servants, and tenants, Constitutionalist recruitment among the ranks of hacienda laborers in Zacatecas continued apace throughout early 1913. By the summer of 1913, the Constitutionalist army had grown to a point where "the governors and military commanders of Zacatecas, San Luis and Coahuila admitted that they could not police beyond the major cities, and they urged landowners to undertake their own defense." Executions and other reprisals against officials, landowners, and merchants were common. Yet some smaller towns and villages, choosing to acknowledge the defeat of the federals, "gave up appealing for troops and made terms with the rebels instead" (45). Lira Pérez apparently attempted this strategy. His brother-in-law Salvador Herrera told Aunt Esther that Francisco's father made an agreement with the rebels in Jerez, paying money to them in return for a guarantee of his safety.

The federals' withdrawal from the countryside during the summer of 1913 was paralleled by a general exodus of middle- and upper-class groups. His own agreement broken in the fall of 1913, Lira Pérez's life was in peril as he was pursued by Maderista soldiers. He next found himself among the thousands of "well-to-do" refugees fleeing to the major cities of the northeast (Knight, 45). He made his way to Torreón, where he hoped his anonymity, as well as the city's distance from Jerez, would provide a measure of protection. Instead, with the arrival of Villa's Division of the North only a few months later in March 1914, Torreón would be the site of one of the bloodiest battles of the revolution, witnessed by Lira Pérez and his family. Later, in August, Natera's Zacatecan forces joined up with Villa's army to lay siege to the city of Zacatecas, killing six thousand federal troops in three days.

By the end of 1913, the Zacatecan Constitutionalists controlled most of the state, with the exception of the capital, where Huertistas remained in power (J. Flores Olague et al., 158). The haciendas surrounding Jerez were "left in the hands of overseers or of peons, sharecroppers and villagers, and most of the smaller towns in the region were stripped of their *caciques,* officials and elite families" (Knight, 46). Lira Pérez's exile thus captures the widespread and random nature of the process of military and political dissolution in Mexico in 1913–14. As Alan Knight observes, "Historians of the Revolution are wont to trace its advance with an eye on the major cities. But their fall came at the end of a long sequence, beginning with the mountains and remote hamlets, then the villages and scattered mining camps, finally the provincial towns and state capitals. The major revolutionary armies of the north, it is true, advanced on Mexico City in 1914 in a roughly progressive, geographical fashion. But long before—and also while—this advance took place, there was a complementary revolutionary advance which cannot be mapped, save metaphorically. This took the form, not of a tide sweeping the country, but rather of an insidiously rising water level, which first inundated the rural areas . . . and finally swamped [the cities] to cover the face of the earth like Noah's flood" (Knight, 46).

By the beginning of 1914, Lira Pérez's situation was desperate. Now in his late fifties, he had several young children to provide for as well as a son by a previous marriage fighting in the federal army. Though freed from the Maderista threat in Jerez, he was now a refugee bereft of property or a means of employment. When by chance he landed in Torreón in time to witness one of the great battles of the civil war, he too must have felt helpless before the flood.

ORPHANS OF HISTORY

If read as a trope embodying the turbulent sociohistorical currents of the revolutionary era, the Róbles narrative suggests that my grandfather's father abused his privileged status in Jerez not only to violate the Róbles daughter sexually but also to try to evade responsibility for his actions. Within the patriarchal, socioeconomically polarized hacienda social order of that era, Lira Pérez's male peers may well have viewed his alleged crime as an "indiscretion." The Porfirian hacienda system in which Lira Pérez lived and worked, controlled by patriarchs who passed their property and status on to the eldest son, had intensified the subordination and exploitation of female peons, servants, and tenants, a condition for centuries endemic to the seigneurial agrarian social order.[35] When local Maderistas rebelled in the summer of 1913, however, Lira Pérez's "indiscretion" may have been only one of many moral transgressions held against the Jerez *hacendados* and their associates.

The silencing of Dominga's voice in my family history is emblematic of that elaborate suppression of submerged social conflict found in many early Mexican American autobiographies. In such texts, nostalgia for an idealized past is often the narrator's dominant self-fashioning technique. Although it is a highly subjective narrative constructed by deeply self-interested individuals over three generations, Berta's anti-nostalgic denunciation of the Pérez patriarch identifies underlying class and gender contradictions buried deep within the "pastoral" sociocultural landscape of "Memorias." If a rape did in fact occur, Lira Pérez's status before the outbreak of civil war—a position that would have been bolstered by the capitalist modernization of the Mexican hacienda economy under the Díaz regime—perhaps would have protected him from any accusation by the Róbles family. This family was apparently of a lower, though not necessarily *campesino,* class whose own situation probably worsened considerably during the war. Working for *hacendados* for more than thirty years would perhaps have ensured for my grandfather's father protection by those men who for decades wielded political and economic authority in the region. Even a university-educated associate of the *hacendados,* however, could not in 1912 have foreseen the uprisings in Jerez only a year later, let alone the coming war and social upheaval.

Just as it has informed my understanding of both Vallejo's "Historical and Personal Memoirs" and Carrillo's *The California I Love,* Padilla's study of early Mexican American autobiographies has illuminated the range of contradictory socioideological and cultural meanings inscribed in my grandfather's "Memorias." Padilla adroitly positions Mexican American autobiographies in relation to their authors' sociohistorical and cultural condition under Anglo American domination. He also traces the complex strategies by which they forge an identity for themselves out of their marginalized status as members of a conquered and displaced ethnic minority. Valuable not only as foundational literary texts, the heroic, self-told stories of formerly unknown Mexican American writers also disclose the monumental injustice Mexican American society has suffered through the exclusion of these works from U.S. literary and historical discourse. The sustained institutional suppression of such texts suggests how great a challenge critics and theorists of Mexican American literature face as they conduct their recuperative and interpretive projects. To those who would dismiss the writers of early autobiographies for their presumed "hacienda syndrome," Padilla replies with a distinctly historicized sense of the complex imbrication of these autobiographers' private and public struggles as Mexican (American) "orphans" in a land that was once their cultural, spiritual, and geographic home.[36]

As Berta Róbles's narrative makes abundantly clear, by failing to address the seigneurial class and caste identities of figures like Vallejo, historicizing such as Padilla's may still leave the voices of other orphans of history suppressed. They must no longer be silenced. Although the story of Dominga Róbles has been elaborately sublimated within my own family consciousness for almost a century, her distant voice, if not yet fully retrieved, has finally been acknowledged. Berta's accusation at the funeral, as well as the other family stories presented in this chapter, should thus remind scholars intent on recovering marginalized texts and establishing the discursive genealogy of suppressed Mexican American literary traditions that the powerfully disruptive autobiographical impulse to self-invention is always at work. The same impulse, of course, shapes other historical texts as well. Finally, Berta's confrontation with my grandfather's narrative, and her implicit challenge to Padilla's autobiography model, possesses a more fundamental meaning. Just as her story has profoundly influenced my understanding of the works discussed in this study, as students of Mexican American autobiography, literature, and history we must recognize and identify the ruptures, omissions, silences, misrepresentations, and lies—both conscious and unconscious—in other foundational Mexican American narratives if we wish to move toward a version of history closer to the "truth" than we can ever approach through "close" readings. Engaging the socioideological suppressions in writings by early Mexican American authors and narrators will help scholars both recuperate and critique how their subjects represent the existential, social, and cultural dilemmas of their fractured subjectivity. Paralleling my grandfather's memoirs, Berta's story is, at one level, one among many partial and subjective tales that constitute my family's cultural memory. But it helped reveal the remarkable energy of my grandfather's retrospective desire, after a life in exile as a cultural "orphan" torn between Mexico and the United States, to resist his community's "present" sociocultural erasure by imaginatively restoring and tenaciously repressing the social history of his Mexican ancestors.

Padilla notes that Vallejo's autobiography operates as a eulogy to a Mexican "social and cultural subjectivity stranded in the past over and against a colonized subjectivity accommodating and acquiescent toward an American social formation that had exploited and displaced [Mexicans]" (Padilla, 87). Like many modern Mexican immigrant narrators, Vallejo and other nineteenth-century Mexican American authors write from the perspective of an aggrieved ethnic community dislocated and excluded by U.S. social institutions. Just as my grandfather's orphaned status symbolizes his immigrant community's sociocultural break with the past *and* a continued separation from both Mexico and the United States, Vallejo and other early autobiographers write as culturally deracinated *huérfanos* (orphans) compelled to remember an earlier "heroic" social landscape that U.S. society has overturned. Undeniably, like Vallejo and other early autobiographers, my grandfather struggled to negotiate his Mexican (American) existence in the United States without rejecting Anglo American society in toto. My grandfather honored this country, and he was in turn very proud of being an American citizen. As a Mexican immigrant laborer, however, he also resisted its political and sociocultural dominance in his life. Along with the family of Dominga Róbles, another orphan of history, one can only wish that my grandfather had also been capable of speaking to similar repressions within the hacienda sociocultural economy of his Mexican forebears. Yet his remembrance of his father's life story today instructs others who continue to seek out our Mexican (American) past.

CONCLUSION

Since October 17, 1994, the day my grandfather left on a trip to Mexico, my family has received no word from him, nor have we received any information that would tell us what may have happened to him. A missing person's report was filed with U.S. and Mexican police, and the disappearance was publicized in several newspapers in Los Angeles and along the United States–Mexico border. In late 1994, the Ventura County Police Department informed us that my grandfather did arrive on October 17 at the downtown Los Angeles bus depot, where he purchased a ticket to the Mexican border city of Tijuana. Though the police could not determine whether he boarded the bus, I and other family members assume that he did. Just as the California and Mexican authorities were confounded by this case, my family has been frustrated in its efforts to find out what may have become of my grandfather. Our relatives in central Mexico heard nothing from him; hospitals, funeral homes, and public institutions that we contacted in Mexico and the United States had no record of his admittance; media announcements of his disappearance yielded no clues. After years of exasperation and grief, we have grown resigned to the likelihood that the circumstances of his death will forever remain a mystery.

When he boarded a bus in Fillmore, at a location just down the road from where, as a young farm worker seeking employment at Rancho Sespe, he had arrived sixty years earlier, my grandfather was not carrying any luggage and, as he was wont to do in his old age, probably had no identification. He was eighty-six years old, underweight, and in poor health. His adopted community of more than half a century must have seemed strangely different to him from the town he had first seen in his youth. After his wife died, he lived alone in a tract house that he never considered his true home because it was far away (two miles) from the Mexican Village at Rancho Sespe where he had raised his children and where, against their wishes, he continued to live until the 1970s. Beginning in the late 1940s, the children had all left the village for Los Angeles; his grandchildren and great-grandchildren, urban and assimilated, were now further removed from Fillmore's Mexican (American) farm worker community.

Some would never know what the workers' camp at Rancho Sespe meant to my grandfather. The Mexican Village, built above the banks of Sespe River amid orange and lemon tree groves, had once been a thriving community filled with well-tended homes and gardens—a place where for decades the language, customs, and culture of Mexico were maintained in the midst of an Anglo-dominated environment that was hostile toward and exploitative of Mexicans. My grandfather loved the village and the people who had been a part of it. When he first arrived there, he knew that the community in its entirety was owned—from its cottages to its trees, gardens, and flowers—by the Spalding family and that Mexican workers and their families could be evicted on short notice at the owners' whim. As I described in chapter 5, during one week in 1941 most of the Mexican families at Sespe were evicted for participating in a labor strike against the ranch, a strike my grandfather did not join.[1] After the strike was broken, my father, who was eleven at the time, recalled seeing his evicted friends and their families waiting on the roadside in the rain. My Uncle David, who was eight, remembers being teased at school by the children of displaced strikers.

Yet Rancho Sespe's rural and pastoral qualities must have attracted my grandfather from the outset, perhaps reminding him of his secure and idyllic childhood alongside his father and grandmother Hipólita at the San Juan de las Calabasas hacienda near Jerez. My Aunt Esther's remembrance of her childhood at Sespe supports this very characterization of the ranch's setting, one endorsed by my father's stories and my own visits there as a child. Though Esther, like my father, is highly critical of the feudal character of the ranch's social relations, in her 1965 college essay, "A Story of Death in Mexican American Culture," she also described it nostalgically as a "little paradise that was surrounded on three sides by lemon and orange orchards and completely isolated from the American community five miles away . . . a place where the skies were clear, the air fresh, the nearby mountains high and majestic, and the river that bordered the village a haven for a man and his three growing sons." My own fondest childhood memories are of visiting my grandparents when they still lived in the village as well as later on, when they resided in Fillmore, the nearby town also set amid citrus farms where my grandmother had separately bought a home. After my grandfather retired from Rancho Sespe

Francisco Róbles Pérez in the 1970s, after retiring from Rancho Sespe.

in 1973, he worked for eight years as the caretaker at another ranch, owned by the Vantree family and situated on the Sespe River at the entrance to Sespe Canyon, a mile or so from town. My grandfather tended the ranch's garden and stables and lived in a small guest house built at the edge of the river—really a tiny frame cabin with only a fireplace for heat—where we often visited. In 1979, winter storms turned the river into a torrent, washing away the cabin. A few years later, when the Vantree ranch house burned to the ground, my grandfather finally returned to live with his wife in Fillmore. Some of us wondered why he had chosen to live and work at another ranch after he had retired, under the authority of yet another wealthy rancher. I now see that it was not only because my grandfather enjoyed the tasks and pleasures of ranch life but also because he missed Sespe.

My grandfather loved Rancho Sespe not only because it was his home and workplace for almost four decades, the place where he and his wife Concepción raised their children and where his family's sweat and tears had commingled with soil. Nor can his attachment be explained entirely by either the socioeconomic circumstances that geographically constrained his life as a farm worker or his desire to return imaginatively to the mythic agrarian landscape of his childhood in rural Zacatecas. He also loved Rancho Sespe—which he always called the last great hacienda in California—because it reproduced for him the agrarian (hacienda) social order that his father Juan Lira Pérez had known in Mexico. Though always exploitative and often brutally so in its treatment of its Mexican laborers, as Esther and my father vividly remember, Rancho Sespe also offered my grandfather a traditional agrarian space of social stability, and hence a measure of Mexican ethnic cultural coherence, that he had not formerly experienced as an immigrant farm worker in the United States. This sense of space and stability may explain why my grandfather never spoke ill of Mr. Spalding, whom he liked and respected. (It took the writing of this book for me to understand and accept my grandfather's affection for a figure whom my father and aunt despised.) Within the limits of Rancho Sespe's racialized social hierarchy, which prohibited union organizing among its largely Mexican work force, my grandfather knew that he would have a secure job and small home in the Mexican Village where he could raise his children without the arduous trials of migrant farm worker life. In return, Mr. Spalding had a loyal worker for life. Hence my grandfather found solace as a displaced Mexican immigrant not only by nostalgically remembering the ancestral agrarian society that he and his family had once known in Mexico but also by adopting as a home a similar paternalistic agrarian space in the United States. The paternalistic bond between Mr. Spalding and my grandfather, strengthened by my grandfather's fierce identification with Rancho Sespe over a span of decades, was never broken. When Mr. Spalding died in 1963, he left three thousand dollars in his will to my grandfather. Mr. Spalding was buried on a hill overlooking his beloved ranch, where his most trusted Mexican employee, my grandfather, dug his grave, set his headstone, and poured the cement for his tomb. In contrast to my grandfather's affective bond with his *patrón*, to this day for my own father Mr. Spalding's headstone stands as a monument to the Mexican American community's long-aggrieved social condition under Rancho Sespe's semifeudal labor system.

My grandfather's immersion in the social world of the hacienda, his irrevocable attachment to the pre-modern rural landscape of his childhood, symbolizes the proximity of the semifeudal and agrarian past of the imagined Mexican American national community. His life as an immigrant buffeted by civil and social turmoil similarly registered that convulsive transformation of Mexican agrarian society generated by the forces of modernity in the late nineteenth and early twentieth centuries. This journey from the pre-capitalist rural "third" world to the modern industrial capitalist "first" world has, of course, been the historical patrimony of immigrants from other populations in other regions throughout the modern era. Though compelled by socioeconomic circumstances to return to a semifeudal social landscape that he would eventually adopt as his home, my grandfather's life journey in this sense captured the struggles of all agrarian populations from traditional cultures plunged into the industrial capitalist "first" world by the modernizing forces of history.

The Russian artist Ilya Repin renders this journey out of the past in his 1883 painting *Religious Procession in the Province of Kursk,* which portrays an outdoor religious procession led by priests who carry above them a religious icon. Representatives of Russia's dispossessed classes, epitomized by two crippled serfs on crutches in the left foreground, stand alongside figures embodying the country's elite: uniformed military officers on horseback, elegantly dressed members of the aristocracy, and robed priests. The expressions in the crowd vary, but most have the grim appearance of refugees, of people escaping from history as much as disciples seeking spiritual redemption. Yet all appear drawn by a common faith in what the religious icon encodes. The icon has not only a religious significance but a secular one as well. It symbolizes the nineteenth-century Russian population's emergent quest for social justice and historical redemption as it entered the modern era bearing the weight of Russia's afflicted feudal past.

As heirs of an equally recent feudal and agrarian past, Mexican Americans similarly carry on our shoulders the weight of the combined memories of Greater Mexico's collective history. This social memory, I have argued in this study, is rooted in the agrarian cultural geography of pre-revolutionary Mexico and the Spanish colonial Southwest. Mexican (American) hacienda writings illustrate the historical immediacy of this inheritance. In these works the hacienda as memory-place resonates with charged meaning as a socially fraught symbol of Mexican (American) identity and origins.[2] Set against a racialized U.S. sociopolitical landscape, the hacienda delineates in these texts an emergent Mexican (American) subjectivity struggling ambiguously against the threat of discursive erasure and material loss. More generally, the hacienda as memory-place serves as a symbolic resolution to social contradictions resulting from the cataclysmic decline of Mexican (American) agrarian ranch society in the late nineteenth and early twentieth centuries, a decline driven by the expansion of (U.S.) industrial capitalism. Though González and Raleigh's *Caballero* stands as a notable exception by overtly identifying the hacienda's social contradictions, in the texts I have examined the hacienda as memory-place works to cement history and memory together into an iconic monument to the past, burying contrary memories in its project to (re)constitute an enabling Mexican (American) historical subjectivity. Hacienda narratives, however, cannot evade the silenced voices of the Mexican past buried deep within the semifeudal agrarian landscape they describe. The ambiguous symbolic meaning of the hacienda as a Mexican American site of memory thus serves as an eloquent illustration of Pierre Nora's conception of memory-places as "fleeting incursions of the sacred [past] into a disenchanted [modern] world; vestiges of parochial loyalties in a society that is busily effacing all parochialisms; de facto differentiations in a society that levels on principle; signs of recognition and group affiliation in a society that tends to recognize only individuals" (Nora, 6–7).

Despite such dissonances and ambiguities within Mexican American cultural memory, scholars and students of the Mexican American past must also remember the hacienda, seeing in it a sign of sociohistorical differences as well as commonality within the imagined Mexican American national community, a sign of the range of cultural identities, rooted in a foundational colonial past, that have emerged through time from disparate sociocultural and economic processes.

This last point suggests my own study's particular relevance to the Recovering the U.S. Hispanic Literary Heritage project. Directed as they are at (re)constructing and legitimating a national (ethnic) community's literary tradition, all ethnic literary recovery projects risk obscuring the historicity of their texts' varied ideological and aesthetic determinants. Because they employ traditional historiographical categories that themselves contributed to the exclusionary model against which the projects rebel, their seemingly transparent recuperative aim is always problematic. This contradiction is highly fraught for ethnic communities that need not only to deconstruct discredited (literary) histories of the past but also to (re)construct and legitimate new (literary) histories in which they are finally represented.[3] And yet, despite many noteworthy exceptions, what Emma Pérez, echoing Foucault, argues about Chicano/a history is equally true of Mexican American historical literary scholarship. Through her elucidation of the "decolonizing" subject, Pérez identifies the ways in which Chicano/a (literary) historiography "has been circumscribed by the traditional historical imagination." Like any other subaltern history, Chicano/a (literary) history, Pérez writes, "will tend to follow traditional history's impulse to cover 'with a thick layer of events the great silent, motionless bases' that constitute the interstitial gaps, the unheard, the unthought, the unspoken. These interstitial gaps interrupt the linear model of time, and it is in such locations that oppositional, subaltern histories can be found." As the negotiating spaces for the "decolonizing" subject, these silences, asserts Pérez, are where agency is articulated.[4] Working against such an expansive articulation, Chicano/a (literary) historiography has employed categories that are themselves problematic, in that they often "deny and negate the voice of the other," the silences, gaps, and suppressions that can and must be uncovered (E. Pérez, 5). The agrarian sociocultural landscape in Mexican American hacienda narratives highlights these contradictions within research for the Recovering the U.S. Hispanic Literary Heritage project. Though posited as a foundational Mexican (American) memory-place, as a contested space embodying difference, discontinuity, dissonance, contradiction, and rupture the hacienda in these early texts stands in antithetical relation to the unitary space of Aztlán claimed by Chicano cultural nationalism as the mythical place of the Chicano nation. As a Spanish colonial site that explodes cultural nationalism's essentialist projection of an unchanging and unproblematic Chicano identity, the hacienda as memory-place validates Pérez's call for a new historiographical paradigm that strives to "decolonize" Mexican American otherness (6).

In the interplay between memory and history ethnic studies scholars have found contradictory ideological imperatives strikingly similar to those identified above by Pérez. "To revise [dominant] history through recourse to [ethnic] cultural memory," writes David Palumbo-Liu, "is not to step outside its functional paradigms, and yet some moment of discontinuity must be introduced." Nevertheless, "*that* discontinuity becomes counterbalanced by another kind of continuity, which lapses back into the same will to know, haunted by the same visions of 'homeland' (both as a cultural 'base' and as a way of knowledge)" (Palumbo-Liu, 219; emphasis in original). Some recovery project scholars share Palumbo-Liu's concerns. In an early essay John M. González, for example, observed that recovered Mexican American literary texts should "immediately [evoke] questions about the institutional sites, contexts and methodologies involved in the production of knowledge" about such texts. The issue of what type of cultural and political work literary recovery projects enact in the dissemination and elaboration of U.S. Latina/o culture, continues González, "comes into focus as a site of contestation over interpretation and pedagogy" (J. M. González, "Romancing Hegemony," 23). As narratives that expose the convoluted interplay between Mexican American history and memory, hacienda texts illustrate the interpretive, methodological, and institutional concerns indicated by González, Palumbo-Liu, and Pérez, among others. Interrogating the hacienda as a site of memory in these works reveals the ways in which acts of historical revision performed by recovered Mexican American literary texts—and by the scholarship about them—may be just as partial, and problematic, as my grandfather's narrative of origins.

The hacienda as memory-place in early Mexican American literature serves as a constant reminder that in ethnic literary recovery research the essentialist impulse to suppress difference and thus cover the unheard and unspoken within ethnic cultural memory is always at work. Drawing from his African Caribbean community's experience of colonialism, the Martiniquian revolutionary theorist Franz Fanon similarly opposed delving narrowly into the histories of aggrieved colonial populations "in order to find coherent elements which [would] counteract colonialism's attempts to falsify and harm." For, as he explains, "a national culture is not a folklore, nor an abstract populism that believes it can discover a people's true nature." Rather, "[a] national culture is the whole body of efforts made by a people in the sphere of thought to describe, justify and praise the action through which that people has created itself and keeps itself in existence."[5] Much as the nostalgic impulse within early Mexican American autobiographies emerges from sociocultural rupture, in the interest of countering U.S. colonialism's depredations recovery project scholarship has often denied or negated the multiform permutations that devolve through time from the ambiguous interplay of Mexican American history and memory.

The essentialist impulse thus also requires erasing the historicity of cultural identities, the ways in which they evolve through a series of mediations over time in relation to changing sociohistorical contexts (Quintana, 76). Projecting a Chicano (ethnic) cultural nationalist identity onto Californio rancher/authors Ruiz de Burton or Vallejo, for example, requires an interpretive sleight of hand that transplants these authors from the Mexican agrarian (hacienda) cultural landscape that shaped their families' histories to a modern capitalist context that obliterates the Spanish colonial past and its distinctive legacies. Such an interpretation forgets that cultural identities have histories and undergo constant transformation, that far from being eternally fixed in some essentialized past they are subject to the continuous "play" of history, culture, and power (S. Hall, "Cultural Identity," 52). Along with the common historical experiences and shared cultural codes that provide Mexican Americans with stable, unchanging, and continuous frames of reference, there are also critical points of significant difference that constitute what Mexican Americans were in the past, and have, through time, become (51–52). Cultural identity, as Stuart Hall reminds us, "is not an essence, an accomplished historical fact that transcends place, time, history, and culture. Rather, it is a *positioning* . . . that has no absolute guarantee in an unproblematic, transcendental 'law of origin'" (53). My readings have similarly traced two vectors of Mexican American cultural identity that are simultaneously operative in the hacienda as memory-place: one that brings to light a common agrarian historical experience and another that exposes discontinuities, fissures, anomalies, and silences within Mexican American cultural memory. Hall's further explication of cultural identity thus expounds my own project's historicist approach to recovered early Mexican American narratives and the scholarship about them: "Far from being grounded in a mere 'recovery' of the past, which is waiting to be found, and which, when found, will secure our sense of ourselves into eternity, identities are the names we give to the different ways we are positioned by, and position ourselves within, the narratives of the past" (52). Hacienda writings demonstrate that if characterizations of Mexican American memory and identity are to be meaningful, critics should address what kind of history Mexican Americans have valued, what in their past they have chosen to remember and forget, how they have disseminated the past they have recalled, and to what uses those memories have been put (Brundage, 3). Nor does recognizing and retrieving the past in this manner diminish the obvious value of restoring the literary patrimony of Mexican Americans. As I have contended throughout this study, this restoration is enhanced, not diminished, by acknowledging and exploring the "play" of difference, the interstitial gaps, ruptures, ambiguities, suppressions, and silences within a Mexican American cultural memory that has evolved since the Spanish colonial era and whose roots extend also into the distant pre-Columbian past. In Mexican American literary and historical scholarship, however, our collective memory often appears static and one-dimensional, the countervailing response to an aggrieved U.S. sociohistorical condition that must, like my grandfather's narrative of origins, erase difference, dissonance, and contradiction. In response to Mexican American writings that affirm a cultural essentialist politics at the expense of memory, multiplicity, and difference, I have posited a poetics of remembrance. Embracing the ambiguous interplay of history and memory, the hacienda as memory-place demonstrates not only how early Mexican (American) authors remembered the colonial past symbolically to reclaim a sense of cultural agency but also how they positioned themselves within, and were positioned by, the narratives that constitute early Mexican American cultural memory. Scholars and readers of recovered Mexican American literary and historical texts today must be constantly aware of their own positionings as they use these narratives to continue the fashioning of Mexican American cultural memory.

Until it was demolished in 1978, the Mexican Village at Rancho Sespe remained a workers' camp for Mexican laborers and their families. Just before the camp was razed, my parents, grandparents, and I visited the village for the last time. Access was the same as it had been forty years earlier: a bumpy dirt road barely visible from the highway and which wound for a half mile through thick groves of orange and lemon trees, then along the Sespe River to the dusty outskirts of the town. Amid the 150 cottages in disrepair and decay we found the house where my father and his brothers and sisters spent their childhoods. My grandparents and my father were upset by the condition of the decrepit house, especially the growth of weeds and vegetation engulfing it. Despite my father's obvious bitterness about conditions at the Spalding citrus ranch, he recalled this home and the Mexican Village of his youth, as he continues to do today, in a manner reminiscent of his father's nostalgic recollection of the bountiful hacienda landscape where my great-grandfather Juan Lira Pérez had lived.

Though most of its full-time residents had already deserted the Mexican Village, as we drove through the town we met an old man, Pancho Casas, Nico's brother-in-law and a close friend of my grandfather, whose family had lived in the village since the time of my grandfather's arrival in 1936. Pancho had been evicted from Sespe for participating in the 1941 strike; he returned to the village several years later. Knowing that the last inhabitants of the workers' camp were young immigrants from Mexico, I was astonished to meet, at that late date, a distant relative and an original resident from my grandfather's generation. Though I had met Pancho before, I had always assumed that he lived in Fillmore. As we continued through the village, I half expected other ghosts from my grandfather's past to appear—perhaps, as I now reflect on that visit, his lost half-brother Paulo, whose distant cousins (Nico and his siblings) had lived at Rancho Sespe from the 1920s through the 1960s. But, as it turned out, Pancho was at that moment preparing to move. His departure marked the end of my family's decades-long residence in the Mexican Village at Rancho Sespe and its century-long habitation within the agrarian (hacienda) social landscape. Although the history of Rancho Sespe's Mexican (American) community was erased from the official record, it lives on in the collective memory of the Mexican Village's Chicano and Chicana descendants.

NOTES

Introduction

1. See chapter 1 for an overview of the scholarly research on the Mexican hacienda. Its designation as "feudal" can be traced to the works of Wistano Orozco, Andrés Molina Enriquez, Frank Tannenbaum, and François Chevalier, whose writings spanned the period from the 1890s to the 1950s (Miller, 229). Their works established the orthodox definition of the Mexican hacienda, rendered here by Simon Miller: "Vast seigneurial properties on a New World scale, dwarfing the equivalents in Europe, and 'feudal' in that they were characterized by archaic methods, introverted autarchy, and systems of coercive debt peonage" (229–30).

2. Though called "Aunt" by my father, Isabel Róbles Pérez was actually my paternal grandfather Francisco Róbles Pérez's first cousin (see the Pérez and Róbles family trees in chapter 5).

3. See Pérez and Róbles family trees, chapter 5.

4. I place the word "rape" in quotation marks because, as described in chapter 5, I was unable to determine whether a rape actually did occur. The Róbles narrative of the "rape," however, shaped my family history at every level.

5. Michel-Rolph Trouillot explains in *Silencing the Past* that human beings participate in history both as actors and as narrators: "In vernacular use, history means both the facts of the matter and a narrative of those facts, both 'what happened' and 'that which is said to have happened.'" The first meaning of history, according to Trouillot, "places the emphasis on the sociohistorical process, the second on our knowledge of that process or on a story about that process." The vernacular use of the word history thus "offers us a semantic ambiguity: an irreducible distinction and yet an equally irreducible overlap between what happened and that which is said to have happened" (Trouillot, 3). In Trouillot's view, "the overlap and the distance between the two [sides of historicity] . . . may not be susceptible to a general formula. The ways in which what happened and that which is said to have happened are and are not the same may itself be historical" (4).

6. As Richard Flores states, the "symbolic work accomplished through 'remembering the Alamo' . . . consists of signifying a radical difference between 'Anglos' and 'Mexicans' so as to cognize and codify the social relations circulating at the beginning of the twentieth century" (R. Flores, "Introduction: Adina De Zavala," xvi).

7. Ensuing chapters will examine this criticism through close readings of the five primary texts that form the subject of my study. See Ramón Gutiérrez and Genaro Padilla's *Recovering the U.S. Hispanic Literary Heritage, Volume I* (1993), and subsequent anthologies of critical essays edited by Erlinda Gonzales-Berry and Chuck Tatum (volume II, 1996), María Herrera-Sobek (volume III, 2000),

and José F. Aranda and Silvio Torres-Saillant (volume IV, 2002), collected and published by the Recovering the U.S. Hispanic Literary Heritage project.

8. See the ensuing chapter readings for illustrations of this model and the conclusion for further elaboration. My model of memory and identity stands in antithetical relation to one premised on cultural nationalism, which fails to acknowledge Mexican Americans' "historical differences in addition to the multiplicity of [their] cultural identities as a people." As Chabram and Fregoso further remind us, cultural nationalism "postulated the notion of a transcendental Chicano subject at the same time that it proposed that cultural identity existed outside of time and that it was unaffected by changing historical processes" (Chabram and Fregoso, 205).

9. See chapter 1 for a description of the hacienda social order. The hacienda was a semifeudal agrarian institution, dependent on a labor force controlled through debt peonage, which "produced subsistence goods as well as a market surplus" (Burkholder and Johnson, 184). Large estates were self-sufficient (i.e., autarkic). These estates "had their crops, their flocks and herds, their wooded areas, their flour mills, forges, and workshops" (311). Haciendas "provided the physical focus for both social life and production. The owner's large house dominated the hacienda's residential core" (184).

10. Faulkner's works have informed my understanding of Mexican American hacienda narratives. Frederick Karl notes that all of Faulkner's major characters "enter the fiction trailing behind them clouds of familial and regional qualifiers . . . the grandparents, parents, and siblings, the hill country or bottom land or tidewater, whose cumulative significance is the indispensable background of identity" (Karl, 133–34). These historical "qualifiers" in Faulkner's works reach back to early plantation society, whereas in many early Mexican American narratives they harken back to the hacienda era.

11. Although all five works are newly recovered literary texts, two of them, Leo Carrillo's *The California I Love* and my grandfather's "Memorias," were composed during or after the 1950s.

12. See chapters 2 and 4 for detailed biographies of these figures. Vallejo was descended from colonists who settled Alta California in the late eighteenth century, whereas Ruiz de Burton was descended on her maternal side from Don José Manuel Ruiz, commander of the Mexican northern frontier in Baja California and later governor (1822–25) of the province.

13. As will be discussed at length chapter 2, colonists from New Spain conquered, displaced, and subjugated the indigenous peoples of these regions.

14. My grandfather's "Memorias" is an unpublished manuscript that I have compiled from my transcription of tape-recorded interviews with him and from several notebooks containing my translation of his original handwritten manuscript.

15. My grandfather disappeared while on a trip to Mexico in 1994. We have not been able to determine when he died. See chapter 5 and the conclusion.

16. Among the works that have foregrounded these concepts are Flores's *Remembering the Alamo: Memory, Modernity, and the Master Symbol*, Mary Pat Brady's *Extinct Lands, Temporal Geographies: Chicana Literature and the Urgency of Space*, and Raúl Homero Villa's *Barrio-Logos: Space and Place in Urban Chicano Literature and Culture*. Also, for a seminal study of early Mexican American history and memory as they evolved during the Spanish colonial era, see Ramón A. Gutiérrez's *When Jesus Came, the Corn Mothers Went Away: Marriage, Sexuality, and Power in New Mexico, 1500–1846*.

17. Stuart Hall, quoted in Brundage, 2.

18. But, as Richard Flores and Marita Sturken both note, history and memory are also "entangled." The Alamo as a cultural symbol has been interwoven with the Southwest's historiography since the early twentieth century and continues to

exert a potent meaning within American national remembrance. As a "master symbol" of Texas and the frontier, explains Flores in *Remembering the Alamo*, the Alamo also "serves as a critical map for the exploitation and displacement of Mexicans" (160). Its effect has been to marginalize Mexican (American) memory within both formal history and American public memory. Similarly, Sturken's *Tangled Memories*, an investigation of the cultural memory of the Vietnam War and other events in modern U.S. history, reveals how American identity is shaped through the interplay of history and memory.

19. Within U.S. ethnic studies, "history" names "the dominant discourse assigning significance and order to things. . . . [It includes] both formal and informal, official and unofficial articulations that affirm and confirm what is taken to be the natural understanding of events and their significance—the 'natural' is, as Raymond Williams tells us, a sign of ideology's work." History "is disseminated much more widely, and perhaps more convincingly, than by 'official historical' texts alone; it is transmitted and reaffirmed by and in a number of representational fields, one of which is literature" (Palumbo-Liu, 212).

20. Corney, quoted in Brundage, 6.

21. The hacienda, however, has served as a defining signifier within late-nineteenth- and twentieth-century Mexican literature. Juan Rulfo's novel, *Pedro Páramo* (1955), whose genealogical landscape has held a lasting influence on my own vision of Mexican history, represents only the most well-known hacienda text within a Mexican literary tradition often concerned with *caciquismo* (bossism or despotism). In their focus on rural *caciquismo* under the Porfirio Díaz regime Mariano Azuela's *Los caciques* (1917) and *Los de abajo* (1916), José López Portillo y Rojas's *La parcela* (1898), and Emilio Rabassa's tetralogy consisting of *La bola* (1887), *La gran ciencia* (1887), *El cuarto poder* (1888), and *Moneda falsa* (1888) can be classified as hacienda texts. A number of early Mexican historical romances, such as Ignacio Altamirano's *El Zarco: episodios de la vida mexicana en 1861–1863* (1901), set in part on rural estates in Mexico, may also be categorized as hacienda literature. As José E. Limón notes, *El Zarco* may have served as a model for González and Raleigh's *Caballero*.

Chapter 1

1. For the quotation about memory, see Faulkner's short story, "A Rose for Emily," 129.

2. Chapter 2 examines the status of California Indians under the hacienda system. Also, see the description of the hacienda social order later in this chapter.

3. Through Don Mariano Alamar, *The Squatter and the Don*'s protagonist, the narrator comments on the role played by settlers and ranchers in the founding of the California missions: "The fact that . . . landowners who established large ranchos were very efficient and faithful collaborators in the foundation of missions was taken into consideration by the Spanish government." In times of Indian outbreaks, "the landowners with their servants would turn out as in feudal times in Europe, to assist in the defense of the missions and the sparsely settled country threatened by the savages" (Ruiz de Burton, *The Squatter and the Don*, 176).

4. The rancher family whose history forms the subject of *Caballero* traces its aristocratic ancestry through its patriarch, Don José Ramón de Mendoza y Robles, who in 1749 built the family's hacienda, Rancho La Palma de Cristo. Don José Ramón may have been modeled after the Spanish colonist Escandón and the *hacendados* Vásquez Borrego and Garza Falcón. The founding colonists were, explains the narrator in the foreword/prologue, "[m]en of courage, of fortitude and of daring, men of wealth in whom was innate the culture of the mother country Spain. . . . Bringing with them small armies of *peons*, herds of cattle and sheep, they crossed the Río Grande in search of the flower-covered plains which their leader Don José de Mendoza y Robles had seen. And so they established themselves in the land between the Nueces and the Río Grande and there built

homes for themselves, their children, and their children's children" (J. González and Raleigh, xxxvii).

5. Alonzo, however, takes the view that "few genuine *haciendas* developed during the Spanish-Mexican period" (Alonzo, 39), contradicting the model put forward by David Montejano in *Anglos and Mexicans in the Making of Texas, 1836–1986*.

6. In *The Squatter and the Don*, Don Mariano Alamar responds to the view that "it was wicked to tolerate the waste, the extravagance of the Mexican government, in giving such large tracts of land to a few individuals." Such gifts, he stresses, "were for the purpose of aiding enterprises for the good of the people" (Ruiz de Burton, *The Squatter and the Don*, 175–76). The Spanish and Mexican governments gave "large tracts of land as an inducement to those citizens who would utilize the wilderness of the government domain—utilize it by starting ranchos which afterwards would originate 'pueblos' or villages, and so on" (176).

7. Californio ranchers used the term *gente de razón* to distinguish themselves from Indians and *mestizos*. See chapter 2.

8. For an analysis of Vallejo's role in the politics of secularization, see chapter 2.

9. As Rosaura Sánchez observes, "At a moment when the hacienda was the dominant mode of production in Mexico, Alta California after 1769 would be returning to a communal form of forced labor [i.e., the mission]. Only later, under Mexican rule, would the rancho and hacienda become the dominant spaces of production in Alta California after secularization of the missions" (Sánchez, *Telling Identities*, 55).

10. By critically interrogating the hacienda mythos, González and Raleigh's *Caballero* constitutes a notable exception. See chapter 3.

11. Chevalier compares the *hacendados* of New Spain to the feudal lords of the Middle Ages. He writes that "[t]he landed proprietor's peculiar mentality was not conducive to thinking in terms of efficient production. He acquired land, not to increase his earnings, but to eliminate rivals and hold sway over an entire region" (Chevalier, 310). Particularly in the northern provinces of New Spain, "the rich and powerful men who . . . concentrated in their persons economic resources, military functions, and judicial powers may be compared to the *ricos omes* of [medieval] Castile" (313). Semo acknowledges the hacienda's feudal origins but argues that from its inception this institution "was a creation suitable to a society in which feudalism and the mercantile economy were inseparably intertwined" (Semo, 155). Over a span of three centuries "there were periods of expansion and contraction that turned the *hacienda* into a predominantly commercial unit during times of market expansion and into a decidedly autarkic one during times of contraction" (155–56). The secret of the hacienda's success and stability, concludes Semo, "lay in its twofold nature . . . and in its adaptability to the fluctuations of a market subject to powerful external pressures" (156).

12. Douglas Monroy, for example, asserts that, though not rigidly feudal, the hacienda system in Alta California retained traces of feudalism as it adapted to the contractions and expansions of the market. While it had "certain characteristics in common with other socioeconomic systems in North America, neither chattel nor market structures adequately describe the way [it] organized production or . . . social relations" (Monroy, *Thrown among Strangers*, 100).

13. José Manuel Salvador Vallejo, "*Notas históricas sobre California*" (1874), BANC MSS C–E 65:10, quoted in Sánchez, *Telling Identities*, 172.

14. Ibid.

15. Symbolically replacing the Spanish colonial official as the arbiter of political and economic power, the *hacendado*, "the main beneficiary of the revolution for independence, the natural representative of large private property and local particularism . . . [made] his interests prevail over those of other social classes" (Semo, 157).

16. Chevalier indicates that hacienda masters "enjoyed considerable discretionary

powers in the dispensing of justice to their workers." Abuses were particularly frequent in the northern provinces, "where many masters were military men called upon to exercise the functions of chief peace officer in their districts" (Chevalier, 295–96).

17. History, as Trouillot reminds us, begins with the "materiality" of the past, with "bodies and artifacts: living brains, fossils, texts, buildings . . . monuments, diaries, censuses, political boundaries, etc." And yet the physical traces that history leaves "limit the range and significance of any historical narrative" (Trouillot, 29).

18. Migration from Mexico to the north during this time must also be understood as an effect of Mexican modernization. As William G. Robbins indicates in his book *Colony and Empire: The Capitalist Transformation of the West*, while the "transforming influences of industrial capitalism (and capitalist agriculture) weighed heavily in laying the groundwork for the revolutionary turmoil that ravaged Mexico," the migration of Mexicans to the north during the revolution "should be placed firmly in the larger context of geopolitics, its most significant features being foreign investments in Mexico during the rule of Porfirio Díaz and the socioeconomic dislocation that followed" (Robbins, 34).

19. Following the U.S. incorporation of Texas, a "structure of peace" between the victorious Anglos and the defeated Mexican elite ensured the survival of the latter, and thus a semblance of the old ranching order, at least until late in the nineteenth century (Montejano, 34). Flores emphasizes, however, that "while some semblance of a 'Mexican' social order persisted in the ranching communities of South Texas, it was now adjudicated through the power of Anglo interests. This relationship of accommodation served to introduce a hierarchical relationship between these two groups . . . along [an] ethnic and racial divide" (R. Flores, *Remembering the Alamo*, 8–9). By contrast, Alonzo contends that by the latter part of the nineteenth century the large landholdings of the old Mexican elite had been subdivided among *ranchero* descendants, indicating that a "landed Mexican elite," as spoken of by Montejano and Flores, did not exist (Alonzo, 256–57).

20. For a description of the status of the Mexican worker during this period, see Emilio Zamora's *The World of the Mexican Worker in Texas*. Zamora shows that, "[a]lthough some Mexicans in places like deep South Texas, the Nueces County area, and San Antonio managed to maintain ownership over their land and businesses . . . the great majority worked as laborers in the farms, railroads, and urban-based low-wage industries throughout the state" (E. Zamora, 10).

21. The population of native peoples in the region suffered a more dramatic decline during the same period. In 1769, when the first colonists from New Spain arrived in the frontier north, the native population of Alta California may have been as high as 300,000. Due to introduced diseases, starvation, relocation, forced labor, warfare, and murder, under both the Hispanic/Mexican order and the American, by 1860 the Indian population had declined to 30,000 (Anderson, Barbour, and Whitworth, 18). In the coastal region where most Spanish and Mexican land grants were situated, the native population had fallen from 135,000 to 98,000 between 1770 and 1832 (Monroy, 244). By the late nineteenth century, the native population had declined to only some 20,000 survivors (Simmons, 48).

22. Robert Cleland's 1940 portrait of the Californios, *The Place Called Sespe: The History of a California Ranch*, reflects the lasting influence of the mission myth in the modern era: "During the period of Spanish-Mexican rule, the Californians were a pastoral people, with simple standards of living and unaffected social customs. Holding the naive philosophy that tranquillity and leisure were among the major virtues, they lived untroubled by the complex problems of the modern world, free from the strain and fret of economic competition, in a 'land of the large and charitable air.'. . . To such a people life presented few problems or vexatious responsibilities" (Cleland, 45).

23. Carey McWilliams finds "astonishing" and "baffling" the presence of an element

NOTES TO PAGES 45–48

of masochism in the legend, "with the Americans, who manufactured the legend, taking upon themselves full responsibility for the criminal mistreatment of the Indian and completely exonerating the Franciscans." The Indian question arose, according to the pastoral myth, "only after American 'civilization' took from the red man their lands and gave them nothing in return" (McWilliams, *Southern California*, 70).

24. The land that Rancho San Francisco occupied was granted in 1839 to the San Fernando mission's administrator, Antonio del Valle. See Richard Griswold del Castillo's "The Del Valle Family and the Fantasy Heritage" for a history of the family from its acquisition of Rancho San Francisco to 1938. Griswold del Castillo discusses the influence of Jackson's visit to Rancho Camulos on the writing of *Ramona*.

25. The Spanish grandee, or don, embodied an agrarian ideal strikingly similar to what the southern cavalier/planter personified for nineteenth-century Americans. Amid the alienating effects of modernity, writes William R. Taylor, Americans "longed for a class of men immune to acquisitiveness, indifferent to social ambition and hostile to commercial life, cities, and secular progress." Many American writers of this era "were attracted by the idea of a conservative country gentry such as England possessed . . . only purer and better" (Taylor, 139). The southern planter seemed "almost perfectly suited to fill the need. His ample estates, his spacious style of life, his Cavalier ancestry and his reputed obliviousness to money matters gained him favor in the eyes of those in search of a native American aristocracy" (140–41). C. Vann Woodward similarly emphasizes that northern writers, such as Herman Melville and Henry James, who took an interest in southern culture "were not very seriously concerned to 'know Southerners' or to bother themselves very deeply about the problem of Southern identity and heritage." To the contrary, "[w]hat they *were* . . . deeply concerned about was what had overtaken their own society since the Civil War, the mediocrity, the crassness, and the venality they saw around them." For these writers "the South or the Southern hero, past or present, was a useful foil for the unlovely present or the symbol of some irreparable loss" (Woodward, 137).

    Carey McWilliams comments on the irony of the Spanish grandee/southern planter parallel: "Today the typical *Californio* occupies . . . a social position that might best be compared with that of the widow of a Confederate general in a small southern town. On all ceremonial occasions, the 'native Californians' are trotted forth, in their faded finery, and exhibited as 'worthy representatives of all that is finest in our Latin-American heritage.'. . . In community after community, the Anglo-Americans genuflect once a year before the relics of the Spanish past" (McWilliams, *North from Mexico*, 39).

26. Consider the following 1890 account by Guadalupe Vallejo, the nephew of Mariano Guadalupe Vallejo: "It seems to me that there never was a more peaceful or happy people on the face of the earth than the Spanish, Mexican, and Indian population of Alta California before the American conquest. . . . [W]e often talk together of the days when a few hundred large Spanish ranches and Mission tracts occupied the whole country from the Pacific to the San Joaquin. No class of American citizens is more loyal than the Spanish Californians, but we shall always be especially proud of the traditions and memories of the long pastoral age before 1840. Indeed, our social life still tends to keep alive a spirit of love for the simple, homely, outdoor life of our Spanish ancestors on this coast" (G. Vallejo, 1).

27. Antonio Coronel appears as a character in Alejandro Morales's intriguing novel, *Reto en el paraíso* (1983), one of the few Mexican American fictions to interrogate the Californio historical legacy. In contemporary Southern California, Dennis Berreyesa Coronel, employed by the white family whose ancestors in the late nineteenth century dispossessed the Coronel family, seeks out his history by reading the memoirs left by his great-grand-uncle, the wealthy rancher Antonio Coronel. But rather than discovering in the manuscript a redemptive (Cali-

fornio) utopian space, Dennis instead uncovers the vexed status of Californio aristocrats in the aftermath of dispossession and displacement. His description of several photographs of Coronel, in which his ancestor appears dressed as a Spanish *caballero* to promote the Old (Spanish) California myth, captures Dennis's profound ambivalence toward the Californio past: "The old man is sitting on a stool in the garden, dressed up like a Spanish caballero, it looks like the photographer dressed him for a costume party. He's very old, you could probably ask the old man to do and say anything, easily manipulated. . . . All the objects in the picture seem to be props, used in an attempt to create a positive image for the consumers of the photograph. Don Antonio is presented as a rare animal dressed in old regalia reminiscent of the glorious past of the Spanish population of Los Angeles. It's a fucking photographic fabrication, a misrepresentation that distorts our history. In effect, Don Antonio is rendered a senile clown who likes to play guitar to pretty women and who lives in the past. He's not at all a danger to the dominant society" (Morales, 309).

Chapter 2

1. All citations of Vallejo's original "Recuerdos históricos y personales tocante a la Alta California" (1874) are to the English translation, "Historical and Personal Memoirs Relating to Alta California," produced by Earl R. Hewitt in 1875. All citations to Ruiz de Burton, *The Squatter and the Don* (1885) are from the Arte Público Press edition (1992).

2. See Aranda's discussion of the politics of recovery project scholarship in "Contradictory Impulses," 553.

3. For criticism that posits Ruiz de Burton and her writings as subaltern, see Sánchez and Pita's introduction to *The Squatter and the Don* or Sánchez's comparative essay on Ruiz de Burton and José Martí, "Dismantling the Colossus: Martí and Ruiz de Burton on the Formulation of Anglo América." See also José David Saldívar's remarks on Ruiz de Burton in *Border Matters* (168–83). For criticism that problematizes the "subaltern" argument, see, for example, the critical essays collected in Amelia María de la Luz Montes and Anne Elizabeth Goldman's *María Amparo Ruiz de Burton*.

4. Comparativist literary scholars identify striking convergences between Spanish America and the U.S. South that derive from these regions' parallel histories of uneven sociopolitical and economic development. Deborah Cohn explains that when Faulkner's works became available in Spanish in the early 1930s, "he and the South that he depicted captured the imagination of Spanish American writers." These writers interpreted the South's experiences, "its Civil War and resulting sense of regional difference and marginalization, its exclusion from the economic and military successes of the rest of the nation, as well as its problems of underdevelopment . . . as analogous to their own nations' struggles" (Cohn, 2). Lois Parkinson Zamora similarly observes that contemporary Latin American writers found in the literature of the U.S. South, and especially in Faulkner's work, "elements kindred to their own national experience" (L. Zamora, 33). Zamora lists these elements as (1) the guilt of the colonist who had profaned his pristine land, (2) the decadence of an irrelevant aristocracy, and (3) the injustice and racial cruelty of the white-skinned usurper (33). For a comprehensive review of recent comparative inter-American criticism, see Jon Smith and Deborah Cohn's anthology, *Look Away!*

Mexican American scholarship has separately charted literary and historical patterns of commonality between the Mexican (American) Southwest and the U.S. South or Spanish America. This body of scholarship includes José E. Limón's *American Encounters;* Ramón Saldívar's "Looking for a Master Plan"; José David Saldívar's *The Dialectics of Our America* and *Border Matters;* Rosaura Sánchez's "Dismantling the Colossus"; Beatrice Pita's "Engendering Critique"; and Luis Leal's *Aztlán y México.* Also, contemporary Chicano and Chicana fiction writers have often drawn upon "southern" literary models. Works by Alejandro

Morales, Anna Castillo, Alicia Gaspar de Alba, and Ron Arias, among many others, testify to the influence of Spanish American and U.S. southern literature on contemporary Chicano/a fiction.

5. The hacienda serves a second function in *The Squatter and the Don* and "Historical and Persoanl Memoirs." While it captures the Californio elite's anticapitalist polemic, it also suggests this group's desire for integration within post–Civil War U.S. (white) society. Hacienda identities in *The Squatter and the Don* and "Historical and Personal Memoirs" thus reflect the Californio oligarchy's contradictory impulses as a "colonized" and displaced aristocracy. At one level, this group questions U.S. rule from the position of a marginalized elite nostalgic for the pre-modern seigneurial era of Mexican national and cultural sovereignty, when it controlled the economic and political institutions of Alta California. By invoking its genteel hacienda class and "Spanish" racial and caste identities, the Californio elite, at another level, imagines a future place for itself within the U.S. (white) nation. Although the hacienda serves as a counter-discursive cultural icon, as a symbol of the Californio elite's pre-conquest racial and class positioning, it also reflects this group's contradictory cultural and political status under the new (U.S.) social order.

6. See my description of the hacienda social order in chapter 1. Monroy observes that although the California hacienda certainly bore remnants of feudalism, many other factors also shaped its agrarian society (Monroy, *Thrown among Strangers*, 182). In this region "[t]he exigencies of the Spanish empire, the profound but ambiguous spiritual and sexual inheritance from the missions, trade with the North Atlantic markets, and the curious and tempestuous bonds between ranchero and Indian laborer all recommend the word *seigneurial*— implying the rule of a 'big' man over family, laborers, and land—instead of simply *feudal*" (182; emphasis in original).

7. Weber notes that, although "many observers compared debt peonage in Mexico to slavery in the southern United States," there were fundamental differences between these two forms of coercive labor. The peon "was not legally a slave nor was peonage limited to one race. Peonage was viewed as a condition of class and bad fortune. A peon could, in theory, end his obligation by paying off his debt, and his condition was not hereditary" (Weber, *The Mexican Frontier*, 212).

8. In Alta California "[a]ffirmation of social standing, not mere accumulation of goods and capital, motivated the [*hacendados'*] aspirations for land, production, and trade. Payment in kind and the relations of reciprocal obligation attached the poor—the landless—to both the wealthy and the middling sort—the landed" (Monroy, "The Creation and Re-creation of Californio Society," 182).

9. M. G. Vallejo, letter to his wife Francisca, February 1865, quoted in Emparan, 113.

10. M. G. Vallejo, letter to his son Platón, October 1876, quoted in Emparan, 139.

11. I draw upon Elizabeth Moss's observation that nineteenth-century "southern domestic fiction essentially duplicated [plantation fiction's] setting and cast of characters." As Moss notes, "the correspondences between plantation and southern domestic fiction extended well beyond [their] superficial similarities" (Moss, 21). Examples of plantation novels include Augustus Baldwin Longstreet's *Georgia Scenes* (1835), John Pendleton Kennedy's *Swallow Barn; or, A Sojourn in the Old Dominion* (1832), and Thomas Nelson Page's *In Ole Virginia* (1887). Representative southern domestic novels include Caroline Gilman's *Oracles for Youth* (1852), Caroline Lee Hentz's *Eoline; or, Magnolia Vale* (1852), Augusta Evans's *Beulah* (1859), and Maria McIntosh's *Charms and Counter Charms* (1848). For a recent study of the plantation novel, see Scott Romine's *The Narrative Forms of Southern Community*. For studies of southern domestic fiction, see Elizabeth Moss, *Domestic Novelists in the Old South*, and Anne Goodwyn Jones, *Tomorrow Is Another Day*.

12. In an earlier piece, González makes a similar argument: "The lingering traces of Reconstruction's dramatic restructuring of U.S. nationalism during a rapidly developing regime of capitalist expansion haunt *The Squatter and the Don*'s pro-

ject of renegotiating the class and racial standing of the Californios within the state's own legal, political and economic processes" (J. M. González, "Romancing Hegemony," 33). The novel, in this view, negotiates the "treacherous parameters of race and class to create a place within the newly ascendant 'white' nation for the Californios" (30). Hence, Ruiz de Burton "contests not the process of incorporation of California's economy and culture into the national core as such, but rather the social position accorded to the Californios within that capitalist order" (31).

13. Coronel is remembered not only for his distinguished political career but also for his contributions to literary discourse, including his influence on the writing of Helen Hunt Jackson's *Ramona*. See chapter 1.

14. This letter is cited in Sánchez and Pita, *Conflicts of Interest*, 186–87.

15. At the beginning of chapter XXII the narrator of the novel hints at its biographical purpose: "Biographies . . . are intended, or should be, admonitory; to teach men by the example of the one held up to view—be this an example to be followed or to be avoided. But if no offense be intended by the biographer, why wait until a man is forevermore beyond hearing what is said of him, before his fellows are told in what and how he surpassed them so much as to be considered worthy of special notice? If he ought to be reproved, let him know it; and if we must worship him as a hero, let him know it also" (Ruiz de Burton, *The Squatter and the Don*, 221).

16. See Sánchez's *Telling Identities* and Padilla's *My History, Not Yours* for analyses of Vallejo's text as a mediated testimonial solicited by Bancroft. Although not a subject of Bancroft's interviews, Ruiz de Burton encouraged Mexican Americans in San Diego to participate. She mailed notes and documents to Bancroft, including some written by her late husband, Henry, and by her late grandfather, José Manuel Ruiz. In a letter to Bancroft on July 15, 1878, Ruiz de Burton wrote of the importance of "historic good name" for Mexican Americans:

> No one seems to care about historic good name, and yet they are very sensitive on the subject and very jealous of any credit given to others. This I mean not only of these families, but of all the Californians in general. The fact of it is (and a very serious fact which you as a conscientious historian must not omit) that "the natives" with the loss of all this property and prestige have also lost all ambition. Without their realizing the fact, or analyzing the cause, they languidly surrender to the effect, and without struggling, or even protesting they allow themselves to be swept away to oblivion by the furious avalanche let loose upon them by the hand of the Anglo-American, the pitiless Anglo-Americans! . . . So, we must not blame the disheartened Californians if they do not rise to the importance of appreciating your work, and you, without resentment for their unambitious indifference, which is the result of their misfortune, must speak kindly of them. You can afford it. And being an American you can say many things that the American people would perhaps not accept from a foreigner. (Ruiz de Burton, *Conflicts of Interest*, 478)

17. M. G. Vallejo, letter to his son Platón, quoted in Emparan, 122.

18. Ibid., 139–40.

19. M. G. Vallejo, letter, quoted in Padilla, *My History, Not Yours*, 103–104.

20. Mrs. Darrell's sympathetic view of Californio ranchers because of their dispossession introduces the novel's central themes in chapter I (Ruiz de Burton, *The Squatter and the Don*, 55–57). She expresses similar views in chapters IV and XVII (78, 187). David Luis-Brown indicates that the "narration implicitly compares the restraint, manners, and Catholicism of Mary and the white South she represents to similar qualities in Don Mariano, contrasting these traits with the Protestant, violent temper of William and the Northeast." In this sense, "Mary's refined manners signal a potential alliance between the Southern and Californio elites" (Luis-Brown, 817).

21. Leonard Pitt notes that "the spirit, if not the letter, of the treaty promised full protection for the conquered population" (Pitt, 84). Griswold del Castillo draws a similar conclusion. "In the six decades following the ratification of the treaty," he explains, "its provisions regarding citizenship and property were complicated by legislative and judicial interpretations." In the end, "the U.S. application of the treaty to the realities of life in the Southwest violated its spirit" (Griswold del Castillo, 63). The treaty stated that Mexicans would be "admitted . . . to the enjoyment of all the rights of citizens of the United States according to the principles of the Constitution . . . [and] shall be maintained and protected in the free enjoyment of their liberty and property" (quoted in Moquin and Van Doren, 185). But its final draft excluded Article X, a proviso that would have protected landowners. Article X stipulated that "[a]ll grants of land made by the Mexican Government or by the competent authorities, in territories previously appertaining to Mexico, and remaining for the future within the limits of the United States, shall be respected as valid, to the same extent that the same grants would be valid, if the said territories had remained within the limits of Mexico" (quoted in Griswold del Castillo, 182). As Rosaura Sánchez comments, despite "assurances in appended explanations that the United States had no intention of annulling land titles that were legitimate under Mexican law," without Article X the treaty provided little legal protection for land claimants (Sánchez, *Telling Identities,* 275).

22. See also John M. González's "Romancing Hegemony" and "The Whiteness of the Blush." Also, see note 4 above.

23. Although the novel invokes the redemptive claims of separateness by marking the boundaries of hacienda "true community," it projects a desire for future Californio integration into the post-Reconstruction United States.

24. See Sánchez, *Telling Identities,* and Padilla, *My History, Not Yours.* Both examine aspects of the text's production as a solicited autobiographical narrative, or testimonial, for Hubert Howe Bancroft's *History of California.* Although excerpts from the text have been published, the five-volume manuscript remains unpublished.

25. This contradiction appears as well in Sánchez's separate readings of *The Squatter and the Don* and "Historical and Personal Memoirs," both of which overlook the works' intertextual relation. Whereas Sánchez reads the novel, and Ruiz de Burton's life, as subaltern, in *Telling Identities* she interprets Vallejo's life and work as displaying all the repressions characteristic of the hacienda elite's class perspective. See Sánchez and Pita, introduction to *The Squatter and the Don,* as well as Sánchez, "Dismantling the Colossus" and *Telling Indentities.*

26. Padilla devotes a chapter to Mexican Californian autobiographical testimonials by María de las Angustias de la Guerra, Eulalia Pérez, and Apolinaria Lorenzana, and another to the New Mexican author Cleofas Jaramillo's *Romance of a Little Village Girl.* In the first, he interrogates Vallejo's identity as (Mexican) patriarch and particularly Vallejo's expressed nostalgic longing for the pre-conquest era when Mexican women conformed to traditional roles as virtuous and obedient wives, daughters, and sisters (Padilla, *My History, Not Yours,* 113–14).

27. Though "race did not stand as a barrier to upward mobility" in Mexican California, according to David J. Weber, the frontier population "denigrated others of darker hue, and tended to 'whiten' themselves as they moved up the social ladder by denying their Indian and black ancestry." Weber points out that "the racial biases of the nouveau riche Californios actually increased . . . in part because they sought to put themselves on an equal footing with the race-conscious Anglo-American newcomers" (Weber, *Mexican Frontier,* 215).

28. This idea should not be construed as emerging from the progressive discourse of Ruiz de Burton's era. To the contrary, as the novel's southern cultural and political affinities indicate, this criticism derives from the novel's subject: that is, the pre-capitalist seigneurial ethos of Mexican agrarian (hacienda) culture. The closing chapter draws upon the seigneurial concepts of "public morality" and

"honor" to construct its argument against (Yankee) capitalism and modernity. The American monopolists "are essentially dangerous citizens in the fullest acceptance of the word," the narrator warns. "They are dangerous citizens, not only in being guilty of violation of the law, in subverting the fundamental principles of public morality, but they are dangerous citizens, because they *lead others* into the commission of the same crimes. Their example is deadly to honorable sentiments" (Ruiz de Burton, *The Squatter and the Don*, 366; emphasis in original).

29. Ruiz de Burton, *Conflicts of Interest*, 273–74 (Ruiz de Burton's emphasis; my translation). *Who Would Have Thought It?* makes a strikingly similar anti-republican argument through the character of Don Felipe de Almenara, a Mexican aristocrat: "I am convinced that a republican form of government is not suited to the Mexicans . . . a monarchy can have nothing—ought to have nothing—objectionable to them. Of course the ideas of this continent are different from those of Europe, but we all know that such would not be the case if the influence of the United States did not prevail with such despotic sway over the minds of the leading men of Hispano-American republics. If it were not for this terrible, this *fatal* influence—*which will eventually destroy us*—the Mexicans, instead of seeing anything objectionable in [a returned monarchy], would be proud to hail a prince who, after all, has some sort of a claim to this land, and who will cut us loose from the leading strings of the United States" (Ruiz de Burton, *Who Would Have Thought It?*, 198; emphasis in original).

30. *The Squatter and the Don* represses California Indian history at two levels. First, its portrait of Don Mariano Alamar erases Vallejo's positions as military commander and hacienda seigneur. Secondly, Ruiz de Burton's husband, Capt. Henry S. Burton, who was the military commander of San Diego during a period of Indian resistance, was involved in U.S. government efforts to subjugate the native peoples of that region. George Harwood Phillips examines Captain Burton's role in Indian relations in his study of Indian resistance in Southern California. In January 1856, "Captain H. S. Burton[,] . . . fearing that hostilities were soon to begin, marched to Temecula." Meeting with Juan Antonio, an Indian leader suspected of fomenting rebellion among local tribes, "Burton advised [him] 'to go home to his people and keep them quiet, and probably something would be done for them; that their wishes would be made known to the general commanding the troops; and that they would be punished if they caused difficulties.' The captain warned him that 'six hundred well-armed men, with plenty cannon, could be brought against him immediately.'. . . Burton recommended to his superiors that Juan Antonio be kept under close surveillance, that once every four to six weeks a detachment of troops, twenty-five to thirty enlisted men under a commissioned officer, be sent to visit him" (Phillips, 133).

31. Vallejo's brother Salvador presents his own account of Mariano's exploits as *caudillo* and conqueror of the Northern California frontier in a separate autobiographical narrative. Salvador notes that after much warfare in Sonoma, his brother's military forces "controlled the great Prince Solano and four hundred natives, [who,] united to eight thousand warriors of that Chieftan [*sic*][,] could easily have taken possession of the whole country." He recalls that "in Sonoma and Petaluma General M. G. Vallejo possessed cattle and grain in such a quantity as to cause admiration; of the small arms and guns I will say nothing for that fact being so generally known does not require for me to enumerate every class of weapons contained in his arsenal of Sonoma." His brother's success as a *caudillo* depended on both military and political prowess. For it was "only through cunning, hard fighting, and diplomacy that M. G. Vallejo succeeded in getting a permanent foothold in the valley of Sonoma, and keeping it afterward by following the astute policy of the ancient Romans, who created dissensions among the neighbors for the purpose of afterwards being called to act as mediators" (J. M. S. Vallejo, 93).

32. Brenner, quoted in Sánchez, *Telling Identities*, 139.

33. See, for example, George Fitzhugh's famous indictment of northern industrialism in *Cannibals All! or, Slaves without Masters* (1857).

Chapter 3

1. Though written in the 1930s and early 1940s, *Caballero* was first published in 1996. Eve Raleigh was the pen name of Margaret Eimer, a Missourian who, according to the novel's recoverer and editor, José E. Limón, "had a considerable hand in the writing of *Caballero*." Though Raleigh's specific role in the writing of the novel remains unclear, Limón states that "the historical material, the plot of ethnic conflict, and the characters" were based on González's "professional research and cultural background" (Limón, "Mexicans," 243). He refers to González's scholarly research as a folklorist and cultural historian who during the late 1920s and early 1930s recorded "the customs and traditions of her native [South Texas] community" (242). *Dew on the Thorn*, a novel written solely by González during the 1920s and 1930s, was published in 1997.

2. *Caballero*'s hacienda theme and setting suggest that González and Raleigh were familiar with southern plantation and domestic narratives, a literary tradition that extends to the early nineteenth century when white southerners first began to shape in writing a distinctive regional identity in opposition to the North. Some of the better-known plantation narratives include John Pendleton Kennedy's *Swallow Barn; or, A Sojourn in the Old Dominion* (1851), Thomas Nelson Page's *In Ole Virginia; or, Marse Chan and Other Stories* (1887), and Thomas Dixon's *The Leopard's Spots* (1902), as well as later narratives of plantation community such as Margaret Mitchell's *Gone with the Wind* (1936) and William Faulkner's *Absalom, Absalom!* (1936). As a professionally trained Texas historian and folklorist, and as an aspiring novelist, González would have had at least some familiarity with these early literary narratives of southern society. González was educated at the University of Texas under the guidance of the romantic folkloristic ethnographer J. Frank Dobie, whose works apologized for the Anglo American colonization of South Texas—one carried out primarily by southerners—during an era when Texas historiography was dominated by folkloristic historian Walter Prescott Webb.

3. Limón writes that "it seems impossible that [González] would not have known Mexico's most famous romance novel and its revered author—Ignacio Altamirano's *El Zarco: Episodes of Mexican Life in 1861–63*—published in 1901 and extremely popular in Mexico in [the] formative years of González's literary life. . . . Like *Caballero* Altamirano's work has as its theme the overcoming of deep social divisions through romance and it foregrounds war, guerrillas, and young lovers of opposed racial backgrounds" (Limón, introduction to *Caballero*, xx).

4. Although he emphasizes the "Texas preference for a western historical heritage," Arnoldo De León describes some of these contemporary southern ties in his analysis of topographical identities in Texas: "Southernness does endure in attitudes toward race relations; literary themes, which include a pastoral past of corn and cotton lands, and of sharecropping farmers in overalls; the popularity of country-and-western music, which, of course, borrows from the blues of the black South; the use of the 'southern drawl'; and the kinship to the fundamentalist South. Texans have also given support to southern-style traditionalism and provincialism, as evidenced in the predominance of the Democratic Party until the 1970s and its faithfulness to states' rights. It is also apparent in a lingering attachment Texans have to the Civil War. Until rather recent times, the Confederate flag waved during some of the Friday-night football games, and teams still go by such names as the Rebels" (De León, 269).

5. The novel's identification of Mexican Texas as a conquered region is "repressed" in the sense that the romances do not validate protagonist Don Santiago's persistent Mexican nationalism. I draw on Limón's observation that González's folklore writings "at times [appear] to be repressing a certain admiration for . . .

[the Mexican lower] classes and an acknowledgment of the state of war" between the Mexican border community and Anglo Americans. "From the beginning," states Limón, "this contradiction is evident in her work" (Limón, *Dancing with the Devil*, 62).

6. I base my view that Mitchell's novel may have served as the inspiration for *Caballero* not only on the striking similarities between their respective stories and settings but also on *Gone with the Wind*'s popularity during the era in which *Caballero* was written. In a letter that González wrote to a friend in June 1978, she mentions having "re-read" *Gone with the Wind* and being favorably impressed. The letter is in the E. E. Mireles and Jovita González de Mireles Papers, Special Collections and Archives, Bell Library, Texas A&M University–Corpus Christi, which contains the original manuscript of *Caballero*, long rumored to exist but seen for the first time since the authors' unsuccessful effort to publish it in the 1940s.

7. Like slaves escaping from the plantation, the hacienda peons, given a chance to flee because of the American occupation, immediately leave Rancho La Palma. The narrator validates their departure as an escape from feudalistic oppression. Earlier, the narrator conveys sympathy for the plight of the hacienda "slave." Don Santiago feels the "gnaw of regret" after whipping an elderly peon. Though he attempts to rationalize the incident, the peon's "grief-stricken eyes" haunt him (J. González and Raleigh, 172). The don then sees a ghostly vision, a man who describes himself as "the part given you by your splendid mother . . . [who once] lived with you." The man "held out a hand and smiled. He had a warming sweet smile. 'Your choice is now. You can be the man you are, or the one I am.'" Rather than embracing this figure, Don Santiago recoils and tries to strike him (173). Cotera calls this figure an "image of compassion and acceptance, the feminine locked within [the don's] masculine identity" (Cotera, "Hombres Necios," 343–44). This ethereal vision, coming just after his act of violence against the helpless peon, "reminds the patriarch that to be the legitimate master of Rancho La Palma, he cannot rule over its inhabitants with his 'heel on their necks'" (343). Disrupting the pastoral motif, in such scenes *Caballero* identifies the class-based iniquities of the hacienda social order.

8. Though not as well known as their male counterparts (mentioned in endnote 2 above), nineteenth-century southern domestic novelists such as Gilman, Evans, and McIntosh "left a lasting impression on the American imagination," according to Elizabeth Moss. "Writing in the language of domesticity," these writers "appealed to the women of America, using the images of home and hearth to make a case for Southern culture" (Moss, 29). Contrasting the (southern) plantation home to the (northern) market world, they sought to defend the South when it faced threats from its powerful regional rival. In Gilman's geography, for example, "the plantation is Home and the city is the Other—not quite the same thing as a dichotomy between good and evil, but a sharp duality of values nonetheless" (MacKethan, 232). While they believed in the fundamental superiority of their native region and its slavery-dependent social order, they placed the southern aristocratic female at the center of the project to define and defend her community. As Moss explains, these women writers believed that "through the development of her physical, intellectual, and moral faculties, the discharge of her feminine responsibilities, and the proper use of her 'influence' . . . the aristocratic Southern female could protect her community from Northern encroachment; conversely, by succumbing to the myriad temptations that [were] associated exclusively with northern society, that same woman could precipitate regional decline" (Moss, 10). For this reason twentieth-century southern women writers such as Ellen Glasgow and Elizabeth Lyle Saxon, who "rebelled against what they perceived as the oppressive bonds of contemporary southern womanhood," invoked "domestic fiction in their literary definition of the South's 'new woman'" (6). *Gone with the Wind* remains the crowning achievement of southern domestic fiction. Mitchell's novel symbolically brought to a climax a decades-long series of pastoral southern literary works and historical,

cultural, and racial developments that helped create the atmosphere in which a hacienda romance like *Caballero* could be written.

9. Richard Slotkin points out that in the typical plantation novel "the sexual identities of the partners suggest that the reconciliation requires the submission of one to the other, with the virile or southern position dominant. The imagery of the plantation novel assimilates to the planter class an abstraction of those heroic traits which had been associated with various figures (and classes) in the Myth of the Frontier" (Slotkin, 144).

10. As Elizabeth Fox-Genovese observes, in *Gone with the Wind* Mitchell "raises all of the questions of female identity, role, and sexuality that figured in American consciousness during the first three decades of the twentieth century" (Fox-Genovese, 393). Scarlett O'Hara stands apart from the other female characters in the novel "because for her alone . . . do the years of the war and its aftermath render problematical the question of appropriate gender role—the definition of being, the aspiration to become, a lady" (399).

11. González summarized in her master's thesis what the seigneurial code of honor meant for Mexican women: "A man was expected to have his escapades, in fact the more conquests, the more of a Don Juan he was, the greater glory to his name. But woe to the woman, wife, daughter or sister, who dared by her actions to besmirch family honor. An action which in a man was overlooked as insignificant was an unpardonable offense for a woman. As the repository of family honor, woman was always under the direct rule of man. When she married she passed from her father's dominion to that of her husband's. As in most Spanish countries, her position was a contradiction. She had complete control in home management, yet she lived a life of conventual seclusion. Married at an early age, and not for love, but for family connections and considerations, she made a submissive wife and an excellent mother" (J. González, "Social Life," 58).

12. Red personifies an "industrialist" ethic antithetical to traditional southern doctrine. W. J. Cash observes that "it was the conflict with the Yankee which really created the concept of the South as something more than a matter of geography, as an object of patriotism, in the minds of Southerners" (Cash, 66). After the Civil War, in southern plantation and domestic fiction the northern carpetbagger served as metonymic foil to everything constructed as traditionally southern. Despite Red's ostensible sympathy for the plight of border Mexicans and relative immersion in their culture, *Caballero* also portrays him as an amoral opportunist who adopts a foreign (i.e., Mexican and Texan) identity to further his business enterprises, particularly his political aspirations in postwar South Texas. Red's political agenda marks him as an analogue to the southern conception of the northern interloper during Reconstruction who meddled in regional politics without regard for the interests of the southern (white) population. Red's political mantra drives home the parallel. As the narrator notes, "The end, [Red] was certain, justified the means, therefore [deception] was entirely fair" (J. González and Raleigh, 214).

13. Note the following passage in González's master's thesis: "Mexicans considered the Americans in Texas as interlopers, no less than vandals, who had by deception and intrigue deprived them of one of their states. They looked indiscriminately upon all Americans as aggressors, waiting for the opportunity to deprive them of their personal possessions as they had deprived the mother country of a whole province. On the other hand, the Americans looked upon the Mexicans as a conquered, inferior race, despised because of their inability to check American advances. Because they were the conquered race the Mexicans were considered cowards and everything that was low and despicable" (J. González, "Social Life," 10–11).

14. At the end of *The Adventures of Huckleberry Finn*, the boy hero intends to "light out" for the territories, bringing him into proximity to Greater Mexico during the period leading up to the U.S.-Mexican War. As a southerner, Huck could possibly

have arrived in Mexico's northern territory of Tejas (Texas) y Coahuila, whose American settlers were predominantly pro-slavery southerners. In *Caballero* Warrener of course embodies this early U.S. southern influence in Texas.

15. See E. Zamora, *The World of the Mexican Worker in Texas*, which covers the late nineteenth and early twentieth centuries. According to Montejano, there was little change in the status of peons in the region in the short or long term. He explains that U.S. "annexation had merely changed the complexion of the landowning elite," which meant that "after the American business elite displaced Mexican ranchers from their land, the life of the landless Mexicans remained generally unaffected and unchanged." Under Anglo American ownership, "the work relations that linked Anglo '*patron*' and Mexican worker remained paternalistic and patriarchal," and the hacienda/ranch "remained the dominant social and economic institution of the border region." The Anglo cattle barons established an "economic, social, and political feudalism" similar to that of the Mexican rancher elite. In short, "the development of the cattle industry required no fundamental changes in traditional labor relations" (Montejano, 80). The longevity of the hacienda as a social institution was due to this resiliency; the paternalism of the former Mexican system was transposed to the later American structure (76).

16. The scholarly research that González did during the 1920s and 1930s as a folklorist and historian of her native border community forms the basis of *Caballero*'s historical tale. See her 1930 master's thesis, "Social Life in Cameron, Starr, and Zapata Counties."

17. As Montejano comments, "Landed Mexicans represented the complicating factor in the Mexican-Anglo relations of the frontier period. Even during the worst times of Mexican banditry, the permanent Mexican residents who were landowners were seen as 'good citizens' while the large 'floating' population employed on ranches were seen as sympathizers of the raiders who opposed the Americans" (Montejano, 52).

18. According to Weber, "After their victory, Anglo-American rebels controlled not only Texas, but the writing of its history. They adopted the story line of their propagandists and added an additional twist—they portrayed themselves as heroic, a superior race of men. Heroes needed villains, and Texas's earliest historians found them full-blown, nurtured in the Hispanic past. . . . Painting the Spanish era in dark hues enabled Texas historians to contrast it with the Texas rebellion" (Weber, *Spanish Frontier*, 339–40).

19. See Limón's discussion of the historical and cultural parallels between Greater Mexico and the U.S. South in *American Encounters*, 7–33.

20. I draw on Limón's comment that "their marriage is to be based not on rapturous love but on what I shall call convenience with consciousness and conscience and on respect and deep mutual admiration" (Limón, "Mexicans," 246).

21. Despite its ambiguities, *Caballero*'s affirmation of the progressive impact of (U.S.) modernity in South Texas differs sharply from Vallejo's conflicted (patriarchal) consciousness in "Historical and Personal Memoirs." *Caballero*'s depiction also underscores the radically divergent views of modernity presented in Carrillo's *The California I Love* as opposed to my grandfather's "Memorias." As both a nostalgic reflection on Old (Spanish) California and Algeresque Hollywood autobiography, Carrillo's text presupposes the benefits of the "American way" in a region once dominated by the semifeudal Mexican ranch system. For my grandfather, however, nostalgia for the Mexican hacienda past served as a statement against his aggrieved socioeconomic condition as a farm laborer within the U.S. social order.

22. In her master's thesis González identifies *Caballero*'s related objectives in her description of the League of United Latin American Citizens (LULAC). González helped found that political organization in the 1920s, and its integrationist platform informs her novel:

[T]here has always existed a group of educated, cultured Mexican families who have always been leaders in their communities. From this class and from the newly created middle class have arisen men who, conscious of the needs of their fortunate fellow citizens, want to bring them out of the political apathy to which they have succumbed. These new leaders are anxious to awake the Mexican-Americans to the realization that they are American citizens and that as such they must demand and exercise their rights. In order to carry this out two things are of the utmost importance[:] they must be educated as to what are their political and civil rights and they must learn the English language. This does not necessarily mean that the Mexican-Americans should forget their racial origin and their language. What these leaders propose to do is to arouse the political pride of these people by reminding them of their past traditions. The educated Mexican-American citizens realize the possibilities of their race and are fired by the desire to organize this element for the sole purpose of hastening the political development of their people. (J. González, "Social Life," 95–96)

Chapter 4

1. Carrillo wrote his memoirs sometime between 1955 and 1961.

2. "Declaration to the Chamber of Deputies . . . Regarding the Reparation and Administration of the Pious Funds." These were thirteen recommendations advocating a program of short-term leases for the mission properties as an alternative to secularization (Cleland, 33).

3. For an analysis of the myth of Old (Spanish) California, see the discussion in chapter 1. For an early work that contributed to the formation of the myth, see Hubert H. Bancroft's *California Pastoral: 1769–1848* (1888). And for a similar example from Carrillo's own era, see Nellie Van de Grift Sanchez's *Spanish Arcadia* (1929).

4. Although recovery project editors have republished Ruiz de Burton's novels, they rejected a recent proposal to republish Carrillo's autobiography.

5. Through his participation in various "Spanish Days" celebrations, as early as the 1930s Carrillo cultivated a public image for himself as the embodiment of the region's Spanish agrarian past. Among such celebrations mentioned in his autobiography are the Rancheros Visitadores and Old Spanish Days Fiesta in Santa Barbara and the "Spanish Vaquero" procession in the Tournament of Roses Parade. Carrillo, because of his screen fame, did more than any other individual to popularize California's Spanish "fantasy heritage" from the 1930s through the 1950s.

6. Flores also recovered and edited De Zavala's work, which was republished in 1996 by Arte Público Press through the Recovering the U.S. Hispanic Literary Heritage project.

7. Between 1929 and 1950 a number of actors played the Cisco Kid in twenty-three motion pictures. He was first portrayed by Warner Baxter, then by Cesar Romero, Gilbert Roland, and Duncan Renaldo. Renaldo returned to the role in the television show. Carrillo did not appear in any of the motion picture versions. Though the Cisco Kid was based on a villainous Anglo character in O. Henry's 1907 short story "The Caballero's Way," he was transformed in the 1929 movie *In Old Arizona* into a cowboy hero of Spanish Castilian heritage. The Latin characterization remains unchanged in films and television.

8. See, e.g., Francisco Lomelí's "Contemporary Chicano Literature, 1959–1990" (88–89), in which he analyzes what is described as Carrillo's "false" representation of Mexican American history and culture in *The California I Love*. Carrillo's film career is briefly referenced in relation to this "false" consciousness. Lomelí's view will be discussed later in the chapter.

9. See Bogle, 36–37.

10. As Donald Bogle explains, the tom "was the first in a long line of socially accept-able Good Negro characters. Always as toms are chased, harassed, hounded, flogged, enslaved, and insulted, they keep the faith, never turn against their white massas, and remain hearty, submissive, stoic, generous, selfless, and oh-so-very kind. Thus they endear themselves to white audiences and emerge as heroes of sorts" (Bogle, 6).

11. Drawing upon Bhabha, José Limón observes that in the Southwest certain stereotypes of Mexicans have functioned at the "intra-psychic" level. In his reading of the "theme of sexualized desire within domination" as projected in the classic western film *High Noon*, Limón notes that as an object of sexual desire "the figure of the Mexican woman . . . represents something repressed but longed for by the dominant culture" (Limón, *American Encounters*, 132). For Limón, "the American cowboy, the Mexican female figure of forbidden sexual-ity, and the 'prim and proper' figure of the Anglo woman represent a scenario of ambivalence played out in partial and unconscious challenge to the ruling cul-tural order" (111).

12. By revealing the "boundaries of colonial discourse" and enabling a "transgres-sion of these limits from the space of that otherness," Bhabha's concept affirms a space of resistance for the "colonized" (Bhabha, 67). Through ambivalence, as Robert Young explains, Bhabha seeks out "the hesitancies and irresolution of what is being resisted" (R. Young, 145). Because "[c]olonial discourse does not merely represent the other . . . so much as simultaneously project and disavow its difference . . . [because it is] a contradictory structure articulated according to fetishism's irreconcilable logic . . . its mastery is always asserted, but is also always slipping, ceaselessly displaced, never complete" (143). Ambivalence thus produces a profound disturbance of the authority of colonial discourse (Lamming, 13).

13. Quinn's autobiography, *The Original Sin: A Self-Portrait* (1972), traces the actor's family history to revolutionary Mexico and foregrounds his working-class *mes-tizo* (i.e., Mexican and Irish) lineage.

14. Mexican American intellectuals such as Arthur Campa, Ramón Ruiz, and Manuel P. Servin also criticized the myth, along with white radicals such as Louis Adamic and Ruth Tuck (Rosales, 81).

15. Carrillo's performance as the genteel hacienda don in an era when the Cali-fornio community had been dispossessed and displaced recalls the U.S. southern response to northern domination in the early twentieth century. As Robert Gray keenly notes, southerners "who benefitted from the changed conditions—the shopkeepers who extended credit, the merchants and bankers who represented Northern interests—lost no time, once they had acquired wealth, in looking back to [antebellum] days and trying to imitate them." This strategy involved "acquiring land with the same indefatigable industry that [planters] once had, discovering ancestors among once-prominent slave-holding families, and in general reinventing their own past along with that of their region" (Gray, 89).

16. For a history of Carrillo's *rancho*, see Dale Ballou May's article, "'The Adobe Is My Birthstone.'" May observes that the widespread popularity of the mission myth made "Spanish" *rancho*-inspired architecture very much in vogue during the 1920s and 1930s. As she explains, "General and specialized literature described ranch house plans, and current magazines capitalized upon, and per-haps even encouraged, the style's popularity. . . . In fact, the style became so popular that architect Cliff May became famous for his western ranch house designs, adapting them to the needs of individual clients" (May, 234).

17. See Mary Sainte Thérèse Wittenburg's history, *The Machados and Rancho La Ballona.*

18. Carrillo's visit to the former Machado ranch would have occurred sometime between 1915 and 1920, at the height of Los Angeles's real estate boom, which was orchestrated in part through promotion of the mission myth.

19. Consider, for example, the following 1890 account by Guadalupe Vallejo, the nephew of Mariano Guadalupe Vallejo: "It seems to me that there never was a more peaceful or happy people on the face of the earth than the Spanish, Mexican, and Indian population of Alta California before the American conquest. . . . [W]e often talk together of the days when a few hundred large Spanish ranches and Mission tracts occupied the whole country from the Pacific to the San Joaquin. No class of American citizens is more loyal than the Spanish Californians, but we shall always be especially proud of the traditions and memories of the long pastoral age before 1840. Indeed, our social life still tends to keep alive a spirit of love for the simple, homely, outdoor life of our Spanish ancestors on this coast" (G. Vallejo, 1).

20. Born in 1861, De Zavala was the granddaughter of Lorenzo de Zavala, a Mexican statesman who served as interim vice-president when the Republic of Texas was proclaimed.

21. Carrillo's performance of the Spanish myth may also have had a pragmatic rationale. Carrillo was an accomplished actor and performer who, in an era when ethnic actors faced racial barriers, forged a long career in Hollywood. Through his performance of the Old California myth Carrillo clearly sought public adulation within U.S. mass culture. He may also have viewed his offscreen *caballero* persona as a strategy for enhancing his acting career. At the end of his life it may have even become an important source of income for him. After his television series ended in 1956, Carrillo assembled and toured in a show entitled *Leo Carrillo and Company* in which he acted as master of ceremonies for a group of Hispanic musicians and other performers (Aaker, 122).

Chapter 5

I would like to acknowledge the assistance and support of my aunt, Esther Pérez Doran, in the writing of this chapter. The daughter and eldest child of Francisco Róbles Pérez, she was also the first Pérez to attend college. Esther retired from the Veterans Administration Medical Center in West Los Angeles, where she worked as a nurse educator and clinical nurse specializing in post-traumatic stress disorder. Now, as a marriage and family therapist, she counsels Spanish-speaking clients who are victims of such crimes as domestic violence and sexual assault. Without Esther's love, guidance, and inspiration the family history brought to light in this chapter could not have been recovered.

1. For two foundational studies of Mexican American autobiography, see Padilla's *My History, Not Yours,* and Sánchez's *Telling Identities.* Padilla's model provides the interpretive framework for my analysis of my grandfather's "Memorias" in this chapter. Chapters 2 and 4 apply Padilla's paradigm to Californio autobiographical narratives, by Vallejo and Carrillo, respectively. For two articles that engage issues linked to Padilla's analysis, see Tey Diana Rebolledo's "Narrative Strategies of Resistance in Hispana Writing" and Anne Goldman's "'I Yam What I Yam.'" The first studies to deal specifically with Chicano autobiography as a genre are Antonio C. Márquez's "Richard Rodriguez's *Hunger of Memory* and the Poetics of Experience," Padilla's "Self as Cultural Metaphor in Acosta's *The Autobiography of a Brown Buffalo.*"

2. See Ramón Saldívar's *Chicano Narrative,* and also his "Ideologies of the Self." Following Juan Bruce-Novoa's analysis of Chicano literary theory in *Retrospace,* as in earlier chapters my examination of Mexican American autobiography takes as its underlying critical assumption the need for "dialectical analysis that takes history into consideration as another text." It also embraces the critical assumption "that true dialectical thought is always self-critical" (Bruce-Novoa, *Retrospace,* 171).

3. This and all subsequent references to Padilla's model come from *My History, Not Yours.*

4. Francisco Róbles Pérez's "Memorias" is an unpublished manuscript. All subsequent paginations refer to the text that I have compiled from my transcription of two notebooks into which I copied and translated the text of the original handwritten manuscript.

5. Because I never knew my maternal grandparents, both of whom died before I was born, I was very close to my paternal grandparents, Francisco Róbles Pérez and Concepción Herrera Pérez.

6. Though my father referred to her as "aunt," Isabel "Chavela" Róbles was actually my grandfather's first cousin, the niece of Juliana Róbles and first cousin of Berta Róbles (see the Róbles family tree in chapter 5).

7. See chapter 2's analysis of Vallejo's "Historical and Personal Memoirs." Raymund A. Paredes uses the term "hacienda syndrome" to highlight contradictions in writings by early New Mexican writers and to call attention to what he identifies as the works' "contrived and derivative romanticism" (R. Paredes, 52–53).

8. Padilla's study includes close readings of women's testimonial autobiographies by Mexican Californians María de las Angustias de la Guerra, Eulalia Pérez, and Apolinaria Lorenzana. Through these readings and particularly his analysis of Angustias de la Guerra's "Ocurrencias en California" Padilla identifies the suppression of Mexican female voices within Vallejo's patriarchal rendering of Alta California history. While nostalgia for the pre-conquest era in Vallejo's "Historical and Personal Memoirs" serves an oppositional function, it also imagines a return to a period and society in which Mexican women conformed to rigidly patriarchal roles as wives, daughters, and sisters. On this point Padilla draws a clear distinction between male and female Mexican Californian autobiographical remembrance:

> Reading the women's narratives against the grain of . . . patriarchal presumption is necessary principally because the gap between women's representation by men and women's self-representation is not only disparate but often directly at odds: men remembering wives, daughters, sisters as domestically devout, cheerfully obedient, and unconcerned about men's political and business dealings before 1848, then as "necias y vanidosas" [stubborn and vain] after; women, however, seldom seating themselves in the domestic sphere but remembering rather their work in the world or, even though confined to the home, describing themselves as more prescient than men at reading the signs of American conquest in the early 1840s, more cognizant of the ways in which political factiousness and fiscal mismanagement throughout California made the country easy prey for the Americans. (Padilla, 114)

9. Because of the Chicana's marginalized social status within a patriarchal (Mexican) cultural tradition, many contemporary Chicana writers and critics have explored the questions that I raise in this chapter. Their writings have, in turn, influenced my effort to historicize my grandfather's narrative. For Chicana feminist approaches to Chicano/Mexicano culture and history, see the distinguished body of writings by Rosaura Sánchez (*Telling Identities*), Norma Alarcón (*Chicana Critical Issues*), Gloria Anzaldúa (*Borderlands/La Frontera*), Ana Castillo (*Massacre of the Dreamers*), Cherríe Moraga (*Loving in the War Years*), María Herrera-Sobek, (*The Mexican Corrido*), Mary Louise Pratt ("Yo soy Malinche"), Tey Diana Rebolledo and Eliana S. Rivero (*Infinite Divisions*), and Adelaida R. del Castillo (*Between Borders*). For two superb Chicana studies anthologies, see Gabriela Arredondo et al., *Chicana Feminisms*, and Adela de la Torre and Beatríz Pesquera, *Building with Our Hands*. A contemporary Chicano novelist who does critically interrogate early Mexican American social history is Alejandro Morales; see especially his novel *Reto en el paraíso* (1983).

10. For an analysis of this question as it has arisen in Chicano poetry, see Pérez-Torres, *Movements in Chicano Poetry*, chapters 2 and 3.

11. Mario Barrera discusses the diverse socioeconomic origins of early-twentieth-

century Mexican immigrants to the United States: "[T]he background of the immigrants prior to migrating is a little-explored topic. The impression most writers have is that the immigrants during this period were largely agricultural workers in Mexico, notwithstanding the fact that the Mexican Revolution of 1910–1920 also caused people of higher occupational categories to migrate. Still, there are indications that the immigrants were not necessarily representative of the largely rural, agricultural population in Mexico at that time" (Barrera, 67). Barrera cites a 1944 survey in San Bernardino, California, of men who had come to the United States from Mexico in the early part of the century that indicated that only about a third of them had been engaged in hacienda work in Mexico.

12. Doroteo Arango (Francisco "Pancho" Villa) (1877–1922) was the legendary general of the Division of the North, which sought to overthrow the Mexican government beginning in 1913. In March and April of 1914, in the town of Torreón, Coahuila, my grandfather and his father crossed paths with Villa's army, as they were caught in "the most grueling and bloody contest in the long annals of the Mexican Revolution" (Knight, 143). "Memorias" describes the artillery and infantry siege by Villa's army from the perspective of a child barricaded in a house with his family. After days of explosions, which included, according to my grandfather, the destruction of a nearby train filled with ammunition, and several more days of street fighting, the battle ended with the Villistas victorious. My grandfather and his family emerged from their house to search for food and water. "In the street there were mountains of dead bodies," my grandfather writes, "both soldiers and their horses, thousands of dead piled on each other in the streets, all shot and covered with blood. . . . [T]he plumes of smoke and soot made the sky look yellow, because all of the *fincas* (ranches) near the town had been burned and all of the businesses and stores in town had been sacked and burned in just a few days" (F. Pérez, 17). As the American journalist John Reed observes in his account of the battle, after the fighting ended there were "vultures gorging themselves on dead horses; the prolific executions of prisoners, the faint smell of corpses and the rising smoke of dozens of funeral pyres" (Reed, quoted in Knight, 143). While my grandfather walked through a street near his house, he discovered a revolver. He recalled dragging the gun home to give to his father. My grandfather's most vivid memory of this incident is of his father, after seeing the gift, angrily throwing it outside. He reprimanded his son harshly for drawing attention to their family during a dangerous time.

13. In a lecture at the University of Texas at Austin ("Time, Space, and Becoming: Narratives of Chicano History," Mar. 11, 1999), the historian Ramón Gutiérrez noted that the "proletarian" historical model, which designates the inception of Chicano/a history as 1910, dominates the written record. For an example of this approach to Mexican American history, see Rodolfo Acuña, *Occupied America*. For two book-length histories by Mexican American scholars that examine the Spanish and Mexican periods, see Ramón Gutiérrez's *When Jesus Came, the Corn Mothers Went Away* and Armando Alonzo's *Tejano Legacy*. Montejano also examines the Mexican period in Texas in his pathbreaking study, *Anglos and Mexicans in the Making of Texas, 1836–1986*. For a critique of Chicano historiography, see Emma Pérez's *The Decolonial Imaginary*, which identifies four Chicano historiographic typologies. The "Ideological/Intellectual" model identifies Chicanos/as as "heroes/intellectuals"; the "Immigrant/Labor" model imagines them as "immigrant laborers" and/or "colonized workers"; the "Social History of the Other" model constructs Chicanos/as as "social beings, not just workers"; and the final category, "Gendered History," argues that "Chicanos are also women, Chicanas" (E. Pérez, 5).

14. Fuentes, quoted in Martin, 260–61.

15. I will refer to "Memorias" throughout as an autobiography rather than as a *testimonio* (testimonial). The collaborative nature of my project implies, however, that my grandfather's account may also be classified as a testimonial. Sánchez has distinguished testimonials from autobiographies by identifying their collab-

orative and mediated qualities. As she explains, while autobiography "offers a self-generated/agential discursive construction of 'self' within particular social spaces," the testimonial is the product of a collaboration involving an interviewer/editor. The production of the testimonial is "mediated and filtered through a second, more powerful agency" so that its narrating voice "is othered in terms of production as well as at the discursive level." In works of this type, "narrating agency . . . is thus not simply that of the speaking subject but also that of the editing and writing subject" (Sánchez, *Telling Identities*, 8). Both the "production" and recuperation of "Memorias" are obviously mediated by my own involvement as an interviewer, editor, and critic—as well as a relative of the interviewee. The final manuscript will, for instance, include transcribed oral responses to questions posed to my grandfather during tape-recorded interviews, from which I have also drawn for my analysis in this chapter.

16. See the conclusion for an account of my grandfather's disappearance. He never returned from a 1994 trip to Mexico.

17. Matt Meier and Feliciano Ribera describe the scale of this socioeconomic cataclysm and its impact on the southwestern United States: "The 1910 revolution, a period of incredible violence and confusion, directly affected the Southwest. Out of fifteen million Mexicans an estimated one million lost their lives in the decade of revolution, and there was a large-scale displacement of people. Thousands fled from the countryside into the larger towns and cities of Mexico; at the same time other thousands fled northward to the United States. No one knows precisely how many Mexicans were involved in this great exodus; one estimate holds that more than one million Mexicans crossed over into the Southwest between 1910 and 1920" (Meier and Ribera, 108–109).

    As for my grandfather, "Memorias" suggests that he was abandoned. Any blood relatives of his father had apparently remained in Jerez during the revolution, and the war prevented communication with them. My grandfather mentions a sister of his father, but she is spoken of only in passing. Except for several half-siblings, no other living Pérez blood relatives are identified in the text. As will be discussed later in this chapter, another family, the Herreras, in-laws to Francisco's father and also from Jerez, were extremely important to my grandfather after his father died in 1919—in fact, Francisco came to the United States with the Herreras. However, my grandfather did not consider them "family"; he always felt like an outsider among them. My grandfather always felt that he had been abandoned by his stepmother, María Herrera, by whom Lira Pérez had three children. Rather than embracing her husband's son after Lira Pérez's death, she "gave" Francisco to her brothers, who were then preparing to emigrate. She and her own children never emigrated. My Aunt Esther believes that María sent Francisco to the United States so that she and her children would be able to claim Lira Pérez's property in Jerez.

    So, although my grandfather was by definition an orphan when he immigrated to the United States, he came here with members of the Herrera family and therefore was not alone and abandoned. Though not mentioned by name in "Memorias," one of the Herreras must have been the person who bought him a pair of shoes at the border (as a child in Mexico, he wore only *huaraches*, or sandals). Francisco eventually lived with the Herreras in California for several years, and, as noted later in this chapter, in 1924 he married María's youngest sister, Concepción. But when my grandfather first arrived in 1921 at the Herrera home in Yorba Linda, he had to explain to them who he was. In the middle of a celebration, as "Memorias" relates, someone pointed at Francisco and asked, "And who is he?"

18. I use "colonial" in quotes because colonialism actually ended in 1821 with Mexican independence form Spain; Lira Pérez was born in 1856. In this and earlier chapters "colonial" also denotes the sociocultural legacy of the Spanish/Mexican hacienda era.

19. The full name of my grandfather's hometown is Jerez de García Salinas. Jerez de

la Frontera, the Andalusian town famous for its sherry wine, was the birthplace of Álvar Núñez Cabeza de Vaca (1490–1560), the first Spaniard to explore North America. Cabeza de Vaca's narrative of his journey, *La relación* (The Account) (1542), is one of the first Spanish descriptions of the New World that "calls for a compassionate and tolerant policy toward the natives of the Western Hemisphere" (Favata and Fernández, 11).

20. As elaborated in chapter 1, the treatment of the indigenous peoples of Mexico took on a distinctly modern (i.e., positivist) cast during the era in which Lira Pérez prospered as a business associate of the Zacatecan *hacendados*. As Meier and Ribera write, between 1880 and 1910, "[t]he economic policies of the government were promoted by a group of positivists, who planned and worked for a modern, scientifically run Mexico which would take its rightful place in the world. They accepted that certain races were less advanced because of heredity and environment; they believed that Indians and their culture were inferior and therefore not a sound base on which to build a modern Mexico. In the name of progress they set out to Europeanize Mexico's Indians; partly as a result of positivist ideas Indians were brutally hounded, and many were sold into virtual slavery to large landowners" (Meier and Ribera, 104).

21. My grandfather's self-description as an "orphan," a trope that suggests alienation from Anglo American as well as Mexican society, contradicts theoretical models positing a transcultural Mexican (American) subject who traverses cultural borders. Several passages in "Memorias," however, indicate that my grandfather recognized in Mexican American cultural formations a new bicultural Mexican subject who did increasingly occupy a "borderland" space. Describing the distinctive "Chicano" language and culture that he encountered in Southern California, my grandfather recalled his first meeting with a group of *pochos* (acculturated, or "faded," Mexicans). On Sundays in 1922, the Mexican American community in Whittier would gather socially. As my grandfather writes, "It was there that I made a few friends, two of whom were young *pochas* born in the United States, Rosa and Luisa. One day while we were talking, one of them asked me, 'Oye, por qué no nos tritéas?' (Hey, why don't ya treat us?) To which I answered, 'Y eso, qué es?' (What do you mean?) The other said, 'Pues, que nos des una raspada o una goma.' (Well, buy us a snow cone or some gum). What they meant to say, of course, was, 'una copa de hielo raspada (a cup of shaved ice) and 'un paquete de chicle' (a pack of gum). The two spoke very poor Spanish. The *pochos* also called automobiles *carruchas*. The following week, I went out on my first date with Rosa. We went to a *borlote*, which is the word the *pochos* used for 'dance'" (F. Pérez, 22).

22. Several passages link my grandfather's personal sense of (cultural) superiority over Anglo Americans—because of his "aristocratic" hacienda past in Mexico— to racism under Jim Crow segregation. "Memorias," for example, depicts the efforts of Mexicans to attend a movie at a local segregated theater in Fillmore, California: "In the movie theater in town, which is still in business today, the racists segregated us from the whites. This, after we had worked perhaps sixty hours during the week—and six days a week. They did the same to the Mexican children; there was a separate school for them. We, of course, protested both of these actions. As we told the whites, we paid money for these services like anyone else in town. . . . In any case, the 'theater' was a cheap little shack compared to the theaters in my own country. . . . You see, almost every large town in Mexico has an opera house, quite unlike the United States" (F. Pérez, 36).

23. There were other recriminations after the 1936 strike. As Gilbert González observes, "The paternalistic attitude of the dominant community toward the villagers waned considerably. The apparent harmony between the dominant and subordinate societies proved to have been built on sand; a good jarring brought it tumbling down. In the past, growers' donations had supported village celebrations and recreational activities. Not so in the aftermath of the strike. The Placentia associations had an unusually good relationship with the village patriotic

committees, having assisted with donations of money and materials. After the strike, petitions for support for the Independence Day celebrations went the way of the union petition—even several years later they were simply ignored" (G. González, 158).

24. Aunt Esther gave me a copy of her essay as I began work on an early version of this chapter. She wrote it as an assignment for a nursing course called "Behavior Patterns" that she took while a student at California State University–Los Angeles. Keith Spalding, a member of the family that owned the Spalding Corporation and *hacendado* of Rancho Sespe, died in 1963. He left several thousand dollars in his will to my grandfather, who had been a worker at the ranch for thirty-six years. I never heard my grandfather criticize Mr. Spalding and certainly not in the manner of Esther or my own father. To the contrary, I now see that my grandfather's relationship with this landowner resembled the seigneurial "bond" between *hacendado* and laborer characteristic of traditional Mexican hacienda society, a point to which I return in the conclusion. My grandfather loved the community of Rancho Sespe as much as he did the space of the Mexican hacienda where he spent his childhood.

25. According to Rodolfo Acuña, "By 1910, foreign investors controlled 76 percent of all corporations [in Mexico], 95 percent of mining, 89 percent of industry, 100 percent of oil, and 96 percent of agriculture. The United States owned 38 percent of this investment, Britain 29 percent, and France 27 percent . . . [and] in contrast, 97.1 percent of the families in [the state of] Guanajuato were without land, 96.2 percent in Jalisco, 99.5 percent in Mexico (state), and 99.3 percent in Puebla" (Acuña, 149–50).

26. Following his father's pro-government stance during the revolution, my grandfather portrays Díaz in a flattering light. He is described in several passages as a benevolent dictator and national hero. The revolutionaries who rose up against Díaz, says my grandfather, "fought against a government that was unique in the history of Mexico . . . one that had maintained the country at the high social and economic level of the other great nations in the western world at that time" (F. Pérez, 4). Not surprisingly, Casimiro—Lira Pérez's first son, the child of his second marriage, to Matilde—joined the federal army and fought against the Maderista and, later, Villista insurrections. See note 31 for my family's theory of what became of Casimiro, whom my grandfather never saw again after he returned for a brief visit during the war.

27. "Memorias" supports its characterization of the "upper-class" status of the Pérezes in Jerez through its portrait of other members of Lira Pérez's extended family:

> My father had three nieces, named Ramirez, who were distinguished, older women in their forties, all unmarried. They were couturiers. They owned a fashion shop in the commercial zone downtown, where they sold dresses for young women and suits for men. Jerez was the [commercial] center for the outlying hacienda community, and so their shop was the only one of its kind for thirty kilometers or more around the town. These women belonged to high society . . . and lived in a mansion—surrounded by bougainvilleas—with electricity, a garden with exotic plants, and a swimming pool. You'll probably ask how they had a pool in the center of town, but I'm one step ahead of you. In that part of Jerez, there was a stream called the Río Chiquito, which passed close to their mansion, and two kilometers away was the Río Grande. But let's return for a moment to the house. My father and I were often invited to go and dine with these sisters. You see, my family had all of the same luxuries as they during the 1890–1912 period. The Ramirez sisters were one of the illustrious families [of Jerez] that have now passed into history, but I remember them as a part of my own family, of whom I am very, very proud. (F. Pérez, 12)

28. See Timothy Dow Adams's *Telling Lies in Modern American Biography*, Paul John Eakin's *Fictions in Autobiography*, and G. Thomas Couser's *Altered Egos*, as well as

Couser and Joseph Fichtelberg's *True Relations*. For a superb study of autobiographies by American women of color, see Barbara Rodríguez's *Autobiographical Inscriptions*. Couser summarizes developments in autobiography studies in the wake of structuralist and poststructuralist critiques: "The trend in autobiography studies has been to erode the distinction between fiction and nonfiction and to deconstruct the apparent relation between the self and its textual embodiment. . . . Autobiography, then, is seen not as produced by a preexistent self but as producing a provisional and contingent one. Indeed, that self is seen as bound and (pre)determined by the constraints of the linguistic resources and narrative tropes available to the 'author'" (Couser, 19).

29. Though Paulo later adopted Pérez as his legal name, he was reared by the Róbleses and never had any contact with the Pérez family. So, while Berta Róbles married a "Pérez," she wed into a family known by her own as Róbleses.

30. In his Last Will and Testament, Lira Pérez names as his only heirs four sons (including Francisco), two daughters, and his fourth wife, María Herrera, who was also his executor. My translation of part of the will reads as follows:

> In the city of Gómez Palacios, the house on North Morelos Street, on the thirteenth day of May, 1919, in the presence of the witnesses Don Filemón Turado and Don Antonio Correa, I state that, being gravely ill, and feeling that I am on the brink of death, it is necessary to set forth the following terms [of my will]. . . .
>
> I am the owner of a house in Jerez, Zacatecas. The house comprises a corner room, bedroom, kitchen, hall, living room, corral, and waterwheel/well. [I own] two tracts of land in San Juan de las Calabasas and a granary in the same location. The granary [is situated] on a smaller piece of land toward the south, but since I do not have the [proper] papers before me, I cannot specify the measurements [of any of these properties].
>
> It is my wish to leave as my only heirs my wife María Herrera and my children, named Casimiro Pérez, Marcos Pérez, Francisco Pérez, Lucas Pérez, [and] Diega and Paula Pérez. I assign to my wife the role of guardian and administrator [of my estate], whose function will be to divide the shares [of my property] in equal parts, in a manner that she is best able to carry out. With nothing more to express, I conclude the present private disposition [of my will]. Since I have no other recourse and am in a foreign region, I have not written this document in the proper legal manner before a Notary Public.

31. See the translated text of Lira Pérez's Last Will and Testament in note 30. Although my grandfather Francisco had two elder half-brothers, the older one, Casimiro, disappeared in 1914 while serving in the federal army and may have died in one of the battles of that year, while the second, Marcos, the one in the photograph taken on Independence Day, 1912, was incapacitated by mental illness and drug addiction during adolescence. My grandfather told me that in 1913, while on leave, Casimiro returned to ask their father for his portion of his inheritance. Lira Pérez sold a tract of land and gave Casimiro the money from the sale. The story from my grandfather is that Casimiro believed he would be killed in the civil war and wanted to spend the money. It seems very likely that he *was* killed in one of the battles of 1914—possibly in Torreón, where his father was living at the time. If Casimiro had survived and returned to Jerez after 1921, my grandfather would have learned of it through his younger half-siblings or perhaps through María Herrera's family. As for Marcos, if he had gone with Lira Pérez when he was forced to leave Jerez, my grandfather probably would have mentioned it. Apparently Marcos was later brought to his father in Torreón. Marcos is mentioned in "Memorias" for his odd behavior as a teenager in Torreón—namely, public nudity and petty crime. The last we hear of this half-brother is when my grandfather, leaving in 1921 to go to the United States, says goodbye to him at the train station. My grandfather says the Herrera family

never knew what became of Marcos; the story I have heard is that he left town when still a teenager and was never heard from again.

32. A number of striking parallels between my grandfather's childhood and Rulfo's early life stand out. Though born in 1918, ten years after my grandfather, Rulfo was from the state of Jalisco, which borders Zacatecas. (The name La Bufa, given to the mountain landmark near the city of Zacatecas described in my grandfather's account, comes from the hill's resemblance to an animal's bladder—an allusion used at the beginning of *Pedro Páramo*.) Both my grandfather and Rulfo were born into the upper class, though their fathers were not landed; rather, both fathers worked in a managerial capacity within the hacienda economy. My grandfather and Rulfo were both orphaned as children during the civil war. Rulfo's hometown, Apulco, was sacked and burned by armed insurgents, and his father was murdered in 1923 while fleeing. According to some scholars, Rulfo's father was killed by peasant insurrectionists, though in an interview the author denied knowing who was responsible. Rulfo's nostalgic depiction of the hacienda community of his childhood in *Pedro Páramo* employs "origins" as a central theme. A more remarkable coincidence is Rulfo's family name. After his mother died in 1927, Rulfo was taken in by her relatives in Mexico City, who required that he use their name—Pérez (the author's full name was Juan Pérez Rulfo).

33. The published version to which I refer appeared as "Heroes and Orphans of the Hacienda: Narratives of a Mexican American Family," *Aztlán* 24, no. 1 (Spring 1999): 33–106. It was reprinted in *I Am Aztlán: The Personal Essay in Chicano Studies*, ed. Chon A. Noriega and Wendy Belcher (Los Angeles: UCLA Chicano Studies Research Center, 2004).

34. Esther later explained why she felt so close to Paulo's daughter Dominga, though they had never met. Not only do she and Dominga share the same grandfather (Lira Pérez), but their grandmothers were sisters *and* their fathers were half-brothers.

35. The aggrieved status of women in nineteenth-century Mexico would certainly support this view. Describing the condition of women in Mexico City during this period, Sylvia Marina Arrom observes that "the pater familias exercised his authority without restraints[;] unencumbered by tradition of competing power; he completely controlled his wife's legal acts, property and person, being able to claim her domestic services, obedience and sexual fidelity (although the double standard granted him sexual freedom); he made all important decisions to enforce his will upon its members using whatever means he deemed necessary" (Arrom, quoted in Griswold del Castillo, "Patriarchy and the Status of Women," 86).

Lira Perez's story demonstrates that an important aspect of the ideal of patriarchal authority in Mexico involved the subordinate position of women, one long defined by tradition. As Richard Griswold del Castillo writes, "In the Iberian Catholic and the pre-Columbian traditions, women were supposed to accept absolute male authority in the household. Spanish laws, including the *Siete Partidas*, frequently described the relationship between husband and wife in monarchical terms. . . . Men were the 'rulers,' women the 'subjects'; husbands were the 'absolute monarchs' of the 'nation' of the family" (Griswold del Castillo, "Patriarchy and the Status of Women," 88).

36. Compare Padilla's model to Sánchez's in *Telling Identities*. Sánchez expands on Padilla's treatment of the socioideological meanings embedded in early Mexican American autobiographical narrative. As she puts it, her study is "rooted in cultural politics," and she thus considers "cultural production as inseparable from structural and agential relations." For that reason, it "takes on and examines the issue of representation by a subaltern population within the context of relations of production, social restructuring, and collective agency" (Sánchez, *Telling Identities*, x). Because Sánchez's model offers a more comprehensive study of that body of testimonials by Californios collected by Bancroft and because it

takes Padilla's historicist premises an important step forward through an analysis grounded in feminist, postcolonial, and especially Marxist theory, it will prove to be indispensable to the future study of nineteenth-century Mexican literature and history. And unlike Padilla's reading of Vallejo's "Historical and Personal Memoirs," Sánchez's analysis does not evade the suppression of class and caste identities characteristic of Californio autobiographical narrative.

Conclusion

1. As noted in chapter 5, the history of this strike is described in scholarly studies on Southern California's agriculture industry. See, for example, Menchaca, *The Mexican Outsiders*, 83–89.

2. "Sites of memory," as Lawrence D. Kritzman explains, are symbolic in nature "because they signify the context and totemic meaning from which collective identity emerges" (Kritzman, x).

3. Brook Thomas argues that poststructuralism is of limited use for those excluded by previous histories, since they "are in a situation in which they need not only to deconstruct discredited histories of the past, but to construct and legitimate new histories in which they are finally represented." He continues, "[I]t may be more than an irony of history that precisely at the moment when women and ethnics in this country sense the possibility of emergence and the establishment of a somewhat autonomous self, a theory is imposed from the still predominantly white, male European academy declaring that notions of emergence and a centered self are bourgeois and reactionary" (Thomas, 192).

4. Pérez identifies four typologies, reflecting the ideological perspective of the historian, that Chicano historiography has traditionally used to structure the past. See note 13, chapter 5.

5. Fanon, quoted in S. Hall, "Cultural Identity," 58.

WORKS CITED

Aaker, Everett. *Television Western Players of the Fifties: A Biographical Encyclopedia of All Regular Cast Members in Western Series, 1949–1959.* Jefferson, N.C.: McFarland, 1997.

Acuña, Rodolfo. *Occupied America: A History of Chicanos.* 2d ed. New York: HarperCollins, 1988.

Adams, Timothy Dow. *Telling Lies in Modern American Autobiography.* Chapel Hill: University of North Carolina Press, 1990.

Alarcón, Norma. *The Sexuality of Latinas.* Berkeley, Calif.: Third Woman Press, 1989.

———. "The Theoretical Subject(s) of *This Bridge Called My Back.*" In *Criticism in the Borderlands: Studies in Chicano Literature, Culture, and Ideology,* edited by Hector Calderón and José David Saldívar, 23–39. Durham, N.C.: Duke University Press, 1991.

———, ed. *Chicana Critical Issues.* Berkeley, Calif.: Third Woman Press, 1993.

Almaguer, Tomás. *Racial Fault Lines: The Historical Origins of White Supremacy in California.* Berkeley: University of California Press, 1994.

Alonzo, Armando C. *Tejano Legacy: Rancheros and Settlers in South Texas, 1734–1900.* Albuquerque: University of New Mexico Press, 1998.

Altamirano, Ignacio. *El Zarco: episodios de la vida mexicana en 1861–63.* 1901. Mexico City: Ediciones Oceano, SA, 1986.

The Americas Review: A Review of Hispanic Literature and Art of the USA 16, no. 3–4 (Fall/Winter 1988). Special issue on U.S. Hispanic autobiography.

Anderson, Benedict. *Imagined Communities: Reflections on the Origin and Spread of Nationalism.* 1983. London: Verso Press, 1983.

Anderson, M. Kat, Michael G. Barbour, and Valerie Whitworth. "A World of Balance and Plenty: Land, Plants, Animals, and Humans in a Pre-European California." In *Contested Eden: California before the Gold Rush,* edited by Ramón A. Gutiérrez and Richard J. Orsi, 12–47. Berkeley: University of California Press, 1998.

Anzaldúa, Gloria. *Borderlands/La Frontera: The New Mestiza.* San Francisco: Spinsters/Aunt Lute, 1987.

Aranda, José F., Jr. "Contradictory Impulses: María Amparo Ruiz de

Burton, Resistance Theory, and the Politics of Chicano/a Studies."
American Literature 70, no. 3 (September 1998): 551–79.

Aranda, José F., and Silvio Torres-Saillant, eds. *Recovering the U.S. Hispanic Literary Heritage, Volume IV.* Houston: Arte Público Press, 2002.

Arredondo, Gabriela F., Aída Hurtado, Norma Klahn, Olga Nájera-Ramírez, and Patricia Zavella, eds. *Chicana Feminisms: A Critical Reader.* Durham, N.C.: Duke University Press, 2003.

Arriaga, Ponciano. "The Dispossessed of Rural Mexico." In *Latin America: Conflict and Creation, A Historical Reader,* edited by E. Bradford Burns, 96–97. Englewood Cliffs, N.J.: Prentice-Hall, 1993.

Arrom, Silvia Marina. *The Women of Mexico City, 1790–1857.* Stanford, Calif.: Stanford University Press, 1985, quoted in Richard Griswold del Castillo, "Patriarchy and the Status of Women in the Late Nineteenth Century Southwest." In *The Mexican and Mexican American Experience in the Nineteenth Century,* edited by Jaime E. Rodríguez O., 85–99. Tempe, Ariz.: Bilingual Press/Editorial Bilingüe, 1989.

Assmann, Jan. "Collective Memory and Cultural Identity." *New German Critique* 65 (Spring/Summer 1995): 125–34.

Bancroft, Hubert Howe. *California Pastoral: 1769–1848.* San Francisco: The History Company, 1888.

———. *History of California.* 7 vols. San Francisco: The History Company, 1884–89.

Barrera, Mario. *Race and Class in the Southwest: A Theory of Racial Inequality.* Notre Dame, Ind.: University of Notre Dame Press, 1979.

Bazant, Jan. *A Concise History of Mexico from Hidalgo to Cardenas, 1805–1940.* Cambridge: Cambridge University Press, 1977.

Bhabha, Homi K. *The Location of Culture.* London: Routledge, 1994.

Bogle, Donald. *Toms, Coons, Mulattoes, Mammies, and Bucks: An Interpretive History of Blacks in American Films.* 1973. 3d ed. New York: Continuum, 1994.

Brady, Mary Pat. *Extinct Lands, Temporal Geographies: Chicana Literature and the Urgency of Space.* Durham, N.C.: Duke University Press, 2002.

Brenner, Robert. "The Social Basis of Economic Development." In *Analytical Marxism,* edited by John Roemer, 23–53. Cambridge: Cambridge University Press, 1986, quoted in Rosaura Sánchez, *Telling Identities: The California testimonios.* Minneapolis: University of Minnesota Press, 1995.

Bruce-Novoa, Juan, ed. *Chicano Authors: Inquiry by Interview.* Austin: University of Texas Press, 1980.

———. *Retrospace: Collected Essays on Chicano Literature.* Houston: Arte Público Press, 1990.

Brundage, W. Fitzhugh. "Introduction: No Deed But Memory." In *Where These Memories Grow: History, Memory, and Southern Identity,* edited by W. Fitzhugh Brundage, 1–28. Chapel Hill: University of North Carolina Press, 2000.

Buffington, Robert M., and William E. French. "The Culture of Modernity." In *The Oxford History of Mexico,* edited by Michael C. Meyer

Works Cited

and William H. Beezley, 397–432. New York: Oxford University Press, 2000.

Burkholder, Mark A., and Lyman L. Johnson. *Colonial Latin America*. New York: Oxford University Press, 1990.

Cabeza de Vaca, Álvar Nuñez. *The Account: Álvar Nuñez Cabeza de Vaca's Relación*. Translated by Martin A. Favata and José B. Fernández.1542. Houston: Arte Público Press, 1993.

Calderón, Hector, and José David Saldívar, eds. *Criticism in the Borderlands: Studies in Chicano Literature, Culture, and Ideology*. Durham, N.C.: Duke University Press, 1991.

Cardoso, Fernando Henrique, and Enzo Faletto. *Dependency and Development in Latin America*. Translated by Marjory Mattingly Urquidi. Berkeley: University of California Press, 1979.

Carrillo, Leo. *The California I Love*. Englewood Cliffs, N.J.: Prentice-Hall, 1961.

Cash, W. J. *The Mind of the South*. 1941. Reprint, New York: Vintage Books, 1991.

Castillo, Ana. *Massacre of the Dreamers: Essays on Xicanisma*. Albuquerque: University of New Mexico Press, 1994.

Chabram, Angie C., and Rosa Linda Fregoso. "Chicana/o Cultural Representations: Reframing Alternative Critical Discourses." *Cultural Studies* 4, no. 3 (October 1990): 203–12.

Chevalier, François. *Land and Society in Colonial Mexico: The Great Hacienda*. Translated by Alvin Eustis. 1963. Berkeley: University of California Press, 1970.

Cleland, Robert G. *The Place Called Sespe: The History of a California Ranch*. 1940. Reprint, San Marino, Calif.: Huntington Library Publications, 1957.

Cohn, Deborah N. *History and Memory in the Two Souths: Recent Southern and Spanish American Fiction*. Nashville, Tenn.: Vanderbilt University Press, 1999.

Conkin, Paul K. *The Southern Agrarians*. Knoxville: University of Tennessee Press, 1988.

Connerton, Paul. *How Societies Remember*. Cambridge: Cambridge University Press, 1989.

Cook, Sherburne F. *The Conflict between the California Indian and White Civilization*. Berkeley: University of California Press, 1976.

Corney, Frederick. "Writing October: History, Memory, Identity, and the Construction of the Bolshevik Revolution, 1917–1927." Ph.D. diss., Colombia University, 1997, quoted in W. Fitzhugh Brundage, "Introduction: No Deed But Memory." In *Where These Memories Grow: History, Memory, and Southern Identity*, edited by W. Fitzhugh Brundage, 1–28. Chapel Hill: University of North Carolina Press, 2000.

Cotera, María. "Hombres Necios: A Critical Epilogue." In *Caballero: A Historical Novel*, by Jovita González and Eve Raleigh, 339–46. College Station: Texas A&M University Press, 1996.

Couser, G. Thomas. *Altered Egos: Authority in American Autobiography*. New York: Oxford University Press, 1989.

Couser, G. Thomas, and Joseph Fichtelberg, eds. *True Relations: Essays on Autobiography and the Postmodern.* Westport, Conn.: Greenwood Press, 1998.

Davis, Mike. *City of Quartz: Excavating the Future in Los Angeles.* 1990. New York: Random House, 1992.

de la Torre, Adela, and Beatríz M. Pesquera. *Building with Our Hands: New Directions in Chicana Studies.* Berkeley: University of California Press, 1993.

Del Castillo, Adelaida R., ed. *Between Borders: Essays on Mexicana/Chicana History.* Encino, Calif.: Floricanto Press, 1990.

De León, Arnoldo. "Region and Ethnicity: Topographical Identities in Texas." In *Many Wests: Place, Culture, and Regional Identity,* edited by David M. Wrobel and Michael C. Steiner, 259–78. Lawrence: University Press of Kansas, 1997.

Deverell, William. "Privileging the Mission over the Mexican: The Rise of Regional Identity in Southern California." In *Many Wests: Place, Culture, and Regional Identity,* edited by David M. Wrobel and Michael C. Steiner, 235–58. Lawrence: University Press of Kansas, 1997.

De Zavala, Adina. *History and Legends of the Alamo and Other Missions in and around San Antonio,* edited by Richard Flores. 1917. Houston: Arte Público Press, 1996.

Dixon, Thomas. *The Leopard's Spots.* 1902. New York: Irvington Publishers, 1979.

Doran, Esther Pérez. "A Story of Death in Mexican American Culture." Unpublished essay, 1965.

Eakin, Paul John. *Fictions in Autobiography: Studies in the Art of Self-Invention.* Princeton, N.J.: Princeton University Press, 1985.

Emparan, Madie Brown. *The Vallejos of California.* San Francisco: The Gleeson Library Associates, University of San Francisco, 1968.

Fanon, Frantz. "On National Culture." In *The Wretched of the Earth.* London: Paladin Press, 1963, quoted in Stuart Hall, "Cultural Identity and Diaspora." In *Identity and Difference,* edited by Kathryn Woodward, 51–59. London: Sage, 1997.

Faulkner, William. *Absalom, Absalom!* 1936. New York: Vintage, 1972.

———. *Light in August.* 1932. New York: Random House, 1959.

———. "A Rose for Emily." In *Collected Stories,* 119–30. New York: Random House, 1956.

Favata, Martin A., and José B. Fernandez. Introduction to *The Account: Álvar Núñez Cabeza de Vaca's Relación.* Houston: Arte Público Press, 1993.

Fentress, James, and Chris Wickham. *Social Memory.* Oxford: Blackwell, 1992.

Flores, Richard. "Introduction: Adina De Zavala and the Politics of Restoration." In *History and Legends of the Alamo and Other Missions in and around San Antonio,* edited by Richard Flores, v–lviii. 1917. Houston: Arte Público Press, 1996.

———. "Public Culture, Privates Spaces: The Making of the Alamo." *Cultural Anthropology* 10 (Jan. 1995): 99–115.

Works Cited

————. *Remembering the Alamo: Memory, Modernity, and the Master Symbol.* Austin: University of Texas Press, 2002.

Flores Olague, Jesús, Mercedes de Vega, Sandra Kuntz Ficker, and Laura del Alizal. *Breve historia de Zacatecas.* Mexico City: El Colegio de México, 1996.

Foner, Eric. *Reconstruction: America's Unfinished Revolution, 1863–1877.* New York: Harper and Row, 1988.

Fox-Genovese, Elizabeth. "Scarlett O'Hara: The Southern Lady as New Woman." *American Quarterly* 33, no. 4 (Autumn 1981): 391–411.

Galarza, Ernesto. *Barrio Boy: The Story of a Boy's Acculturation.* Notre Dame, Ind.: University of Notre Dame Press, 1971.

García Márquez, Gabriel. *The Autumn of the Patriarch.* 1975. New York: Harperperennial, 1999.

————. *One Hundred Years of Solitude.* 1970. New York: HarperCollins, 1991.

Goldman, Anne. "'I Yam What I Yam': Cooking, Culture, and Colonialism." In *De/Colonizing the Subject: Politics and Gender in Women's Autobiographical Practice,* edited by Sidonie Smith and Julia Watson, 170–82. Minneapolis: University of Minnesota Press, 1992.

González, Gilbert G. *Labor and Community: Mexican Citrus Worker Villages in a Southern California County, 1900–1950.* Urbana: University of Illinois Press, 1994.

González, John M. "Romancing Hegemony: Constructing Racialized Citizenship in María Amparo Ruiz de Burton's *The Squatter and the Don.*" In *Recovering the U.S. Hispanic Literary Heritage, Volume II,* edited by Erlinda González-Berry and Chuck Tatum, 23–39. Houston: Arte Público Press, 1996.

————. "The Whiteness of the Blush: The Cultural Poetics of Racial Formation in *The Squatter and the Don.*" In *María Amparo Ruiz de Burton: Critical and Pedagogical Perspectives,* edited by Amelia María de la Luz Montes and Anne Elizabeth Goldman, 153–86. Lincoln: University of Nebraska Press, 2004.

González, Jovita. *Dew on the Thorn.* Houston: Arte Público Press, 1997.

————. "Social Life in Cameron, Starr, and Zapata Counties." Master's thesis, University of Texas, 1930.

González, Jovita, and Eve Raleigh. *Caballero: A Historical Novel.* Edited by José E. Limón and María Cotera. College Station: Texas A&M University Press, 1996.

González, Michael J. "'The Child of the Wilderness Weeps for the Father of Our Country': The Indian and the Politics of Church and State in Provincial California." In *Contested Eden: California before the Gold Rush,* edited by Ramón A. Gutiérrez and Richard J. Orsi, 147–72. Berkeley: University of California Press, 1998.

González-Berry, Erlinda, and Chuck Tatum, eds. *Recovering the U.S. Hispanic Literary Heritage, Volume II.* Houston: Arte Público Press, 1996.

Gray, Richard J. *Writing the South: Ideas of an American Region.* 1986. Baton Rouge: Louisiana State University Press, 1997.

Griswold del Castillo, Richard. "The Del Valle Family and the Fantasy Heritage." *California History* 59, no. 1 (1980): 2–15.

———. "Patriarchy and the Status of Women in the Late Nineteenth-Century Southwest." In *The Mexican and Mexican American Experience in the Nineteenth Century*, edited by Jaime E. Rodríguez O., 85–99. Tempe, Ariz.: Bilingual Press/Editorial Bilingüe, 1989.

———. *The Treaty of Guadalupe Hidalgo: A Legacy of Conflict*. Norman: University of Oklahoma Press, 1990.

Gutiérrez, David G. *Walls and Mirrors: Mexican Americans, Mexican Immigrants, and the Politics of Ethnicity*. Berkeley: University of California Press, 1995.

Gutiérrez, Ramón A. *When Jesus Came, the Corn Mothers Went Away: Marriage, Sexuality, and Power in New Mexico, 1500–1846*. Stanford, Calif.: Stanford University Press, 1991.

Gutiérrez, Ramón, and Genaro Padilla, eds. *Recovering the U.S. Hispanic Literary Heritage*. Houston: Arte Público Press, 1993.

Haas, Lisbeth. *Conquests and Historical Identities in California, 1769–1936*. Berkeley: University of California Press, 1995.

Hackel, Steven W. "Land, Labor, and Production: The Colonial Economy of Spanish and Mexican California," In *Contested Eden: California before the Gold Rush*, edited by Ramón A. Gutiérrez and Richard J. Orsi, 111–46. Berkeley: University of California Press, 1998.

Halbwachs, Maurice. *On Collective Memory*. Edited and translated by Lewis A. Coser. Chicago: University of Chicago Press, 1992.

Hall, Jacquelyn Dowd. "'You Must Remember This': Autobiography as Social Critique." *Journal of American History* 85, no. 2 (September 1998): 439–65.

Hall, Stuart. "Cultural Identity and Diaspora." In *Identity and Difference*, edited by Kathryn Woodward, 51–59. London: Sage, 1997.

———. "Introduction: Formations of Modernity." In *Modernity: An Introduction to Modern Societies*, edited by Stuart Hall, David Held, Don Hubert, and Kenneth Thompson, 3–18. London: Blackwell, 1996.

———. "The Narrative Construction of Reality: An Interview with Stuart Hall." *Southern Review* 17 (March 1984): 3–17, quoted in W. Fitzhugh Brundage, "Introduction: No Deed But Memory." In *Where These Memories Grow: History, Memory, and Southern Identity*, edited by W. Fitzhugh Brundage, 1–28. Chapel Hill: University of North Carolina Press, 2000.

Hart, John Mason. "The Mexican Revolution, 1910–1920." In *The Oxford History of Mexico*, edited by Michael C. Meyer and William H. Beezley, 435–65. New York: Oxford University Press, 2000.

Herrera-Sobek, María. *The Mexican Corrido: A Feminist Analysis*. Bloomington: Indiana University Press, 1990.

———, ed. *Reconstructing a Chicano/a Literary Heritage: Hispanic Colonial Literature of the Southwest*. Tucson: University of Arizona Press, 1993.

Herrera-Sobek, María, and Virginia Sánchez Korrol, eds. *Recovering the U.S. Hispanic Literary Heritage, Vol. III*. Houston: Arte Público Press, 2000.

Herrera-Sobek, María, and Helena Viramontes, eds. *Chicana Creativity and Criticism: New Frontiers in American Literature.* Rev. ed. Albuquerque: University of New Mexico Press, 1996.

Homer, Sean. *Fredric Jameson: Marxism, Hermeneutics, Postmodernism.* New York: Routledge, 1998.

Hurtado, Albert L. *Intimate Frontiers: Sex, Gender, and Culture in Old California.* Albuquerque: University of New Mexico Press, 1999.

Jackson, Helen Hunt. *Ramona.* 1884. New York: Avon Books, 1970.

Jones, Anne Goodwyn. "The Cash Nexus." In *The Mind of the South: Fifty Years Later,* edited by Charles W. Eagles, 23–51. Jackson: University Press of Mississippi, 1992.

———. *Tomorrow Is Another Day: The Woman Writer in the South, 1859–1936.* Baton Rouge: Lousiana State University Press, 1981.

Kanfer, Stefan. *A Journal of the Plague Years.* New York: Atheneum, 1973.

Karl, Frederick R. *William Faulkner, American Writer: A Biography.* New York: Grove Press, 1988.

Katz, Friedrich. "Labor Conditions on Haciendas in Porfirian Mexico: Some Trends and Tendencies." *Hispanic American Historical Review* 54, no. 1 (February 1974): 1–47, quoted in Mario Barrera, *Race and Class in the Southwest: A Theory of Racial Equality.* Notre Dame, Ind.: University of Notre Dame Press, 1979.

Keller, Gary D. *Hispanics and United States Film: An Overview and Handbook.* Tempe, Ariz.: Bilingual Review/Press, 1994.

———. "The Image of the Chicano in Mexican, United States, and Chicano Cinema: An Overview." In *Chicano Cinema: Research, Reviews, and Resources,* edited by Gary D. Keller, 13–58. Binghamton, N.Y.: Bilingual Review/Press, 1985.

Kennedy, John Pendleton. *Swallow Barn: or, A Sojourn in the Old Dominion.* Rev. ed. New York: G. P. Putnam, 1851.

Knight, Alan. *The Mexican Revolution.* Vol. 2, *Counter-revolution and Reconstruction.* Reprint, Lincoln: University of Nebraska Press, 1990.

Kritzman, Lawrence D., ed. Foreword to *Realms of Memory: Rethinking the French Past,* by Pierre Nora. Vol. 1, *Conflicts and Divisions,* ix–xiv. New York: Columbia University Press, 1996.

Lamming, George. "The Occasion for Speaking." In *The Postcolonial Studies Reader,* edited by Bill Ashcroft, Gareth Griffiths, and Helen Tiffin, 12–17. London: Routledge, 1995.

Larralde, Carlos M., and Richard Griswold del Castillo. "San Diego's Ku Klux Klan, 1920–1980." *Journal of San Diego History* 46, no. 2–3 (Summer 2000): 3–24.

Leal, Luis. "Mexican American Literature: A Historical Perspective." In *Modern Chicano Writers: A Collection of Critical Essays,* edited by Joseph Sommers and Tomás Ybarra-Frausto, 18–30. Englewood Cliffs, N.J.: Prentice-Hall, 1979.

———. *Juan Rulfo.* Boston: Twayne, 1983.

———. *Aztlán y México: perfiles literarios e históricos.* Tucson: University of Arizona Press, 1979.

Le Goff, Jacques. *History and Memory.* 1977. Translated by Steven Rendall and Elizabeth Claman. New York: Columbia University Press, 1992.

Limón, José E. *American Encounters: Greater Mexico, the United States, and the Erotics of Culture.* Boston: Beacon Press, 1998.

———. *Dancing with the Devil: Society and Cultural Poetics in Mexican-American South Texas.* Madison: University of Wisconsin Press, 1994.

———. Introduction to *Caballero: A Historical Novel,* by Jovita González and Eve Raleigh, xii–xxvi. College Station: Texas A&M University Press, 1996.

———. *Mexican Ballads, Chicano Poems: History and Influence in Mexican-American Social Poetry.* Berkeley: University of California Press, 1992.

———. "Mexicans, Foundational Fictions, and the United States: *Caballero,* a Late Border Romance." In *The Places of History: Regionalism Revisited in Latin America,* edited by Doris Sommer, 236–48. Durham, N.C.: Duke University Press, 1999.

Lomelí, Francisco. "Contemporary Chicano Literature, 1959–1990: From Oblivion to Affirmation to the Forefront." In *Handbook of Hispanic Cultures in the United States.* Vol. 1, *Literature and Art,* edited and introduced by Francisco Lomelí, 86–108. Houston: Arte Público Press, 1993.

Longstreet, Augustus Baldwin. *Georgia Scenes: Characters, Incidents, etc. in the First Half Century of the Republic.* 1835. Savannah, Ga.: Beehive Press, 1975.

López, Ana M. "Are All Latins from Manhattan? Hollywood, Ethnography and Cultural Colonialism." In *Mediating Two Worlds: Cinematic Encounters in the Americas,* edited by John King, Ana M. López, and Manuel Alvarado, 67–80. London: British Film Institute, 1993.

Luis-Brown, David. "'White Slaves' and the 'Arrogant *Mestiza*': Reconfiguring Whiteness in *The Squatter and the Don* and *Ramona.*" *American Literature* 69, no. 4 (December 1997): 813–39.

MacKethan, Lucinda H. "Domesticity in Dixie: The Plantation Novel and *Uncle Tom's Cabin.*" In *Haunted Bodies: Gender and Southern Texts,* edited by Anne Goodwyn Jones and Susan V. Donaldson, 223–42. Charlottesville: University Press of Virginia, 1997.

Márquez, Antonio C. "Richard Rodriguez's *Hunger of Memory* and the Poetics of Experience." *Arizona Quarterly* 39, no. 4 (Winter): 130–41.

Martí, José. *Inside the Monster: Writings on the United States and American Imperialism.* Translated by Elinor Randall. Edited Philip S. Foner. New York: Monthly Review Press, 1975.

Martin, Gerald. *Journeys through the Labyrinth: Latin American Fiction in the Twentieth Century.* London: Verso Press, 1989.

Marx, Leo. "Pastoralism in America." In *Ideology and Classic American Literature,* edited by Sacvan Bercovitch and Myra Jehlen, 36–69. Cambridge: Cambridge University Press, 1986.

May, Dale Ballou. "'The Adobe Is My Birthstone': Leo Carrillo's Rancho de los Quiotes." *Journal of San Diego History* 35, no. 4 (Fall 1989): 230–47.

McWilliams, Carey. *North from Mexico: The Spanish-Speaking People of the United States.* 1948. New York: Greenwood Press, 1968.

Works Cited

———. *Southern California: An Island on the Land*. 1946. Salt Lake City: Peregrine Smith Books, 1988.

Meier, Matt S., and Feliciano Ribera. *Mexican Americans, American Mexicans: From Conquistadors to Chicanos*. Rev. ed. New York: Farrar, Straus & Giroux, 1993.

Menchaca, Martha. *The Mexican Outsiders: A Community History of Marginalization and Discrimination in California*. Austin: University of Texas Press, 1995.

Meyer, Michael C., and William L. Sherman. *The Course of Mexican History*. New York: Oxford University Press, 1979.

Miller, Simon. "Mexican Junkers and Capitalist Haciendas, 1810–1910: The Arable Estate and the Transition to Capitalism between the Insurgency and the Revolution." *Journal of Latin American Studies* 22, no. 2 (May 1990): 229–63.

Milner, Clyde A., ed. *A New Significance: Re-Envisioning the History of the American West*. New York: Oxford University Press, 1996.

Mitchell, Margaret. *Gone with the Wind*. 1936. New York: Warner Books, 1993.

Monroy, Douglas. "The Creation and Re-creation of Californio Society." In *Contested Eden: California before the Gold Rush*, edited by Ramón A. Gutiérrez and Richard J. Orsi, 173–95. Berkeley: University of California Press, 1998.

———. *Rebirth: Mexican Los Angeles from the Great Migration to the Great Depression*. Berkeley: University of California Press, 1999.

———. *Thrown among Strangers: The Making of Mexican Culture in Frontier California*. Berkeley: University of California Press, 1990.

Montejano, David. *Anglos and Mexicans in the Making of Texas, 1836–1986*. Austin: University of Texas Press, 1987.

Montes, Amelia María de la Luz, and Anne Elizabeth Goldman, eds. *María Amparo Ruiz de Burton: Critical and Pedagogical Perspectives*. Lincoln: University of Nebraska Press, 2004.

Moquin, Wayne, and Charles Van Doren. "The Treaty of Guadalupe Hidalgo." In *A Documentary History of the Mexican Americans*, edited by Wayne Moquin with Charles Van Doren, 181–87. New York: Praeger, 1971.

Moraga, Cherríe. *Loving in the War Years: lo que nunca pasó por sus labios*. Boston: South End Press, 1983.

Moraga, Cherríe, and Gloria Anzaldúa, eds. *This Bridge Called My Back: Writings by Radical Women of Color*. Watertown, Mass.: Persephone Press, 1981.

Morales, Alejandro. *Reto en el paraíso*. Ypsilanti, Mich.: Bilingual Press/Editorial Bilingüe, 1983.

Moss, Elizabeth. *Domestic Novelists in the Old South: Defenders of Southern Culture*. Baton Rouge: Louisiana State University Press, 1992.

Nora, Pierre. "General Introduction: Between Memory." In *Realms of Memory: Rethinking the French Past*, by Pierre Nora. Vol. 1, *Conflicts and Divisions*, 1–20. New York: Columbia University Press, 1996.

Noriega, Chon A. "Birth of the Southwest: Social Protest, Tourism, and

D.W. Griffith's *Ramona.*" In *The Birth of Whiteness: Race and the Emergence of U.S. Cinema,* edited by Daniel Bernardi, 203–26. New Brunswick, N.J.: Rutgers University Press, 1996.

Oden, Frederick Bryant. "The Maid of Monterey: The Life of Maria Amparo Ruiz de Burton, 1832–1895." Master's thesis, University of San Diego, 1992.

Padilla, Genaro M. "Self as Cultural Metaphor in Acosta's *The Autobiography of a Brown Buffalo.*" *Journal of General Education* 35 (1984): 242–58.

——. *My History, Not Yours: The Formation of Mexican American Autobiography.* Madison: University of Wisconsin Press, 1993.

Page, Thomas Nelson. *In Ole Virginia; or, Marse Chan and Other Stories.* 1887. Chapel Hill: University of North Carolina Press, 1969.

Palumbo-Liu, David. "The Politics of Memory: Remembering History in Alice Walker and Joy Kogawa." In *Memory and Cultural Politics: New Approaches to American Ethnic Literatures,* edited by Amritjit Singh, Joseph T. Skerrett Jr., and Robert E. Hogan, 211–26. Boston: Northeastern University Press, 1996.

Paredes, Américo. *"With His Pistol in His Hand": A Border Ballad and Its Hero.* Austin: University of Texas Press, 1958.

Paredes, Raymund A. "The Evolution of Chicano Literature." *Three American Literatures: Essays in Chicano, Native American, and Asian-American Literature for Teachers of American Literature,* edited by Houston A. Baker Jr., 33–79. New York: Modern Language Association, 1982.

Percy, William Alexander. *Lanterns on the Levee: Recollections of a Planter's Son.* New York: Knopf, 1941.

Pérez, Emma. *The Decolonial Imaginary: Writing Chicanas into History.* Bloomington: Indiana University Press, 1999.

Pérez, Francisco Róbles. "Memorias." Unpublished manuscript, 1992.

Pérez Firmat, Gustavo. "Introduction: Cheek to Cheek." In *Do the Americas Have a Common Literature?,* edited by Gustavo Pérez Firmat, 1–5. Durham, N.C.: Duke University Press, 1990.

Pérez-Torres, Rafael. *Movements in Chicano Poetry: Against Myths, against Margins.* Cambridge: Cambridge University Press, 1995.

Pettit, Arthur G. *Images of the Mexican American in Fiction and Film.* College Station: Texas A&M University Press, 1980.

Phillips, George Harwood. *Chiefs and Challengers: Indian Resistance and Cooperation in Southern California.* Berkeley: University of California Press, 1975.

Pita, Beatrice. "Engendering Critique: Race, Class, and Gender in Ruiz de Burton and Martí." In *José Martí's "Our America": From National to Hemispheric Cultural Studies,* edited by Jeffrey Belnap and Raúl Fernández, 129–44. Durham, N.C.: Duke University Press, 1998.

Pitt, Leonard. *The Decline of the Californios: A Social History of the Spanish-Speaking Californians, 1846–1890.* Berkeley: University of California Press, 1966.

Porter, Carolyn. "Reification and American Literature." In *Ideology and*

Classic American Literature, edited by Sacvan Bercovitch and Myra Jehlen, 188–217. Cambridge: Cambridge University Press, 1986.

Pratt, Mary Louise. "Yo soy Malinche: Chicana Writers and the Poetics of Ethnonationalism." *Callaloo* 16, no. 4 (1993): 859–73.

Prenshaw, Peggy Whitman. "Southern Ladies and the Southern Literary Renaissance." In *The Female Tradition in Southern Literature,* edited by Carol S. Manning, 73–88. Urbana: University of Illinois Press, 1993.

Quinn, Anthony. *The Original Sin: A Self-Portrait.* Boston: Little, Brown, 1972.

Quintana, Alvina E. "Ana Castillo's *The Mixquiahuala Letters:* The Novelist as Ethnographer." In *Criticism in the Borderlands: Studies in Chicano Literature, Culture, and Ideology,* edited by Hector Calderón and José David Saldívar, 72–83. Durham, N.C.: Duke University Press, 1991.

Ransom, John Crowe, et al. *I'll Take My Stand: The South and the Agrarian Tradition.* 1930. Baton Rouge: Louisiana State University Press, 1977.

Rebolledo, Tey Diana. "Narrative Strategies of Resistance in Hispana Writing." *Journal of Narrative Technique* 20, no. 2 (Spring 1990): 134–46.

———. *Women Singing in the Snow: A Cultural Analysis of Chicana Literature.* Tucson: University of Arizona Press, 1995.

Rebolledo, Tey Diana, and Eliana S. Rivero, eds. *Infinite Divisions: An Anthology of Chicana Literature.* Tucson: University of Arizona Press, 1993.

Revueltas, José. *Human Mourning* [El luto humano]. Translated by Roberto Crespi. 1943. Minneapolis: University of Minnesota Press, 1990.

Reyes, Luis, and Peter Rubie. *Hispanics in Hollywood: A Celebration of One Hundred Years in Film and Television.* Hollywood, Calif.: Lone Eagle, 2000.

Robbins, William G. *Colony and Empire: The Capitalist Transformation of the American West.* Lawrence: University of Kansas Press, 1994.

Robinson, Cecil. *Mexico and the Hispanic Southwest in American Literature.* Tucson: University of Arizona Press, 1977.

Rodríguez, Barbara. *Autobiographical Inscriptions: Form, Personhood, and the American Woman Writer of Color.* New York: Oxford University Press, 1999.

Romine, Scott. *The Narrative Forms of Southern Community.* Baton Rouge: Louisiana State University Press, 1999.

Rosales, F. Arturo. "'Fantasy Heritage' Revisited: Race and Class in the Writings of the Bandini Family Authors and Other Californios, 1828–1965." In *Recovering the U.S. Hispanic Literary Heritage, Volume II,* edited by Erlinda González-Berry and Chuck Tatum, 81–104. Houston: Arte Público Press, 1996.

Rosenus, Alan. *General M. G. Vallejo and the Advent of the Americans: A Biography.* Albuquerque: University of New Mexico Press, 1995.

Ruiz, Ramón Eduardo. *The Great Rebellion: Mexico, 1905–1924.* New York: Norton, 1980.

Ruiz de Burton, María Amparo. *Conflicts of Interest: The Letters of María Amparo Ruiz de Burton.* Edited by Rosaura Sánchez and Beatrice Pita. Houston: Arte Público Press, 2001.

———. *The Squatter and the Don.* 1885. Houston: Arte Público Press, 1992.

———. *Who Would Have Thought It?* 1872. Houston: Arte Público Press, 1995.

Rulfo, Juan. *Pedro Páramo.* Translated by Lysander Kemp. 1955. New York: Grove Press, 1987.

Saldívar, José David. *Border Matters: Remapping American Cultural Studies.* Berkeley: University of California Press, 1997.

———. *The Dialectics of Our America: Genealogy, Cultural Critique, and Literary History.* Durham, N.C.: Duke University Press, 1991.

Saldívar, Ramón. *Chicano Narrative: The Dialectics of Difference.* Madison: University of Wisconsin Press, 1990.

———. "Ideologies of the Self: Chicano Autobiography." *Diacritics* (Fall 1985): 25–34.

———. "Looking for a Master Plan: Faulkner, Paredes, and the Colonial and Postcolonial Subject." In *The Cambridge Companion to William Faulkner,* edited by Philip M. Weinstein, 96–120. New York: Cambridge University Press, 1995.

Sánchez, Rosaura. "Dismantling the Colossus: Martí and Ruiz de Burton on the Formulation of Anglo América." In *José Martí's "Our America": From National to Hemispheric Cultural Studies,* edited by Jeffrey Belnap and Raúl Fernández, 115–28. Durham, N.C.: Duke University Press, 1998.

———. *Telling Identities: The Californio testimonios.* Minneapolis: University of Minnesota Press, 1995.

Sánchez, Rosaura, and Beatrice Pita. Introduction to *The Squatter and the Don,* by María Amparo Ruiz de Burton, 5–51. Houston: Arte Público Press, 1992.

———. Introduction to *Who Would Have Thought It?* by María Amparo Ruiz de Burton, vii–lxv. Houston: Arte Público Press, 1995.

———, eds. *Conflicts of Interest: The Letters of María Amparo Ruiz de Burton.* Houston: Arte Público Press, 2001.

Sandos, James A. "'Because He Is a Liar and a Thief': Conquering the Residents of 'Old' California, 1850–1880." In *Rooted in Barbarous Soil: People, Culture, and Community in Gold Rush California,* edited by Kevin Starr and Richard J. Orsi, 86–112. Berkeley: University of California Press, 2000.

———. "Between the Crucifix and Lance: Indian-White Relations in California, 1769–1848." In *Contested Eden: California before the Gold Rush,* edited by Ramón A. Gutiérrez and Richard J. Orsi, 196–229. Berkeley: University of California Press, 1998.

Semo, Enrique. *The History of Capitalism in Mexico: Its Origins, 1521–1763.* Austin: University of Texas Press, 1993.

Sharpe, Jenny. "Figures of Colonial Resistance." In *The Postcolonial Studies Reader,* edited by Bill Ashcroft, Gareth Griffiths, and Helen Tiffin, 99–103. London: Routledge, 1995.

Shohat, Ella, and Robert Stam. *Unthinking Eurocentrism: Multiculturalism and the Media.* London: Routledge, 1994.

Simmons, William S. "Indian Peoples of California." In *Contested Eden:*

Works Cited

California before the Gold Rush, edited by Ramón A. Gutiérrez and Richard J. Orsi, 48–77. Berkeley: University of California Press, 1998.

Singh, Amritjit, Joseph T. Skerrett Jr., and Robert E. Hogan, eds. *Memory and Cultural Politics: New Approaches to American Ethnic Literatures.* Boston: Northeastern University Press, 1996.

———. *Memory, Narrative, and Identity: New Essays in Ethnic American Literatures.* Boston: Northeastern University Press, 1994.

Slotkin, Richard. *The Fatal Environment: The Myth of the Frontier in the Age of Industrialization, 1800–1890.* Norman: University of Oklahoma Press, 1998.

Smith, Jon, and Deborah Cohn, eds. *Look Away!: The U.S. South in New World Studies.* Durham, N.C.: Duke University Press, 2004.

Sommer, Doris. *Foundational Fictions: The National Romances of Latin America.* Berkeley: University of California, 1991.

———. "Irresistible Romance: The Foundational Fictions of Latin America." In *Nation and Narration,* edited by Homi K. Bhabha, 71–98. London: Routledge, 1990.

———, ed. *The Places of History: Regionalism Revisited in Latin America.* Durham, N.C.: Duke University Press, 1999.

Starr, Kevin. *Americans and the California Dream, 1850–1915.* New York: Oxford University Press, 1973.

———. *Embattled Dreams: California in War and Peace, 1940–1950.* New York: Oxford University Press, 2002.

———. *Inventing the Dream: California through the Progressive Era.* New York: Oxford University Press, 1985.

Stein, Stanley J., and Barbara H. Stein. *The Colonial Heritage of Latin America: Essays on Economic Dependence in Perspective.* New York: Oxford University Press, 1970.

Sturken, Marita. *Entangled Memories: The Vietnam War, the AIDS Epidemic, and the Politics of Remembering.* Berkeley: University of California Press, 1997.

Taylor, William R. "Cavalier and Yankee: Synthetic Stereotypes." In *Myth and Southern History.* Vol. 1, *The Old South,* edited by Patrick Gerster and Nicholas Cords, 133–45. 2d ed. Urbana: University of Illinois Press, 1989.

Thomas, Brook. "The New Historicism and Other Old-fashioned Topics." In *The New Historicism,* edited by H. Aram Veeser, 182–203. New York: Routledge, 1989.

Trouillot, Michel-Rolph. *Silencing the Past: Power and the Production of History.* Boston: Beacon Press, 1995.

Tuck, Ruth D. *Not with the Fist: Mexican-Americans in a Southwest City.* New York: Harcourt, Brace, 1946.

Tuttle, Jennifer. "Symptoms of Conquest: Race, Class, and the Nervous Body in *The Squatter and the Don.*" In *María Amparo Ruiz de Burton: Critical and Pedagogical Perspectives,* edited by Amelia María de la Luz Montes and Anne Elizabeth Goldman, 56–72. Lincoln: University of Nebraska Press, 2004.

Vallejo, Guadalupe. "Ranch and Mission Days in Alta California." *The Century Magazine* 41, no. 2 (December 1890): 1–18.

Vallejo, José Manuel Salvador. "Notas históricas sobre California." 1874. In *Nineteenth Century Californio Testimonials,* edited by Rosaura Sánchez, Beatrice Pita, and Barbara Reyes, 92–105. La Jolla, Calif.: UCSD Ethnic Studies/Third World Studies, 1994.

Vallejo, Mariano Guadalupe. "Historical and Personal Memoirs Relating to Alta California." 1874. Translated by Earl R. Hewitt, 1875. 5 vols. Unpublished testimonial, BANC MSS C-D 17, 18, 19, 20, 21. Bancroft Library, University of California at Berkeley.

Van de Grift Sanchez, Nellie. *Spanish Arcadia.* Los Angeles: Powell Publishing Company, 1929.

Vidal, Gore. *Palimpsest: A Memoir.* New York: Random House, 1995.

Villa, Raúl Homero. *Barrio-Logos: Space and Place in Urban Chicano Literature and Culture.* Austin: University of Texas Press, 2000.

Villarreal, José Antonio. *Pocho.* 1959. Garden City, N.Y.: Doubleday, 1970.

Weber, David J. *The Mexican Frontier, 1821–1846: The American Southwest under Mexico.* Albuquerque: University of New Mexico Press, 1982.

———. *Myth and the History of the Hispanic Southwest: Essays.* Albuquerque: University of New Mexico Press, 1998.

———. *The Spanish Frontier in North America.* New Haven, Conn.: Yale University Press, 1992.

Wittenburg, Mary Sainte Thérèse. *The Machados and Rancho La Ballona: The Story of the Land and Its Ranchero, José Agustín Antonio Machado, with a Genealogy of the Machado Family.* Los Angeles: Dawson's Book Shop, 1973.

Woll, Allen L. *The Latin Image in American Film.* Los Angeles: UCLA Latin American Center Publications, 1977.

Woodward, C. Vann. *The Burden of Southern History.* 1960. 3d ed. Baton Rouge: Louisiana State University Press, 1993.

Woolsey, Ronald C. *Migrants West: Toward the Southern California Frontier.* Claremont, Calif.: Grizzly Bear Publishers, 1996.

Wyatt-Brown, Bertram. *Honor and Violence in the Old South.* New York: Oxford University Press, 1986.

Young, Eric Van. "Mexican Rural History since Chevalier: The Historiography of the Colonial Hacienda." *Latin American Research Review* 18, no. 3 (1983): 5–61.

Young, Robert. *White Mythologies: Writing History and the West.* London: Routledge, 1990.

Zamora, Emilio. *The World of the Mexican Worker in Texas.* College Station: Texas A&M University Press, 1993.

Zamora, Lois Parkinson. "The Usable Past: The Idea of History in Modern U.S. and Latin American Fiction." In *Do the Americas Have a Common Literature?* edited by Gustavo Pérez Firmat, 7–41. Durham, N.C.: Duke University Press, 1990.

INDEX

Index

Index